30 LIFE PRINCIPLES

BIBLE STUDY

A 90-Day Action Plan for
Living These Principles

CHARLES F. STANLEY

Harper*Christian*
Resources

30 Life Principles Bible Study, Updated Edition
Copyright © 2016, 2023 by Charles F. Stanley

Published in Grand Rapids, Michigan, by HarperChristian Resources. HarperChristian Resources is a registered trademark of HarperCollins Christian Publishing, Inc.

Requests for information should be sent to customercare@harpercollins.com.

ISBN 978-0-310-16377-0 (softcover)
ISBN 978-0-310-16378-7 (ebook)

HarperChristian Resources titles may be purchased in bulk for church, business, fundraising, or ministry use. For information, please e-mail ResourceSpecialist@ChurchSource.com.

Cover Photography: Charles F. Stanley
Cover design: Veldheer Creative Services
Interior design by InsideOut Creative Arts

First Printing September 2023 / Printed in the United States of America

CONTENTS

INTRODUCTION

The Principles

Your life as a Christian is a wondrous adventure filled with twists and turns, good times, and also *difficult* challenges. Through it all, the Bible is your greatest resource for insight, wisdom, hope, and guidance. God has given you hundreds of life principles in His Word to help you become everything He designed you to be. These are the tenets of the Christian faith that have been tried and proven throughout history—truths that have never failed and will never disappoint. You can see their impact on the lives of the saints—from Old Testament times to the present day—and God has promised that if you follow His commands, He will bless your obedience.

During his sixty years of ministry, Dr. Charles Stanley faithfully highlighted the 30 Life Principles that guided his life and helped him to grow in his knowledge, service, and love of God. Dr. Stanley taught them so others can find God's wisdom, receive His comfort and peace, and grow into mature followers of the Lord Jesus Christ. Perhaps you've been inspired by these 30 Life Principles and are wondering how you can further make them a part of your life. You might be asking what the Bible teaches about having a lifetime of spiritual success and avoiding the traps of ineffectiveness and spiritual misery. You may be considering how these Life Principles apply to the circumstances and challenges you face on a daily basis.

The *30 Life Principles Bible Study* has been developed to help you answer these questions, put these principles from God's Word into action, and encourage you to grow in your relationship with Jesus. Of course, these principles were never meant to take the place of God's Word, but serve as guidelines for discovering the richness of God's truth and knowing Him in a deeper way. By following these Life Principles, you will be on the road to the life that He designed for you. And as you submit yourself to Him more fully, God will reveal Himself to you. That's what makes the journey of obedience so exciting.

How to Use this Study

This study has been designed to help you discover the 30 Life Principles and put them to action in your life over the course of 90 days. You can use it for individual study or as a resource for a small group. Each lesson in the Bible study will contain the following elements:

LIFE'S QUESTIONS: Each lesson opens with an insight into the principle and a brief overview of what you will be studying.

DAILY BIBLE STUDY: Each lesson includes three days' worth of Bible study for you to complete during the week. If you are doing this Bible study with a small group, you will discuss your responses to these questions during your meeting time. Before you begin each day's study, take a few moments to ask God to open your heart to His Word, help you better understand His principles, and learn how to apply them to your life in practical ways.

LIVING THE PRINCIPLE: In addition to studying each principle in God's Word, it is also important to put what you have learned into action. This section contains ideas for further reflection on the principle, how to ask God to make it more a part of your daily walk with Him, how to share what you have discovered about it with others, and other ways to put the principle into practice.

LIFE LESSONS TO REMEMBER: Each lesson includes a summary of three key items to remember for the Life Principle you have studied.

PRINCIPLE IN ACTION: The names of people in the Bible who put the principle into action have been listed in the margin of each lesson. Use the Scripture references provided to learn more about their lives and the ways in which they followed—or failed to follow—God's instruction.

SCRIPTURE QUOTATIONS: Additional Scripture quotations, key concepts, and related quotes have been provided in the margins to give you further insight into each principle, cement the key ideas in your mind, and help you follow along.

In addition to answering the questions in the daily Bible study portions, you will also want to make notes of what comes to mind as you read the selected passage(s) of Scripture. Be sure to have a pen and paper for writing, and ask the Lord to reveal Himself to you as you work through each of the lessons. Remember that every problem you will face has its solution in the Word of God. It will offer you the wisdom and insight you seek at every turn. You cannot and will not encounter anything that is beyond God and His principles in Scripture!

If you would like to lead a group through this material, please see the section at the end of this book for a basic design of how to set up your group time, navigate problems and opportunities that may arise during your discussion time, and to get the most out of the study as a group.

Knowing Christ

It is important to note that putting God's principles into action begins with *knowing Jesus Christ as your Lord and Savior*. There is simply no substitute for a personal relationship with Jesus Christ. It is the core of God's message to each of us, and the Bible is clear you cannot know God without first knowing the One who reconciles you to Him. As Paul writes, "When we were enemies we were reconciled to God through the death of His Son, much more, having been reconciled, we shall be saved by His life" (Romans 5:10).

God's Son, Jesus Christ, provides a relationship with Him—and He also provides eternal life if you trust Him. As Paul again writes, "If you confess with your mouth the Lord Jesus and believe in your heart that God has raised Him from the dead, you will be saved" (Romans 10:9). To start a personal relationship with God—the One who created you and loves you no matter what—all you need to do is tell God you are trusting in Him for salvation. Tell Him in your own words or use this sample prayer:

Lord Jesus, I know that Your death on the cross was enough to forgive all of my sin and restore my relationship with God. I ask You to forgive my sin and be my Savior. Thank You for providing the way for me to have a growing relationship with my heavenly Father, and thank You for giving me eternal life. I know that You hear my prayers, and I praise You for loving me unconditionally and saving me. In Jesus' name, Amen.

If you have just received Christ as your Savior, congratulations! You've just made the best decision of your life! We would love to know about your decision. Please contact In Touch's Customer Care center at (800) 789-1473, so that we can rejoice with you and send you our *New Believer's Kit* to help you take the next step in your walk with God.

Your Intimacy with God—His Highest Priority for Your Life—Determines the Impact of Your Life

Then God said, "Let Us make man in Our image, according to Our likeness."

GENESIS 1:26

Life's Questions

At the beginning of any journey, you must set out in the right direction to reach your destination. That is why this Bible study begins with God's wonderful purpose for bringing you into this world. To find the life that's worth living—one that makes a *real* difference in this world—you first must understand that you're a special, beloved person. What's more, God has a unique and wonderful plan for you that will give you all the love, satisfaction, fulfillment, and significance you're looking for in life.

True success in God's eyes is not measured in terms of wealth, accomplishments, or popularity. Some of the richest, most talented, and best-known people in the world have little or no real impact on the world around them. On the other hand, countless people who are "average" by cultural standards—regardless of their unique limitations—make an enormous impact on the world simply by serving in the place that God has called them to serve. It is people's relationship and obedience to God that determine their impact.

Have you wondered what motivated God to design the universe or why He created you? It was love . . . pure and simple. Even before the

PRINCIPLE IN ACTION
Phinehas (Numbers 25:10–13)
Deborah (Judges 4:1–5:31)
Mary of Bethany (John 12:1–8)
Timothy (1 Timothy 1:2, 18)
James (James 1:1)

Success is desiring to be the person that God has called you to be and to achieve those goals that God has helped you to set.

—CHARLES F. STANLEY

beginning of the world, God loved you and wanted to have a close, personal relationship with you that would bring great joy, fulfillment, and power to your life (see Ephesians 1:4). Therefore, Life Principle 1 is this: *Your intimacy with God—His highest priority for your life—determines the impact of your life.*

Day 1: Made In God's Image

God created you like Himself so you could have fellowship with Him.

When God created you, He made you like Himself. Why? So you would have the capacity for fellowship with Him. Without that commonality, you would have no way to comprehend Him on a personal level. However, because you have this commonality, you can recognize His perfections. You can appreciate His limitless love, mercy, grace, wisdom, and power because of the (extremely) limited versions of those attributes you see in yourself. Worship, of course, is the only sensible reaction to God when faced with this realization.

The world tends to sum up a person's impact based on the fame and fortune that he or she possesses. But God sums up a person's impact in terms of relationship, character, and obedience to Him. God wants you to succeed first and foremost in your relationship with Him, then in your relationships with others, and finally in your vocations and ministries. His highest priority and purpose for your life is intimacy with Him. Therefore, the depth of your relationship with Him will determine the impact of your life in this world.

Each of us has a need to know that we are loved.

Thanks to God's design, this relationship simultaneously fills your deepest personal needs—especially the need to know that you are loved. Each one of us has to feel certain, deep down in our hearts, that someone cares for us and has our best interests at heart. When your relationship with God is strong, you experience His love with a passionate intensity too deep for words. So it is that God created you with fellowship in mind—with Himself and others. But you cannot fully love others until you have yourself experienced the love of God.

God said, "Let Us make man in Our image, according to Our likeness; let them have dominion over the fish of the sea, over the birds of the air, and over the cattle, over all the earth and over every creeping thing that creeps on the earth" (Genesis 1:26).

1. Read Genesis 1. God is spirit. He is eternal, all-powerful, and all-knowing. He exists out of time, and the laws of physics don't apply to Him. He is sovereign, answers to no one, and can't be defeated. In what ways, then, are you created in His image (26)? Where is the resemblance?

_____

_____

_____

_____

_____

2. What impact does the fact you were created in God's image have on your dominion over the animal world (26)?

_____

_____

_____

3. What impact does the fact you were created in God's image have on your relationship with other people?

_____

_____

_____

4. Is it possible to catch a "glimpse of God" in other people? Explain.

_____

_____

_____

5. After the first five days of creation, God declared His work to be "good" (4, 10, 12, 18, 21, 25). After the sixth day—the day He created humankind in His own image—He declared His work to be "very good" (31). Why do you think He said this?

_____

_____

_____

_____

The word image _in the Old Testament also means_ a _likeness, model, semblance, or shadow._ This is what you have in common with God and why you can know Him more deeply.

Day 2: A Willing Surrender

You experience God's love when you willingly surrender to His call to be your Savior, Lord, and Friend. _Surrender_ is a loaded word. In military terms, it means that all is lost. In spiritual terms, however, it means that all is gained. To _surrender_ to God is to let go of the steering wheel of your life and leave the driving to the One who not only designed the car but also plotted the course. To surrender control to God is to gain confidence and faith.

In spiritual terms, to surrender to God means that all is gained.

There are at least three reasons why God seeks your surrender. First, *He loves you and desires your fellowship and worship.* As long as you hold something back from God, you cannot know Him completely or fully experience His love. However, when you surrender all that you are to Him, you get all of Him.

Second, *He wants your service to be effective and fruitful.* Regardless of your particular situation or the limitations you might have, the more you love Jesus and serve Him in the place He has called you to serve, the more effective that service will be. The closer you draw to God, the more impact your life will have. The more energetically you nurture your relationship with the Lord, the greater the positive mark you will leave behind.

Third, *He waits for the freedom to bless you.* God is omnipotent, but He will not violate His own principles. He draws you to Himself so you can experience His love and forgiveness. He asks for your willing surrender so He can give you the best blessings He has to offer.

6. Read Psalm 37. Why does the prosperity of evildoers make it difficult for people to surrender to God (1)?

_____

_____

_____

7. What is the connection between surrendering to God and leaving justice and vengeance to Him (6)?

_____

_____

_____

8. What is the connection between surrendering to God and waiting patiently for Him (7)?

_____

_____

_____

_____

9. What does it say about God that He waits for you to surrender instead of forcing you to submit to His will?

_____

_____

_____

_____

10. What does it say that we sometimes choose to wait to surrender until circumstances escalate beyond our control?

_____

_____

_____

Humble yourselves in the sight of the Lord, and He will lift you up (James 4:10).

The word good *in the Old Testament also means* well-pleasing, proper, pleasant to the senses, useful, profitable, *or a general* state of well-being and happiness. *Everything good that comes to you is from God (see James 1:17).*

Day 3: Resistance Is Foolish

If God loves you more than anyone else ever could—and if He knows better than anyone else what will bring you ultimate joy, satisfaction, and fulfillment—why would anyone resist surrendering to Him? Why would anyone refuse to give himself or herself completely to Him and enjoy the blessings He has in store for His faithful followers?

Pride is one of the most obvious explanations. Many people flatter themselves into thinking they know better than God and can handle their lives better than He can. So they keep Him at a distance. Others choose not to surrender because they fear what God will do (or not do) for them. They think if they give Him control, He'll make them do exactly what will make them most miserable. Still others refuse to surrender because they believe Satan's lies, which tell them God is judgmental and only seeks to punish them for their mistakes.

All of this is completely false! God *always* has your best interests in mind. He will refuse you no good thing when you gladly submit to His will (see Romans 8:32). He has said, "I know the thoughts that I think toward you . . . thoughts of peace and not of evil, to give you a future and a hope" (Jeremiah 29:11). Given this, it only makes sense to surrender to God. And when you do, you grow close to Him and begin to make an impact on this world.

God knows what will bring you ultimate joy, satisfaction, and fulfillment.

God *always* has your best interests in mind.

11. Read Jonah 1. How did Jonah respond to God's call to go to Nineveh (3)? How might his story have unfolded if he had submitted to God's will from the start?

_____

_____

_____

Jonah arose to flee to Tarshish from the presence of the LORD. He went down to Joppa, and found a ship going to Tarshish; so he paid the fare (Jonah 1:3).

So they picked up Jonah and threw him into the sea, and the sea ceased from its raging. Then the men feared the LORD exceedingly, and offered a sacrifice to the LORD and took vows (Jonah 1:15–16).

12. Jonah's resistance was rather blatant. He booked a journey in a different direction from the one God told him to take (1:3)—and faced the consequences for his actions (15). What are some of the subtle ways today that people resist surrendering to God?

_____

_____

_____

13. If Jonah's story proves anything, it's that God ultimately accomplishes His will—whether you like it or not. You can learn that the hard way, as Jonah did, or the easy way. How would you convince a skeptical friend that the easy way is better?

_____

_____

_____

God saw their works, that they turned from their evil way; and God relented from the disaster that He had said He would bring upon them, and He did not do it (Jonah 3:10).

14. Read Jonah 3. What is the future to which you can look forward if you submit to God's will? What are some examples of the impact you might have on the world around you?

_____

_____

_____

It displeased Jonah exceedingly, and he became angry. So he prayed to the LORD, and said, "Ah, LORD, was not this what I said when I was still in my country? Therefore I fled previously to Tarshish; for I know that You are a gracious and merciful God, slow to anger and abundant in lovingkindness, One who relents from doing harm (Jonah 4:1–2).

15. Read Jonah 4:1–2. What was Jonah's reason for refusing to surrender to God? In what ways have you refused to follow God because of a lack of compassion for others?

_____

_____

_____

Throughout modern times, the story of Jonah often has been ridiculed as myth, but the Hebrew people accepted it as historical. Jesus Christ Himself also vouched for the truth of the book and the remarkable story it relates (see Matthew 12:39–41).

Living the Principle

You were created for intimacy with God.

How will you live out Life Principle 1 this week? Remember, you were created for intimacy with God. The impact that your relationship with Him makes in your life cannot be overstated. His highest priority for you is to be involved with Him in prayer, the study of His Word, and worship and praise. So, if you want to lead a life that is fulfilling, significant, and makes a difference, the secret is to surrender yourself completely to Christ and open your heart to His love and mercy.

It's only through your fellowship and communion with God that you will be able to truly affect other people's lives in a way that lasts eternally. It's only through your connection with Him that you will be able to leave a lasting spiritual legacy for your children, grandchildren, and the generations that come after you. As you spend time with God and get to know Him intimately, it will become evident in every area of your life—and this will positively affect the life of every person you encounter.

So, with this in mind, ask yourself some difficult questions this week. Begin by asking yourself what impact, if any, you are having on the world around you. If you find that you are having little impact, or that your life seems to lack meaning, consider your relationship with God. Would you describe it as strong and vibrant? Are you letting other things get in the way of your time with Him and study of His Word? If so, what can you eliminate so that your intimacy with God will grow? What other steps can you take to restore the intimacy? Spend time in prayer, asking God to draw you into communion with Himself and transform your life.

Fellowship with God enables you to affect others in a way that lasts eternally.

Life Lessons to Remember

❖ God loves you and desires your fellowship and worship (see Deuteronomy 6:5).
❖ God wants your service for Him to be effective and fruitful (see John 15:5).
❖ God waits for you to invite Him to bless you (see Revelation 3:20).

You can never know the mind of God fully because you are a finite creature and He is infinite, but you can grow in your understanding about who God is, how He operates in your world, and why He does things He does. You can grow in your understanding by reading more of God's Word, gaining more maturity in Christ Jesus, and learning how to read the Bible with spiritual understanding. "The Helper, the Holy Spirit, whom the Father will send in My name, He will teach you all things, and bring to your remembrance all things that I said to you"
(John 14:26).

Notes AND Prayer Requests

Use this space to write any key points, questions,
or prayer requests from this week's study.

Obey God and Leave All the Consequences to Him

Now therefore, if you will indeed obey My voice and keep My covenant, then you shall be a special treasure to Me above all people for all the earth is Mine.

EXODUS 19:5

Life's Questions

God is the Creator of all that exists. "All things were made through Him, and without Him nothing was made that was made" (John 1:3). As the Creator and Orderer of the universe, He has the right and the power to conform all circumstances to His will. He is also entitled to expect a certain standard of behavior from those who believe in Him.

Of course, because His standard is higher than that of the culture in which you live, obeying His commands will set you apart from the crowd. In certain circumstances, it will make you a target for scorn from a world that denies His authority. As you strive to meet God's standard, you might be accused of intolerance and narrow-mindedness, or singled out on social media or in social settings. The consequences can be severe . . . which is why God instructs you to leave them to Him. He can bring ultimate good from even the direst consequences.

How do you relate to God, His commands, and the challenges and temptations that confront you? When God directs you to do something, how do you respond? Do His commands seem too difficult or costly for you to obey? Are you facing a decision that seems overwhelming? Are you torn about whether to follow God's instructions? If so, Life Principle 2 will help you: *Obey God and leave all the consequences to Him.*

PRINCIPLE IN ACTION
Noah (Genesis 6:22)
Aaron (Leviticus 8:2–3)
Shadrach, Meshach, and Abed-Nego (Daniel 3:19–29)
Amos (Amos 7:14–15)
Mary (Luke 1:31–38)

Great faith does not blossom overnight. It is the result of years of trusting and obeying the Lord.
—CHARLES F. STANLEY

Day 4: Staring Down the Challenges

Obedience can be a challenge, especially when you're tempted to believe you stand to lose more through your obedience than you might gain. However, obeying God is essential to pleasing Him. When God commands you to obey Him, it's with your best interests in mind. He knows the outcome of every possible choice you might make, and He steers you to the path of the greatest good. In the process, He gives you key principles by which to live. He also sets a framework around your life that forms a hedge of protection from evil (see Job 1:10).

Can you remember the last time you were tempted to do the opposite of what you knew God desired you to do? Most likely, a struggle erupted within your heart. The questions arose: *Will obeying God cost me more than disobeying Him? Can I experience greater happiness by committing this sin than I would by obeying God? What will happen if I disobey?* If you chose to obey God in that situation, you took the way of wisdom and undoubtedly realized that in the end, the blessing of obedience outweighed any possible consequences.

God asks you to submit your life to Him and leave whatever happens to His loving care. As you grow in your walk with the Lord, obedience becomes the avenue by which you come to know Him better. Your experiences teach you that obeying Him produces positive results. Your bond of trust in Him becomes stronger and stronger. In turn, He pulls you closer to Himself and teaches you more about His precepts and His love.

Obeying God is essential to pleasing Him.

Obedience is the avenue by which you know God better.

Nebuchadnezzar the king made an image of gold. . . . When all the people heard the sound of the horn, flute, harp, and lyre, in symphony with all kinds of music, all the people, nations, and languages fell down and worshiped the gold image (Daniel 3:1, 7).

1. Read Daniel 3. Shadrach, Meshach, and Abed-Nego were Hebrew captives who had made names for themselves in Babylon. King Nebuchadnezzar had appointed them to serve as governors, which gave them great status and privilege. Given this, why might it have seemed to make sense for them to ignore God's law and comply with Nebuchadnezzar's order to bow down to his gold image (1–7)?

   _____

   _____

   _____

   _____

Shadrach, Meshach, and Abed-Nego answered . . . "Our God whom we serve is able to deliver us from the burning fiery furnace, and He will deliver us (Daniel 3:16–17).

2. What was Shadrach, Meshach, and Abed-Nego's reply to King Nebuchadnezzar's order (16–18)? What did they acknowledge about God? What kind of relationship would you need to have with God in order to say—and *mean*—those words?

   _____

   _____

   _____

3. Shadrach, Meshach, and Abed-Nego stated they had no guarantee God would save them from the fiery furnace—yet still they refused to bow to the golden image. Why was death preferable to disobedience for them?

_____

_____

_____

_____

"But if not, let it be known to you, O king, that we do not serve your gods, nor will we worship the gold image which you have set up" (Daniel 3:18).

4. What are some of the likely results of Shadrach, Meshach, and Abed-Nego's bold acts of obedience in their own lives, among their circles of influence, and throughout Babylon?

_____

_____

_____

_____

5. Consider a time in your life when it seemed to make sense to ignore God's law—or the Holy Spirit's prompting in your conscience—in favor of a more popular course of action. What can you take away from the story of Shadrach, Meshach, and Abed-Nego?

_____

_____

_____

_____

Do not be conformed to this world, but be transformed by the renewing of your mind (Romans 12:2).

The word obey *in the Old Testament primarily means to* listen. *It can also mean to* heed, agree, consent, understand, *and* yield to. *To obey God means that you must listen for His voice and trust what He's telling you. Obeying God is absolutely essential to pleasing Him.*

Day 5: To Trust or Not to Trust

Disobedience says to the Lord that you know better than He does when it comes to your life and the circumstances surrounding it. Nothing could be further from the truth. God loves you and is committed to you. He commands your obedience not because He is a strict

Disobedience says to God that you know better than He does when it comes to your life.

taskmaster but because He knows the devastating effect that disobedience and sin will have on your life.

You were created to have fellowship with Him. Disobedience disrupts that fellowship and puts obstacles in the way of your relationship. It creates spiritual distance between you and God and makes you vulnerable to temptation. That vulnerability doesn't go unnoticed by Satan. He encourages disobedience by telling you the Lord's promises cannot be trusted and you can enjoy life more if you ignore His commands. Satan will skew your perspective by causing you to doubt the most secure and trustworthy thing in the world: God's Word.

You were created to have fellowship with God.

The key to resisting Satan's temptation is to remember that disobedience *always* produces consequences—including feelings of guilt, shame, and worthlessness; broken lives; destroyed marriages; and bitter disputes. While sin can never change God's eternal love for His children, it can certainly disrupt your fellowship and alienates you from His blessings. In times of disobedience, you become spiritually weak and unable to discern right from wrong. You sink deeper into sin's grasp and find it impossible to reverse your sinfulness on your own.

Disobedience always leads to consequences.

Now the serpent was more cunning than any beast of the field which the LORD God had made. And he said to the woman, "Has God indeed said, 'You shall not eat of every tree of the garden'?" (Genesis 3:1).

6. Read Genesis 3. Notice that Satan began his temptation of Eve with the question, "Has God indeed said . . . ?" (1). Why was this question such an effective tool when it came to temptation? What did it cause Eve to consider?

   _____

   _____

   _____

   _____

The serpent said to the woman, "You will not surely die. For God knows that in the day you eat of it your eyes will be opened, and you will be like God, knowing good and evil" (Genesis 3:4–5).

7. Satan followed up his question to Eve with a declaration that God had lied to her (4). What did he say that made this lie sound like the truth in her ears (5)? What decision concerning who to trust did Eve and Adam (who was with her) have to make?

   _____

   _____

   _____

   _____

The eyes of both of them were opened, and they knew that they were naked (Genesis 3:7).

8. What was the immediate consequence of Adam and Eve's sin (7)? How did it affect their relationship with God (8–9)? How does your sin cause you to hide from God?

   _____

   _____

   _____

9. What were some of the long-term consequences for Adam and Eve (16–19)? Why did God have to drive them out of the Garden of Eden (22–24)?

_____

_____

_____

"I will greatly multiply your sorrow and your conception. . . . Cursed is the ground for your sake; in toil you shall eat of it" (Genesis 3:16–17).

10. What are some examples of how being obedient to God might present a challenge in the following areas: your friendships, your dating relationships, your entertainment choices, your career path, your reputation, and your comfort zone?

_____

_____

_____

The LORD God said, "Behold, the man has become like one of Us, to know good and evil. And now, lest he put out his hand and take also of the tree of life, and eat, and live forever"—therefore the LORD God sent him out of the garden of Eden to till the ground from which he was taken. So He drove out the man (Genesis 3:22–24).

Satan often begins his temptations by questioning God's commands and suggesting obedience is not necessary. You do great harm to yourself when you believe you will find greater blessing in doing your own thing than in obeying God. Obedience always results in blessings.

Day 6: Confidence-Building Strategies

When God called out to Moses from a burning bush and said, "I will send you to Pharaoh that you may bring My people, the children of Israel, out of Egypt" (Exodus 3:10), Moses was understandably concerned that he was not up to the task. "Who am I that I should go to Pharaoh?" he asked (11). God had to build Moses' confidence by giving him the words to say and promising to be with Him. He does the same in your life.

The Bible provides you with many principles that will help you obey God with all your heart and give you confidence that you can always trust Him to keep His promises. For instance, Paul writes in Romans 8:28, "We know that all things work together for good to those who love God." When you trust God with your life, you can be certain that even when circumstances seem dire, *God is leading you and directing you*—and He will work things out for your good.

The Bible also tells you that "those who wait on the LORD shall renew their strength" (Isaiah 40:31). When in doubt, you can *choose to wait on God* for an answer to your problem. When you do, you can be confident that He will lead you in the best direction.

By faith [Moses] forsook Egypt, not fearing the wrath of the king; for he endured as seeing Him who is invisible (Hebrews 11:27).

God is always leading you and directing you.

When in doubt, choose to wait on God for an answer.

Meditating on Scripture will build your confidence in God.

Trials and challenges will build your confidence in God.

Trust in the LORD with all your heart, and lean not on your own understanding; in all your ways acknowledge Him, and He shall direct your paths. Do not be wise in your own eyes; fear the LORD with your possessions, and with the firstfruits of all your increase; so your barns will be filled with plenty, and your vats will overflow with new wine. My son, do not despise the chastening of the LORD, nor detest His correction; for whom the LORD loves He corrects, just as a father the son in whom he delights. Happy is the man who finds wisdom, and the man who gains understanding; for her proceeds are better than the profits of silver, and her gain than fine gold. She is more precious than rubies, and all the things you may desire cannot compare with her. Length of days is in her right hand, in her left hand riches and honor. Her ways are ways of pleasantness, and all her paths are peace. She is a tree of life to those who take hold of her, and happy are all who retain her (Proverbs 3:1–18).

Meditating on God's Word will also help build your confidence in Him. Joshua noted the importance of this when he said to the Israelites, "Meditate in [God's laws] day and night, that you may observe to do according to all that is written in it. For then you will make your way prosperous, and then you will have good success" (Joshua 1:8). When you saturate your mind with Scripture, you gain God's viewpoint and know right from wrong when temptation comes.

Even *times of trial and challenges can build your confidence* in God. When the people of Israel entered the Promised Land at God's direction, they had to face strong enemy opposition. God will rarely empty your life of trouble and conflict, for if He did, you would not have any reason to depend on Him. He allows enough difficulty to keep you turned toward Him.

11. Read Proverbs 3:1–18. How can you know when you are starting to "lean . . . on your own understanding" (5)? What steps can you take to "acknowledge" God instead (6)?

_____

_____

_____

_____

12. What does God promise when you choose to seek His wisdom, honor Him with your possessions, and yield to His correction (7–12)? How difficult or easy do you find this is to do in your life? Explain.

_____

_____

_____

_____

13. When was the last time you felt the Holy Spirit give you direction or wisdom in making a decision? What did you learn from the experience? What is the true value of such godly wisdom (13–18)?

_____

_____

_____

_____

14. What's the longest you've ever waited for direction from God in a certain situation or circumstance? What did you learn from the experience about yourself and about God?

_____

_____

_____

_____

15. If you were to make obeying God the number one priority in every area of your life, where do you think you would see the most opposition, conflict, or temptation? Explain.

_____

_____

_____

_____

"Behold, to obey is better than sacrifice, and to heed than the fat of rams" (1 Samuel 15:22).

In Exodus 3:14, God said His name is "I AM WHO I AM." This is also translated as, "I WILL ALWAYS BE WHO I HAVE ALWAYS BEEN." God never changes! He will be as faithful and loving to you as He was to Moses and the Israelites all those many years ago.

Living the Principle

How will you live out Life Principle 2 this week? Consider the challenges you may be facing as a result of your obedience to God. One strategy for successfully dealing with those challenges is to think of them as badges of honor for your faithfulness. Remember, if you're being targeted for standing with God, there's no better place in the world to be!

If you find that you are struggling with obedience in a certain area, ask yourself what God is leading you to do—and what is standing in your way. With the help of the Holy Spirit, weigh the pros and cons of obedience. Ask God to help you recognize the potential that lies in following His will. Ask Him to expose the consequences that cause you to fear as the ineffective threats that they really are. And ask Him to remind you of the promises He has made in the Bible to help you grow in confidence that His way is always the best way.

Life Lessons to Remember

❖ God wants you to trust Him with your life and all that concerns you (see Proverbs 3:5–6).
❖ At times you will need to wait on the Lord for an answer to your problem or situation (see Psalm 37:9).
❖ At other times you must be willing to endure conflict (see Matthew 5:10–12).

Notes AND Prayer Requests

USE THIS SPACE TO WRITE ANY KEY POINTS, QUESTIONS,
OR PRAYER REQUESTS FROM THIS WEEK'S STUDY.

God's Word Is an Immovable Anchor in Times of Storm

God is not a man, that He should lie, nor a son of man, that He should repent. Has He said, and will He not do? Or has He spoken, and will He not make it good?

NUMBERS 23:19

Life's Questions

If you've made the decision to seek an intimate relationship with God and obey Him no matter what, you will undoubtedly experience seasons of difficulty and uncertainty. Some challenges you will see coming long before they actually hit. Others will blindside you with the suddenness of a lightning strike. Some challenges that may seem manageable at first will later reveal themselves as much more difficult and serious than you imagined. Others have the potential to turn your life upside down immediately.

Your walk with God is a journey of faith, and there will be situations in which your trust in Him will be tested. If you've read the stories of Joseph, Job, and countless other heroes of the faith in the Bible, you know what a dark night of the soul looks like. Jesus Himself said, "In the world you will have tribulation." But He also added this promise: "Be of good cheer, I have overcome the world" (John 16:33).

What will you cling to when a deluge of trouble rains on your life and everything you know to be true seems to be swept away by winds of adversity? What will you hold on to when the waves of doubt threaten to crash down on you? Where can you find a firm foundation when everything around you is sinking? The answer is found in Life Principle 3: *God's Word is an immovable anchor in times of storm.*

PRINCIPLE IN ACTION
Ezra (Ezra 7:10)
Job (Job 10:12)
Jehoiakim
    (Jeremiah 36:20–32)
Habakkuk
    (Habakkuk 3:17–19)
Joshua the Priest
    (Zechariah 6:9–13)

We need to read the Bible daily to give our minds and hearts the spiritual nutrition they need to face life's daily demands.
—CHARLES F. STANLEY

Day 7: A Guidebook for Life's Journey

God knows when you need encouragement, guidance, and hope. After all, He created you and understands your inner workings better than you do. What's more, He is able to meet your every need. That's why He provides promises in His Word so you can understand His nature and trust Him. The more time you spend in Scripture—reading about people who claimed His promises, as well as those who rejected them—the stronger your bond with Him grows.

In emotionally devastating times, that bond may prove to be a lifeline and essential to your spiritual welfare. God's Word is therefore a compass, a guide, and an instruction book to life. Just as you use instruction manuals at work or in the kitchen, you can use God's Word as your resource for wisdom and truth. No one would think of baking a cake without a recipe, nor would a mechanic rebuild a car engine without a manual. Likewise, you shouldn't attempt to tackle the complexities of life without instructions from the One who makes each day possible.

As with most things, preparation is the key to success. A wise strategy is to familiarize yourself with God's Word before an emergency arises. Spend as much time as possible acquainting yourself with its stories, its promises, and its wisdom. The more time you spend in study, the better prepared you'll be to apply the wisdom of Scripture when you need it most.

1. Read Psalm 119:97-104. These words were written by King David, the only person God ever described as "a man after [His] own heart" (Acts 13:22). Based on David's words in these verses, how would you describe his heart?

   _____

   _____

   _____

   _____

   _____

2. David said he meditated on God's Word "all the day" (97). What do you think this looked like in his life? Is it still possible to meditate on God's Word continuously today—or was that something that could only be done in simpler times? Explain.

   _____

   _____

   _____

   _____

   _____

The more time you spend in Scripture, the stronger your bond with God grows.

Don't tackle life without instructions from the One who makes each day possible.

Oh, how I love Your law! It is my meditation all the day (Psalm 119:97).

3. In what ways is God's wisdom superior to the wisdom of this world (98)? How have you witnessed this in your own life?

_____

_____

_____

_____

4. When was a time that God's Word "restrained" you from following an evil way (101)? How did you know God was guiding you in that situation?

_____

_____

_____

_____

5. How has the Bible given you understanding (104)? What are you doing to gain more understanding from God's Word on a daily basis?

_____

_____

_____

You, through Your commandments, make me wiser than my enemies; for they are ever with me. I have more understanding than all my teachers, for Your testimonies are my meditation. I understand more than the ancients, because I keep Your precepts. I have restrained my feet from every evil way, that I may keep Your word. I have not departed from Your judgments, for You Yourself have taught me. How sweet are Your words to my taste, sweeter than honey to my mouth! Through Your precepts I get understanding; therefore I hate every false way (Psalm 119:98–104).

Left to ourselves, we often don't know which path leads to life and which ends in death. But through His Word, God sheds light on our situation and leads us to safety.

Day 8: The Value of a Discerning Eye

Discernment is the ability to decide between God's truth and the world's error. In your life as a believer, it is important for you to have discernment so you can understand God's Word and apply it in ways that honor Him. Reading the Bible is the first step in this process. The second step is to consider the *context* in which the passage was written by asking these questions:

❖ Who did God choose to write this particular passage?
❖ What were the historical circumstances of its writing?
❖ To whom was the passage written—and why?

Discernment is the ability to decide between God's truth and the world's error.

❖ What is the tone of the passage?

❖ How does it connect to the passages around it?

❖ How do respected Christian scholars and teachers interpret the passage?

❖ What relevance does the passage have for believers today?

You can't just name and claim promises in Scripture that look good to you.

It's important not to fall into the trap of lifting individual passages and verses out of context to serve your need in a particular situation. You cannot, for example, simply name and claim promises that look good to you. Some of God's promises are conditional; you have to meet certain criteria before you can claim them. And those promises that aren't conditional may be claimed only with prayer and an earnest desire to know God's will for your life.

While God wants you to experience His best, He also wants you to know Him and enjoy His presence in a personal way that expresses His sufficiency. In order to enjoy His presence fully, you need the assistance of the Holy Spirit. So, before you open God's Word, ask the Holy Spirit to guide your study and application. Claiming a promise from God's Word without guidance from the Holy Spirit will lead to disappointment, disillusionment, and frustration.

Ask the Holy Spirit to guide your study of God's Word.

6. Read Matthew 4:1–11. How did Jesus respond each time Satan tried to tempt Him (4, 7, 10)? What enabled Him to have these verses ready when needed (see Luke 2:46–49)?

_____

_____

_____

_____

_____

_____

Now when the tempter came to Him, he said, "If You are the Son of God, command that these stones become bread." But He answered and said, "It is written, 'Man shall not live by bread alone, but by every word that proceeds from the mouth of God.'" Then the devil took Him up into the holy city, set Him on the pinnacle of the temple, and said to Him, "If You are the Son of God, throw Yourself down. For it is written: 'He shall give His angels charge over you,' and 'In their hands they shall bear you up, Lest you dash your foot against a stone.'" Jesus said to him, "It is written again, 'You shall not tempt the LORD your God'" (Matthew 4:3–7).

7. Why do you think Satan chose to quote Scripture in his second attempt to tempt Christ (6)? How did Satan misuse this passage from Psalm 91:11–12?

_____

_____

_____

_____

8. What can you learn from Jesus' response to Satan's temptation (7)?

_____

_____

_____

_____

9. How have you learned to interpret, discern, and apply God's Word wisely?

_____

_____

_____

_____

10. Why are wisdom and discernment necessary when it comes to statements like these?

❖ "The Bible says God wants you to be rich."
❖ "The Bible says God wants you to be happy."
❖ "The Bible says God is punishing you if you're suffering."

_____

_____

_____

_____

Again, the devil took Him up on an exceedingly high mountain, and showed Him all the kingdoms of the world and their glory. And he said to Him, "All these things I will give You if You will fall down and worship me." Then Jesus said to him, "Away with you, Satan! For it is written 'You shall worship the LORD Your God, and Him only you shall serve.'" Then the devil left Him, and behold, angels came and ministered to Him (Matthew 4:8–11).

Jesus responded to each of Satan's three temptations by appealing to the unchanging Word of God. If we want to successfully overcome temptation, we must do the same.

Day 9: Firmly Anchored

At times, God will bring a specific Scripture to mind to deliver His hope and reassurance to your heart. At other times, He will challenge you to pray and seek His wisdom on a certain issue. When you look to God in faith, He will always lead you according to His will. This may not happen overnight. Many times, God will want you to meditate on a certain Scripture passage over a period of time before He gives His guidance.

In 1 Samuel 7:1–3, we read that when David wanted to build the temple for the Lord, he first expressed his desire to Nathan the prophet. David didn't order his men to begin construction but *waited* for God's leadership. And it was a good thing he did, because the Lord wanted David's son Solomon to do the job instead (see 1 Chronicles 28:6).

Later, after hearing God's words from Nathan, he "sat before the LORD" (1 Samuel 7:18). This means he spent time alone in God's presence, communicating with God from the depths of his heart, asking Him questions, and listening quietly for His answers. This was a pattern David developed throughout his life. Being a man after God's own heart,

God will always lead you according to *His* will.

In Your presence is fullness of joy; at Your right hand are pleasures forevermore (Psalm 16:11).

21

he sought to know the mind and heart of God so he could do what the Lord desired of him.

God honored David's attitude by giving him a wonderful promise: "Your house and your kingdom shall be established forever before you. Your throne shall be established forever" (2 Samuel 7:16). The Lord will likewise honor your desire to seek His guidance and wisdom. If you come to Him expecting Him to answer, He will never disappoint you. If you are true to His Word and understand it within its context, you will recognize how to apply God's principles and promises. You will find strength to cling to the Lord as an anchor during difficult times.

God will honor your desire to seek His wisdom.

Your word is a lamp to my feet and a light to my path. . . . I do not forget Your law. The wicked have laid a snare for me, yet I have not strayed from Your precepts. . . . You are my hiding place and my shield; I hope in Your word (Psalm 119:105, 109–110, 114).

11. Read Psalm 119:105–135. Nighttime travelers in David's day had no streetlights to illuminate their way, so they carried lanterns. These handheld lights helped travelers avoid making wrong turns and revealed potential dangers and obstacles in their path. Spiritually speaking, how does God's Word serve similar purposes (105, 130, 133)?

    _____

    _____

    _____

12. How does David say that he avoided the snare of the wicked (109–110)? How did he anchor his life in the Lord (114)?

    _____

    _____

    _____

I am Your servant; give me understanding, that I may know Your testimonies. . . . The entrance of Your words gives light; it gives understanding to the simple. . . . Direct my steps by Your word, and let no iniquity have dominion over me (Psalm 119:125, 130, 133).

13. When was a time in your life that God's Word revealed a path you should take or an obstacle you wouldn't have otherwise seen (125)? How did you act on that knowledge?

    _____

    _____

    _____

14. In what ways has the Word of God served as an anchor for your soul? How has God been your hiding place and your shield?

    _____

    _____

    _____

    _____

"This hope we have as an anchor of the soul, both sure and steadfast, and which enters the Presence behind the veil" (Hebrews 6:19).

15. In what ways are you "sitting before the Lord" as King David did? How has a daily Bible study routine, an active prayer life, an accountability group, or a plan for memorizing passages of Scripture helped to anchor you in your faith?

_____

_____

_____

> *You will seek Me and find Me, when you search for Me with all your heart* (Jeremiah 29:13).

Living the Principle

What storm are you currently facing? Is trouble striking you like a tidal wave? Are you finding yourself disheartened by your situation? If so, remember that God will never fail you, and He'll never change His mind about the promises He's made to you. So this week when the crises come—and they *will* come—lay your heart out to God and ask for His love and comfort. Ask Him to show you His will and lead you to His message of encouragement.

But don't stop there. Continue on by reading God's Word and meditating on it every day this week. A good place to start is the book of Psalms, or, if you're a new believer, the gospel of John. Ask godly friends what Scripture passages have been meaningful and inspiring to them. As you do this, the Lord will bring His Word to your mind at the moment you most need a reminder of His love and comfort. His Word will serve as an anchor of strength, guidance, and comfort to keep you steady when the waves of adversity rise. He will serve as a lamp to your feet and a light to your path.

How will you live out Life Principle 3 this week? Discuss with a trusted Christian friend some ways that you can keep God's Word as your anchor during difficult times. Talk about how the Bible has encouraged you and kept your focus on God in the past. Then spend time in prayer, asking God to draw you into intimate communion with Himself and to transform your life so you can grow closer to Him and affect the world for the sake of His kingdom.

> God will never fail you and never change His mind about the promises He's made.

Life Lessons to Remember

❖ God's promises are the anchors of your spiritual life (see Hebrews 6:18–20).
❖ God always fulfills the promises He makes (see Joshua 21:45).
❖ God will reward you as you patiently wait for Him to fulfill His promises (see Habakkuk 2:2–3).

Notes AND Prayer Requests

USE THIS SPACE TO WRITE ANY KEY POINTS, QUESTIONS,
OR PRAYER REQUESTS FROM THIS WEEK'S STUDY.

_____

_____

_____

_____

_____

_____

_____

_____

_____

_____

_____

_____

_____

_____

The Awareness of God's Presence Energizes You for Your Work

My elect shall long enjoy the work of their hands.
They shall not labor in vain.

ISAIAH 65:22-23

Life's Questions

In the book of Ecclesiastes, Solomon writes, "Nothing is better for a man than that . . . his soul should enjoy good in his labor. This also, I saw, was from the hand of God" (2:24). This may be a challenging verse for you, especially if your profession fails to fully engage you, fulfill you, or use your skills. You may do an enormous amount of work and receive little compensation and acknowledgment in return. Or maybe you're a caregiver to your children, spouse, or aging parents, and you do an immense amount of work that is sometimes thankless and exhausting.

Even if you really like your job, you may not always find it enjoyable because every occupation brings with it certain difficulties and frustrations. Likewise, you may not always recognize God's hand in what you are doing or appreciate the work deep down in your soul. You may feel like crying out, as Solomon himself once did, "Meaningless! Meaningless . . . Utterly meaningless! Everything is meaningless" (Ecclesiastes 1:2 NIV).

So, how *do* you feel about the work you do? Is it your dream job or just something that pays the bills? Whatever your situation may be, God expects you to do your best at whatever you do. But how can you stay motivated and honor God in your labors when people, politics, and other problems cause you distress? Life Principle 4 provides the answer and gives you this encouragement: *The awareness of God's presence energizes you for your work.*

PRINCIPLE IN ACTION
Joseph (Genesis 39:1–6)
Micaiah (2 Chronicles 18)
Israelites (Haggai 2:4)
Zacchaeus (Luke 19:1–10)
Luke (2 Timothy 4:11)

Servanthood is to be our attitude and our motivation as we follow Christ Jesus our Lord.

—CHARLES F. STANLEY

Day 10: The Power of Servanthood

If your goal is to get the most out of your work—to embrace its potential to bring you closer to God and make an impact on others—then your first step is to follow Jesus' lead and view yourself as a servant. Jesus came to earth not to be served but to serve, and He instructed everyone who calls Him "Lord" to adopt the same attitude. He said that whoever desires to be great must be a servant, and He modeled this lifestyle to His disciples (see Matthew 20:25–28).

The apostle Paul later instructed, "Bondservants, obey in all things your masters according to the flesh, not with eye-service, as men-pleasers, but in sincerity of heart, fearing God" (Colossians 3:22). Paul instructed servants to do their work heartily, even though they received no paycheck for their efforts. Given this, how much more powerfully should his words resonate for those who get paid to work?

Many people would argue they are not compensated adequately for their work. Some may try to even the score by taking longer lunch hours, clocking out early, or coming in late. But this is not the approach God has in mind. If you are compensated for eight hours of work, you need to give your employer eight full hours. You are a servant of God, and as His representative, you have a responsibility to do quality, conscientious work.

The best pathway to promotion is servanthood. Whoever wants to be a leader must adopt an attitude of humility (see Mark 9:35). Never doubt the impact of a humble spirit and eager-to-work attitude on everyone around you—the boss included!

As God's representative, you have a responsibility to do quality work.

The LORD was with Joseph, and he was a successful man; and he was in the house of his master the Egyptian. And his master saw that the LORD was with him and that the LORD made all he did to prosper in his hand (Genesis 39:2–3).

1. Read Genesis 39. Joseph had been the favorite son of a wealthy patriarch, but due to the treachery of his brothers, he was now working as a lowly servant in a foreign country. How did Joseph respond to this change in his situation (2–3)?

_____

_____

_____

_____

_____

So it was, from the time that he had made him overseer of his house and all that he had, that the LORD blessed the Egyptian's house for Joseph's sake; and the blessing of the LORD was on all that he had in the house and in the field (Genesis 39:5).

2. What was the result of Joseph's diligence (4–6)? How might he have demonstrated his character and potential in the way he went about his work?

_____

_____

_____

_____

3. The Bible says "the LORD was with Joseph" during this time (2), but this doesn't mean that he didn't face adversity. What happened to Joseph because he chose not to betray his master (8, 19–20)? What does this tell you about what you might face when you choose to do your work for God and bring honor to Him?

_____

_____

_____

_____

4. How do you approach a job that—on the surface—appears to be "beneath" you? What lessons can you learn from Joseph's example?

_____

_____

_____

_____

5. What are some recent opportunities you've had to demonstrate your character and potential in your workplace? What were the results?

_____

_____

_____

_____

But he refused and said to his master's wife, "Look, my master does not know what is with me in the house, and he has committed all that he has to my hand. . . . So it was, when his master heard the words which his wife spoke to him, saying, "Your servant did to me after this manner," that his anger was aroused. Then Joseph's master took him and put him into the prison, a place where the king's prisoners were confined. And he was there in the prison (Genesis 39:8, 19–20).

Joseph spent at least a decade in prison, but none of it was wasted time. God used that invaluable experience to teach him the principles that he would need when governing Egypt and to position him for maximum impact and blessing.

Day 11: Who's the Boss?

Your second step in getting the most out of your work is to recognize that you ultimately work for the Lord Himself. Your employer may exercise supervisory authority over you, but Jesus Christ is your Lord. You labor for Him. As Paul wrote, "Whatever you do, do it heartily, as to the Lord and not to men, knowing that from the Lord you will receive the reward of the inheritance; for you serve the Lord Christ" (Colossians 3:23).

If you're a Christian, Jesus is your supervisor. For that reason, you have a responsibility to give a full day's labor, regardless of your feelings

Ultimately, you work for the Lord Himself.

toward the people who sign your paycheck. One of the mistakes people often make in their approach to work is to try to "segment" life. They think of Monday through Friday as workdays, Saturday as a play day, and Sunday as a day of worship. But God did not design life in this manner. If Jesus Christ is your Savior, you can't exclude Him from *any* part of your life.

In other words, it isn't right to teach a Sunday school class with everything you have and then meander into your job halfheartedly the rest of the week. Jesus wants you to honor and glorify Him in everything you do. Likewise, ministry isn't just what you do at church. You worship God every day of the week. On Sunday, you do it in church, while on Monday through Friday you worship with the quality of your work.

Do you have a good testimony for the Lord in the marketplace? Are you an exemplary employee because you serve God? Does your attitude reflect the joy you have in considering Jesus as your true CEO? How is the awareness of God's presence energizing your work?

> *Jesus wants you to honor and glorify Him in everything you do.*

6. Read Genesis 40. At this point, Joseph had been demoted from servant to prisoner. Whatever career arc he may have envisioned for himself had now been destroyed. He had no friends who could help him, no recourse in the Egyptian legal system, and no reason to believe he would ever be a free man again (1–3). What thoughts do you suppose were going through his head at this time?

> *It came to pass after these things that the butler and the baker of the king of Egypt offended their lord, the king of Egypt. And Pharaoh was angry with his two officers, the chief butler and the chief baker. So he put them in custody in the house of the captain of the guard, in the prison, the place where Joseph was confined. And the captain of the guard charged Joseph with them, and he served them; so they were in custody for a while (Genesis 40:1–4).*

_____
_____
_____
_____

7. In spite of this setback, how did Joseph demonstrate that he still viewed God as his boss? In what ways do you think his work ethic made an impact on his fellow prisoners and on his jailer (4)?

_____
_____
_____
_____

> *They said to him, "We each have had a dream, and there is no interpreter of it." So Joseph said to them, "Do not interpretations belong to God? Tell them to me, please" (Genesis 40:8).*

8. As the story progresses, we see that Joseph did not give in to despair but chose to embrace the challenges before him. What did he offer to do for the butler and the baker (8)? Why do you think he chose to do this for the two men?

_____
_____
_____
_____

9. What request did Joseph make for his act of service (14)? What was the result (23)?

_____

_____

_____

_____

Remember me when it is well with you, and please show kindness to me; make mention of me to Pharaoh, and get me out of this house. . . . Yet the chief butler did not remember Joseph, but forgot him (Genesis 40:14, 23).

10. How do you handle these types of repeated setbacks in your work? What can you learn from Joseph about being effective and making a difference, even under the most difficult of circumstances?

_____

_____

_____

_____

Joseph was faithful, and it cost him greatly. Yet God did not forget Joseph's obedience.

Day 12: Deferred Benefits

Your third step in coming to grips with the role of work in your life is to recognize that your pay comes both now and in the hereafter. The truth of this statement can be a tough sell in the culture of instant gratification in which you live. The world will tell you that you deserve to get what is coming to you in a timely and fair manner.

Certainly, there is a reason to concern yourself with the amount of financial compensation you receive for your labor. You have household expenses that must be paid. You have budgets that must be met. You have savings and investment responsibilities that cannot be ignored. You will find, however, that even if you have done your very best and given all you have, you will never really get paid all you are worth. Your value as an employee cannot be accurately measured . . . let alone compensated.

That's when you must look to the hereafter. The apostle Paul wrote, "From the Lord you will receive the reward of the inheritance" (Colossians 3:24). No one's pockets are as deep as God's. He sees not just the hours you put in but also the heart, soul, and determination you pour into your work. He sees every time you go above and beyond the call of duty. He sees the difference you make in the lives of your clients and coworkers.

Your pay comes both now and in the hereafter.

No one's pockets are as deep as God's.

God knows exactly what you are worth and will reward you far beyond measure—and certainly beyond what any human employer ever could. That's a promise you can trust forever.

11. Read Genesis 41. Two years passed before the king's butler finally remembered Joseph (9–13). For two full years Joseph remained in prison, managing the day-to-day events of his fellow prisoners. What does this tell you about God's plans and His timing?

_____

_____

_____

"Now there was a young Hebrew man with us there, a servant of the captain of the guard. And we told him, and he interpreted our dreams for us. . . . And it came to pass" (Genesis 41:12–13).

12. How did Joseph respond when he was summoned from prison to appear before the king of Egypt (16)? Why do you think he was able to demonstrate such confidence?

_____

_____

_____

Joseph answered Pharaoh, saying, "It is not in me; God will give Pharaoh an answer of peace" (Genesis 41:16).

13. How did Joseph's experiences as a servant and prisoner prepare him for the appointment the king gave him as second-in-command of Egypt (37–41)?

_____

_____

_____

Then Pharaoh said to Joseph, "Inasmuch as God has shown you all this, there is no one as discerning and wise as you. You shall be over my house, and all my people shall be ruled according to your word" (Genesis 41:39–40).

14. What was the end result of Joseph's faithfulness to the Lord (54–57)? How did God use him to save many lives, not only in Egypt, but also in the surrounding region?

_____

_____

_____

The famine was over all the face of the earth, and Joseph opened all the storehouses and sold to the Egyptians. And the famine became sever in the land of Egypt. So all countries came to Joseph in Egypt to buy grain, because the famine was severe in all lands (Genesis 41:56–57).

15. When you look at God's perfect plan for Joseph—how his challenges, trials, and suffering ultimately put him in a position to do extraordinary things on God's behalf—what lessons can you apply to your own life? What might your challenges, trials, and suffering be preparing you to do?

_____

_____

_____

_____

If you are giving your best effort at work and are trusting God to give you wisdom in all of your endeavors, then watch for the ways in which the Lord will cause others to bless you.

Living the Principle

The story of Joseph reveals how you can stay motivated and honor God in your work. Joseph did this by remembering God was with him, no matter what happened. He set his heart to serve God faithfully, whether he was in the prison or the palace, and regardless of whether he was experiencing famine or fruitfulness. The same should be true for you.

Like Joseph, you may not know why God has allowed the difficulties you face in your labors. It's possible you have a certain goal in mind with regard to your profession. But it's also possible—even likely—that God's plan for you is much greater than you have for yourself. Like Joseph, you might not be able to see that plan at the time, but you must continue to obey God nonetheless and never lose heart (see Galatians 6:9).

Whether it's a battle with an enemy, an overwhelming challenge, or a personal crisis that appears impossible to overcome, remember that God is with you. He is your energy, your strength, your wisdom, and your creativity. He is also your boss. So do your very best for His sake and allow Him to work through you. He's got a great victory and a wonderful reward in store for you if you'll trust Him and do as He says.

How will you live out Life Principle 4 this week? Begin by identifying one area of your work in which you struggle—whether it involves your attitude, your integrity, your motivation, or your interaction with a coworker. Brainstorm three specific steps you can take to improve in that area and keep your mind focused on God's presence. Ask God to help you grow as a servant in your work, honor Him with what you do, and always view Him as your boss.

God was with [Joseph] and delivered him out of all his troubles, and gave him favor and wisdom in the presence of Pharaoh, king of Egypt (Acts 7:9).

Life Lessons to Remember

❖ You are a servant and should view yourself that way (see Philippians 2:5–7).
❖ You ultimately work for the Lord Himself (see Ephesians 2:10).
❖ Your pay comes both now and in the hereafter (see 1 Corinthians 3:13–14).

Notes AND Prayer Requests

USE THIS SPACE TO WRITE ANY KEY POINTS, QUESTIONS,
OR PRAYER REQUESTS FROM THIS WEEK'S STUDY.

_____

_____

_____

_____

_____

_____

_____

_____

_____

_____

_____

_____

_____

_____

_____

_____

God Does Not Require You to Understand His Will, Just Obey It, Even If It Seems Unreasonable

You shall walk in all the ways which the LORD your God has commanded you, that you may live and that it may be well with you, and that you may prolong your days in the land which you shall possess.

DEUTERONOMY 5:33

Life's Questions

Are things in your life not going the way you planned? Do you feel out of step with your heavenly Father? Is it difficult for you to understand what went wrong in a particular situation or why God doesn't seem to be blessing you? If so, it may be time for a careful self-evaluation.

Sometimes, it may feel as if God is no longer working in your life because you've insisted on doing things your way instead of His way. Perhaps you've placed a condition on God, and you'll only obey Him when you think His instructions are logical. What this really means is you've failed to commit yourself to Him completely and failed to trust in His will with your whole heart. This is bound to cause frustration in your life.

Or perhaps you are hesitant to obey God because He's commanded you to do something you're not comfortable doing or that you think is irrational. As a result, your prayers seem to be going unanswered, and the path ahead appears to be blocked. In such cases, it could be that

PRINCIPLE IN ACTION
Gideon (Judges 6:36–40)
Jonah (Jonah 3:3)
Jeremiah (Jeremiah 13:1)
Simeon (Luke 2:25–35)
Simon (Luke 5:5–11)

When we honor and obey God in a situation, He works to bring our emotions in line with our faith.

—CHARLES F. STANLEY

God is waiting for you to take the step of faith that He's commanded you to take. He may be asking you to embrace Life Principle 5: *God does not require you to understand His will, just obey it, even if it seems unreasonable.*

Day 13: Putting the "I" in Obedience

Gauging your level of obedience to God can be a difficult task. Unless you're in close contact with Him, you may not be aware of certain areas of disobedience in your life. This may explain why God doesn't answer your prayers or why, despite all your best efforts, the circumstances of your life are still not working out.

Any area of disobedience in your life needs to be addressed because such sin will prevent you from experiencing God's best. Perhaps God has asked something of you and, in response, you have either ignored His words or done only part of what He asked. True obedience to God means doing what He says, when He says it, how He says it should be done, and as long as He says to do it. It means doing what God says, regardless of whether or not you understand the reasons for it—until His will has been accomplished.

Now, before you try to make a list of everything God has ever asked you to do or not do, consider this: *Is there one particular area of your life in which you struggle to obey the Lord? As you read Scripture, does He continually bring a specific sin to mind? When you go to Him in prayer, does the same issue surface repeatedly?* If the Lord is bringing something to your mind right now, it could be that you have been living in the same uncomfortable situation for years because at some point, you chose to do things your way instead of His way.

You may not be aware of certain areas of disobedience in your life.

True obedience is doing what God says, regardless of you understanding the reasons.

1. Read Luke 5:1–11. What were the fishermen in this story doing when Jesus approached them (2)? How does Simon (Peter) describe their situation (5)?

   _____

   _____

   _____

   _____

[Jesus] saw two boats standing by the lake; but the fishermen had gone from them and were washing their nets. . . . [Peter] said to Him, "Master, we have toiled all night and caught nothing" (Luke 5:2, 5).

2. What unusual request did Jesus make (4)? How did Peter respond? Why do you think Peter was willing to obey Christ in this matter?

   _____

   _____

   _____

   _____

[Jesus said], "Launch out into the deep and let down your nets for a catch" (Luke 2:4).

3. What was the result of the fishermen following Jesus' instructions (6–7)? What did this reveal to Peter and the others (8–9)?

_____

_____

_____

_____

4. It is interesting to note that Jesus could have approached the men before they went out in the evening. Why do you suppose He waited until their own efforts had failed?

_____

_____

_____

_____

5. What does this story tell you about the kinds of requests God will make of you? When is a time in your life that God worked in such unpredictable ways?

_____

_____

_____

_____

When they had done this, they caught a great number of fish, and their net was breaking. So they signaled to their partners in the other boat to come and help them. And they came and filled both the boats, so that they began to sink. When Simon Peter saw it, he fell down at Jesus' knees, saying, "Depart from me, for I am a sinful man, O Lord!" For he and all who were with him were astonished at the catch of fish which they had taken (Luke 5:6–9).

---

*True obedience means doing what God says,
when He says it, how He says it should be done,
until what He says is accomplished—
whether you understand the reasons for it or not.*

Day 14: Preparing for Rain While the Sun's Shining

Following God's will instead of your own will make a tremendous difference in your life, which is why you must make obedience to Him your top priority. But to do so, you need to understand why submission plays such an important role in your relationship with God. An excellent biblical example to illustrate this point is Noah. God called Noah to build an enormous ark, which was a request that must have seemed both impossible and illogical to him. Yet Noah complied without asking questions (see Genesis 6–9).

Obedience to God must be your top priority.

Obeying God will not always be a popular decision.

Obeying God will not always be a popular decision. People will criticize you. They will laugh at you. But think about this: *Noah chose to walk with God in the midst of a corrupt society.* In fact, the world had grown so wicked that God determined to destroy every living human being on the face of the earth, with the exception of one family—Noah's. We can only imagine what those evil people must have said to Noah as they watched him day after day. As Jesus said, "They were eating and drinking, marrying and giving in marriage, until the day that Noah entered the ark" (Matthew 24:38).

Soon after the raindrops started falling, all the mocking stopped. Noah had obeyed God in spite of what other people thought of him, and the Lord had spared him from the great flood that covered the earth. If Noah had listened to his critics, he would not have built the ark, and he would have been swept away with everyone else. Instead, he chose to obey God.

The word of the LORD came to Elijah . . . saying, "Go, present yourself to Ahab, and I will send rain on the earth." So Elijah went to present himself to Ahab; and there was a severe famine in Samaria (1 Kings 18:1–2).

6. Read 1 Kings 18. What was the situation in Israel as this story opens (1)? What did God tell Elijah to do? How did Elijah respond (2)?

_____

_____

_____

_____

*"As the LORD your God lives, there is no nation or kingdom where my master has not sent someone to hunt for you"
(1 Kings 18:10).*

7. Why would it have been difficult for Elijah to obey this command (10)?

_____

_____

_____

_____

*Elijah said to Ahab, "Go up, eat and drink; for there is the sound of abundance of rain." . . . Then it came to pass the seventh time, that he said, "There is a cloud, as small as a man's hand, rising out of the sea!" So he said, "Go up, say to Ahab, 'Prepare your chariot, and go down before the rain stops you'"
(1 Kings 18:41–44).*

8. As a result of Elijah's obedience, the Lord brought a great victory against the prophets of Baal (20–40). What did Elijah instruct Ahab to do next (41)? What sign was there that God was bringing an end to the drought (43)?

_____

_____

_____

_____

9. What did Elijah do as soon as his servant saw a small cloud in the sky (44)? How does this demonstrate Elijah's faith in God?

_____

_____

_____

_____

10. How did Elijah prepare for rain while the sun was still shining? What does this story tell you about your need to obey God, even when there is no evidence that what He promises is going to come to pass?

_____

_____

_____

_____

_____

_____

Now it happened in the meantime that the sky became black with clouds and wind, and there was a heavy rain (1 Kings 18:45).

It had not rained for three years, yet Elijah was absolutely certain the Lord would honor the promise He had given him. You must likewise not grow impatient in prayer. You should keep asking, seeking, and knocking, knowing God will answer you (see Luke 11:9–10).

Day 15: Bracing for the Impact

When you choose the path of obedience, you must be prepared for the negative responses you will undoubtedly receive. You must remind yourself that God has an excellent reason for His instructions and will help you in extraordinary ways. You must never focus on the things or the people who try to distract you from doing God's will but rely on the Holy Spirit, who enables you to obey God's commandments and directs you in how to walk in His ways.

As the stories of Noah, Joseph, Elijah, and others reveal, whatever God requires of you—whether it be painful or joyful, profitable or costly, reasonable or peculiar—He will give you the ability and strength to be faithful. Even when it seems as if God is calling you to step into an impossible situation, He will always provide a way out. Often, He will use such situations to increase your trust and obedience in Him. In this way, He shapes you into the person He wants you to be so you can achieve the things He has so wonderfully prepared for you.

With the help of the Holy Spirit, you *can* walk obediently before the Lord in His strength and His power. So choose to obey Him, even if you don't understand why He is asking you to do something. Walk boldly in faith, even if you feel you are bracing for an impact, and trust His instructions are for your good (see Jeremiah 29:11). That way, as you become the person He wants you to be, you will also bear the fruit He wants you to bear.

Be prepared for negative responses when you choose the path of obedience.

God will always provide a way out.

[They] laid their hands on the apostles and put them in the common prison (Acts 5:18).

When they heard that, they entered the temple early in the morning and taught (Acts 5:21).

Then the captain went with the officers and brought them without violence, for they feared the people, lest they should be stoned. And when they had brought them, they set them before the council. And the high priest asked them, saying, "Did we not strictly command you not to teach in this name? And look, you have filled Jerusalem with your doctrine, and intend to bring this Man's blood on us!" But Peter and the other apostles answered and said: "We ought to obey God rather than men" (Acts 5:26–29).

11. Read Acts 5:12–33. What caused the Jewish religious leaders to be filled with indignation toward the apostles (12–16)? What did they do as a result (18)?

_____

_____

_____

12. At night, an angel of the Lord opened the prison and freed the apostles. What instruction did he then give to them (20)? How did they respond (21)?

_____

_____

_____

13. In what ways did obeying this instruction require the apostles to brace for the negative impact they knew would be coming? How did this come to pass (26–33)?

_____

_____

_____

14. What is an example of something God is calling you to do that makes you feel uncomfortable? What can you learn about God's faithfulness from this story?

_____

_____

_____

15. If all acts of obedience to God resulted in immediate and obvious rewards, the world likely would be a much more obedient place. But that's not the case. Obedience to God is always rewarded—but not always immediately and not always obviously. What are some of the longer-term and less dramatic rewards for obeying God?

_____

_____

_____

_____

The Bible consistently recognizes that when people try to disgrace you because you confess Christ, you are receiving one of the greatest possible blessings—you have been given the privilege of identifying with your Savior.

Living the Principle

What has God called you to do? Do His instructions seem extreme or confusing? Has He challenged you to do something you don't feel capable of doing? Remember, it is not your job to understand God's plan, just to obey Him. God sees the beginning, middle, and end of your situation, and His perspective is far more complete than yours. If you could just see things from His point of view, you would be highly motivated to obey Him.

Unfortunately, if you disobey God, you will continue to struggle in the same area repeatedly, and you will lose out on His blessings. God's goal is to grow your trust in Him, so He will give you assignments that test your heart and mature your faith. The good news is that when you submit to God, He shows you His faithfulness and empowers you to do everything He calls you to do. Your obedience—even though you might not always understand what He is doing—exercises your faith and makes it stronger.

How will you live out Life Principle 5 this week? Think of something specific you believe God has been calling you to do—or perhaps an area of your life that He wants you to turn over to Him. Spend some time in prayer, talking to Him about your concerns. Be honest about your fears and reluctance. Ask Him to strengthen your resolve and help you embrace the risks that come with obeying Him. Understand the goal isn't to comprehend God's will but to step forward in obedience. Then, after you pray, take that step. What that looks like will depend on what God is calling you to—but it should be bold, take you out of your comfort zone, and bring you measurably closer to God's will for your life.

> *"I am the Alpha and the Omega, the Beginning and the End," says the Lord, "who is and who was and who is to come, the Almighty" (Revelation 1:8).*

Life Lessons to Remember

❖ Obedience must be the top priority of your life (see Psalm 119:145).
❖ The Holy Spirit enables you to walk obediently before God (see John 14:26).
❖ Obedience produces desirable fruit in your life (see Jeremiah 29:11).

One of the main reasons people doubt is because they lack understanding that God is with them always. Anytime you experience momentary doubt, get on your knees, open your Bible, and begin to read God's Word.

Notes AND Prayer Requests

USE THIS SPACE TO WRITE ANY KEY POINTS, QUESTIONS,
OR PRAYER REQUESTS FROM THIS WEEK'S STUDY.

You Reap What You Sow, More Than You Sow, and Later Than You Sow

You have not obeyed My voice. Why have you done this?
Therefore . . . 'I will not drive them out before you;
but they shall be thorns in your side,
and their gods shall be a snare to you.'"

JUDGES 2:2–3

Life's Questions

When you think of how farmers operate, Life Principle 6 makes perfect sense: *You reap what you sow, more than you sow, and later than you sow.* Picture a farmer at the start of the growing season, plowing his field to get it ready for that year's crops. Whatever seed the farmer plants is what the field will produce. If he plants tomato seeds, he will grow tomatoes. If he plants pumpkin seeds, he will grow pumpkins. He will always harvest the product of the kind of seed that he has planted.

The farmer will always take more from the ground than he put into it. The tiny seed he planted in the spring will sprout and become a plant that produces fruit in the fall, which will then yield many more seeds for the next years' harvests. Of course, this is not an instantaneous process. The farmer must wait for the crop to mature in its time. He must be patient and care for the seeds he has planted in the earth. It is a long process that takes months, but the farmer knows the rewards of the harvest always come later than the initial investment.

What seeds are you planting? What would you like to accomplish with your life? Those questions are inevitably linked. Every decision you make, every word you speak, every temptation you resist, every urge you

PRINCIPLE IN ACTION
Adam and Eve
  (Genesis 3:15–19)
Naomi (Ruth 1:16–17)
David (1 Samuel: 17:48–51)
Nebuchadnezzar
  (Daniel 4:30–37)
Tychicus (Ephesians 6:21)

We cannot sow disobedience to God and expect to reap His blessing. What we sow, we reap.
—CHARLES F. STANLEY

give in to, every thought you express, and every opinion you allow to flourish sows a seed. For this reason, it's important to be conscious of what you are sowing with your thoughts, words, and actions, because they set the direction of your life.

Day 16: Plant the Seeds for Tomorrow

What you are today is the result of your thinking and the way you lived in the past. If you foster a strong work ethic when you are young, it prepares you to take on the responsibilities of a career when you grow older. If you make wise decisions today, it gives you the ability to continue making God-honoring decisions in the future.

This is true even with your finances. If you save and invest wisely today, you will have plenty for tomorrow. But if you spend everything you have today, you will have little or nothing to show for your efforts in the future. Shortsighted people are like the servant in Jesus' parable of the talents who buried his money in the ground (see Matthew 25:14–30). Unlike the master's first two servants, this man sowed nothing for the future. The master had only this to say to him: "You wicked and lazy servant . . . you ought to have deposited my money with the bankers, and at my coming I would have received back my own with interest" (verses 26–27).

The lesson of reaping what you sow is a difficult one for many to comprehend. Even God's chosen people, the nation of Israel, struggled with the concept. Their waywardness and failure to do what God instructed them to do often placed them in the position of forfeiting His blessings. Their never-ending cycle of sowing obedience and reaping blessing, and then sowing disobedience and reaping punishment, would be comical if it weren't so tragic.

The good news for believers today is that the Lord offers clear, concise, and practical principles in Scripture to serve as warnings and encouragement regarding sowing and reaping.

1. Read Galatians 6:6–10. Paul says, "Do not be deceived" (7). How are people often deceived into thinking they won't reap what they sow?

_____

_____

_____

_____

_____

_____

_____

Making wise decisions today enables you to make wise decisions tomorrow.

Failure to follow God's instructions can lead to forfeiting His blessings.

Let him who is taught the word share in all good things with him who teaches. Do not be deceived, God is not mocked; for whatever a man sows, that he will also reap (Galatians 6:6–7).

2. Why does it seem so much easier to sow in the flesh than "to the Spirit" (8)?

_____

_____

_____

_____

_____

For he who sows to his flesh will of the flesh reap corruption, but he who sows to the Spirit will of the Spirit reap everlasting life. And let us not grow weary while doing good, for in due season we shall reap if we do not lose heart. Therefore, as we have opportunity, let us do good to all, especially to those who are of the household of faith (Galatians 6:8–10).

3. What does it mean to not "grow weary while doing good" (9)? What do good works and acts of service to others have to do with sowing and reaping?

_____

_____

_____

_____

_____

_____

_____

4. What opportunities have you had this week to "do good" to others—to sow to the Spirit (10)? How many of those opportunities did you pursue? Explain.

_____

_____

_____

_____

_____

_____

_____

5. As you look at your life today, what type of "seeds" are you sowing for the future?

_____

_____

_____

_____

_____

Sow for yourselves righteousness; reap in mercy; break up your fallow ground, for it is time to seek the Lord, till He comes and rains righteousness on you (Hosea 10:12).

It's a dangerous thing to think, God won't mind. He does mind when you disobey. You may not immediately see the consequences of your actions, but they are coming.

Day 17: A Universal Truth

The principle of reaping what you sow, more than you sow, and later than you sow, applies to everyone—both Christians and non-Christians. It is a law of life. Notice what Paul says in Galatians 6:7: "Do not be deceived, God is not mocked." This is the root cause of the careless and indulgent lifestyle of many people: They are deceived. People who reject the notion either do not believe the truth or think they will somehow be the exceptions to God's laws.

To *mock God* is to turn up one's nose at Him and hope to outwit Him. It is a foolish thought because, as Paul explains in 2 Corinthians 5:10, "We must all appear before the judgment seat of Christ, that each one may receive the things done in the body, according to what he has done, whether good or bad." The author of Hebrews adds, "It is appointed for [all] men to die once, but after this the judgment" (9:27).

The fact that you reap what you sow is good news if you sow good habits, but it's a frightening thought if you are currently involved in ungodly activities. Just as you cannot sow crabgrass and expect to reap pineapples, you cannot sow disobedience and expect to reap God's blessings. So do not be deceived: You *will* reap the harvest of your life.

6. Read Hosea 8. How would you describe the relationship between God and the people of Israel based on this passage?

_____

_____

_____

_____

7. What specific actions had the people of Israel sown that had aroused God's anger (4–5)?

_____

_____

_____

_____

8. What does God mean when He says of His people, "They sow the wind, and reap the whirlwind" (7)?

_____

_____

_____

_____

The principle of sowing and reaping is a law of life.

You cannot sow disobedience and expect blessings.

"They set up kings, but not by Me; they made princes, but I did not acknowledge them. From their silver and gold they made idols for themselves—that they might be cut off. Your calf is rejected, O Samaria! My anger is aroused against them—how long until they attain to innocence? For from Israel is even this: a workman made it, and it is not God; but the calf of Samaria shall be broken to pieces. They sow the wind, and reap the whirlwind. The stalk has no bud; it shall never produce meal. If it should produce, aliens would swallow it up" (Hosea 8:4–7).

9. What did God say would be the result of what the Israelites had reaped (14)?

_____

_____

_____

_____

_____

10. The Israelites had a long history of reaping what they sowed. When they sowed faithfulness and obedience to God, they reaped blessings. When they sowed idolatry and disobedience, they reaped judgment. Why do you think it is so difficult for each generation to learn the lessons of the past?

_____

_____

_____

_____

When Israel chose her kings without the Lord's guidance, they ultimately regretted it. God wants to be intimately involved in all the details of our lives, especially in the major decisions that shape our futures.

Day 18: The Coming Yield

Farmers plant seed because they expect to harvest a great deal more than they sow. A single seed can yield dozens and even hundreds of seeds. It is the same way with righteousness and sin. A small decision to do either *good* or *bad* reaps a much bigger crop . . . for either joy or sorrow. As Jesus illustrated in the parable of the soils, when you allow God's Word to produce good things in you, the results multiply: "He who received seed on the good ground is he who hears the word and understands it, who indeed bears fruit and produces: some a hundredfold, some sixty, some thirty" (Matthew 13:23).

As a follower of Christ, you may become discouraged when the present seed you are sowing does not appear to be producing an immediate crop. Maybe, for example, you have been sharing the gospel with a loved one and praying for him or her to come to Christ. You have been waiting for the seeds you have sown to come to harvest . . . but nothing

"Ephraim has made many altars for sin, they have become for him altars for sinning. I have written for him the great things of My law, but they were considered a strange thing. For the sacrifices of My offerings they sacrifice flesh and eat it, but the Lord does not accept them. Now He will remember their iniquity and punish their sins. They shall return to Egypt. For Israel has forgotten his Maker, and has built temples; Judah also has multiplied fortified cities; but I will send fire upon his cities, and it shall devour his palaces" (Hosea 8:11–14).

A small decision to do good or bad reaps a bigger crop.

has happened. What you must remember is that unlike the crops of the field, which get harvested at the same time each year, there is no timetable for the harvest of life.

The truth is that some crops are reaped quickly, while others take time. The harvest season will come, but it will be according to God's timetable. So let Paul's words in Galatians 6:7, "Whatever a man sows, that he will also reap," be a comfort and assurance to you today as you faithfully labor to sow godly seeds. Know that your faithfulness *will* produce a rich harvest in the future, for your heavenly Father always keeps His promises.

The harvest will come according to God's timetable.

11. Read Matthew 25:31–40. To what is Jesus referring when He says He will "sit on the throne of His glory" (31)? What event does He mean?

_____

_____

_____

_____

"All the nations will be gathered before Him, and He will separate them one from another, as a shepherd divides his sheep from the goats. And He will set the sheep on His right hand, but the goats on the left. Then the King will say to those on His right hand, 'Come, you blessed of My Father, inherit the kingdom prepared for you from the foundations of the world'"
(Matthew 25:32–34).

12. What do the *sheep* and the *goats* represent in this parable (33–34)?

_____

_____

_____

_____

13. What does Jesus say to those on His right (34–36)? What is their response (37–39)?

_____

_____

_____

_____

"Then the righteous will answer Him, saying, 'Lord, when did we see You hungry and feed You, or thirsty and give You drink? When did we see You a stranger and take You in, or naked and clothe You? Or when did we see You sick, or in prison, and come to You' And the King will answer and say to them, 'Assuredly, I say to you, inasmuch as you did it to one of the least of these My brethren, you did it to Me'"
(Matthew 25:37–40).

14. In what ways did this group sow good seed (40)?

_____

_____

_____

15. What does this parable tell you about the godly seeds you sow in your life? Why is it important to continue serving God, even if you don't see the results?

_____

_____

_____

_____

What you do with the good news of Jesus has enormous consequences because the punishment of those who reject Jesus is just as eternal as the reward of those who serve Him.

Living the Principle

Do you seek God's leadership when you make a decision? Do you obey Him as soon as you know His will? Each choice you make for good or evil is a seed you are planting for your future. Sometimes, it will be the smallest decisions that will affect you the most. This is because sin turns your heart away from God, while obedience turns your heart toward Him.

If you fill your life with God's Spirit and Word, you will reap the fruit of the Spirit (see Galatians 5:22–23). But if you're disobedient, greedy, and selfish, then you're going to reap the terrible consequences of your ungodly lifestyle. So it's time to get serious about following God. You must decide *today* what kind of life you are going to live for God—and then commit yourself to doing it. One day soon you will see the return on what you've planted over the years. Make sure that will be a crop you will be proud to claim.

How will you live out Life Principle 6 this week? Talk with some trusted Christian friends about what God is calling you to sow with your life. Ask them to tell you if there are any areas in your life where they are already seeing a harvest. Encourage them to be open and honest with you. Spend some time in prayer, talking to God about the results of your conversation.

Sometimes it will be the smallest decision that will affect you the most.

Life Lessons to Remember

❖ You always reap what you sow (see Luke 6:43–45).
❖ You always reap more than you sow (see John 12:23–25).
❖ You always reap later than you sow (see Isaiah 49:4; Mark 9:41).

There is no regular timetable for the harvest of life. Some crops we reap quickly; others take a long time. But do not be deceived— their season will come. And by going the second mile now and giving more than is required, we will reap rich dividends later.

Notes AND Prayer Requests

USE THIS SPACE TO WRITE ANY KEY POINTS, QUESTIONS,
OR PRAYER REQUESTS FROM THIS WEEK'S STUDY.

_____

_____

_____

_____

_____

_____

_____

_____

_____

_____

_____

_____

_____

_____

Dark Moments Last as Long as Necessary for God to Accomplish His Purpose

*Now David was greatly distressed, for the people spoke of
stoning him, because the soul of all the people was grieved,
every man for his sons and his daughters.
But David strengthened himself in the LORD his God.*

1 SAMUEL 30:6

Life's Questions

Sometimes it can seem as if the trials in life will never really end. You're either beginning a season of difficulties, in the middle of one, or just ending one. Whether the trial is relational, financial, physical, or spiritual, it can be draining and discouraging. What's more, the problems don't happen in a vacuum. There are always new emergencies and troubles to deal with that make life even more difficult!

Yet the Bible says that God is always good. As He Himself said to His people, "The LORD [is] merciful and gracious, longsuffering, and abounding in goodness and truth, keeping mercy for thousands, forgiving iniquity and transgression and sin" (Exodus 34:6–7). Of course, this may be a difficult truth to accept when you're going through a trial, but it's one to cling to if you want to make it through. It's also helpful to remember Life Principle 7: *The dark moments of your life will last as long as is necessary for God to accomplish His purpose in you.*

The disadvantage you face is that you have a limited perspective on your dark moments. You can see how you are being affected in the

PRINCIPLE IN ACTION
Joseph (Genesis 40)
Moses (Exodus 3:1–4)
Hannah (1 Samuel 1:1–20)
Esther (Esther 9:22)
Ezekiel (Ezekiel 37:1–14)

*It takes adversity to call us back
to our sense of values about
what is truly important.*
—**CHARLES F. STANLEY**

49

moment . . . but that's about it. What you can't see is the bigger picture of what God is accomplishing during those dark times—until He reveals it to you. In the meantime, you will have to trust that God wants only what is (ultimately) best for you.

Day 19: Learning to Stand

If you want God's best for your life and desire to be used by Him, at some point you will have to travel the road of adversity. This means God can and will use adversity in your life for a good purpose. God will use adversity, regardless of its source, to help you take great leaps forward in spiritual growth—and He will allow that adversity to remain in your life until He accomplishes His purpose in you. He will not keep it in your life one minute longer than is necessary.

Look at the life of any hero of the Christian faith, and you will see that the person went through a season of adversity—and oftentimes, more than one. Abraham and Sarah remained childless until they were well into their nineties. Moses spent forty long years in the wilderness before God called him to lead the Israelites out of Egypt. David hid in caves to avoid the wrath of King Saul. Daniel was tossed into a lions' den. Peter had to live with the guilt of having denied that he was a follower of Jesus.

When a trial does come your way, you can know that God will be with you in the midst of it. You can choose not to be discouraged but to "glory in tribulations, knowing that tribulation produces perseverance; and perseverance, character; and character, hope" (Romans 5:3–4). And you can be absolutely certain that God is going to see you through the heartache and bring you out whole, joyful, and more mature on the other side.

1. Read 1 Peter 1:1–12. The apostle Peter was writing to believers who were being physically persecuted for their faith—people who were risking their lives to follow Christ (1–2). What encouragement did he first provide to them (3–5)? How do you think they reacted to these words?

_____

_____

_____

_____

_____

_____

_____

_____

God will use adversity in your life for a good purpose.

God will be with you in the midst of every trial.

Blessed be the God and Father of our Lord Jesus Christ, who according to His abundant mercy has begotten us again to a living hope through the resurrection of Jesus Christ from the dead, to an inheritance incorruptible and undefiled and that does not fade away, reserved in heaven for you, who are kept by the power of God through faith for salvation ready to be revealed in the last time (1 Peter 1:3–5).

2. Why did Peter say believers should rejoice when dark times come and they face opposition from others (6–7)?

_____

_____

_____

3. What are the elements of a genuine faith (7)?

_____

_____

_____

4. What is the "bigger picture" that Peter is calling believers to consider when they suffer for the sake of Christ (8–9)?

_____

_____

_____

5. What are some trials you have been through lately? How have you seen God use those trials to build your faith in Him?

_____

_____

_____

_____

In this you greatly rejoice, though now for a little while, if need be, you have been grieved by various trials, that the genuineness of your faith being much more precious than gold that perishes, though it is tested by fire, may be found to praise, honor, and glory at the revelation of Jesus Christ, whom having not seen you love. Though now you do not see Him, yet believing you rejoice with joy inexpressible and full of glory, receiving the end of your faith—the salvation of your souls. Of this salvation the prophets have inquired and searched carefully, who prophesied of the grace that would come to you, searching what, or what manner of time, the Spirit of Christ who was in them was indicating when He testified beforehand the sufferings of Christ and the glories that would follow (1 Peter 1:6–11).

If you're walking with God and want to be used by Him, you will go through difficult times in your life.

Day 20: Adversity and Endurance

When trouble comes, do you tend to doubt God's mercy? Or do you thank Him for His faithfulness during the heart-wrenching time? Do you trust that He will never leave or forsake you? Adversity will reveal where you stand in your faith. It will reveal how much you are willing to endure for God. You never know how much difficulty you can withstand until you are tried.

Right now—right where you are—remember this: God has put a limit on all adversity. Because you are a child of God, the Holy Spirit is living

Adversity will reveal where you stand in your faith.

inside of you, and He knows how much you can bear. The psalmist said, "Many are the afflictions of the righteous, but the LORD delivers him out of them all" (Psalm 34:19), and, "As a father pities his children, so the LORD pities those who fear Him. For He knows our frame; He remembers that we are dust" (103:13–14).

Many times, what you will discover is that your ability to handle adversity is greater than you first thought. You find that you are stronger and more resilient than you imagined. You are able to not only *survive* difficult circumstances but also *thrive* in the midst of them. When you learn and mature in the midst of trials, God is pleased because He sees His purpose being fulfilled in you. You are growing spiritually and increasingly being conformed to the likeness of Christ. God is thrilled when you respond wisely to adversity!

> You are able to not only survive but also thrive in the midst of adversity.

6. Read 2 Corinthians 12:7–10. In this passage, Paul shared a personal struggle with his readers. He didn't explain what his "thorn in the flesh" was (7), but it was likely a chronic problem. What impact might this have had on Paul's day-to-day activities?

_____
_____
_____
_____

> *Lest I should be exalted above measure by the abundance of the revelations, a thorn in the flesh was given to me, a messenger of Satan to buffet me, lest I be exalted above measure. Concerning this thing I pleaded with the Lord three times that it might depart from me (2 Corinthians 12:7–8).*

7. Why do you suppose Paul prayed *three* times for God to remove it (8)? What was God's answer to his requests (9)?

_____
_____
_____
_____

8. How would you explain the phrase, "My strength is made perfect in your weakness," to a new believer who is struggling with a chronic health issue (9)?

_____
_____
_____
_____

> *And He said to me, "My grace is sufficient for you, for My strength is made perfect in weakness." Therefore most gladly I will rather boast in my infirmities, that the power of Christ may rest upon me. Therefore I take pleasure in infirmities, in reproaches, in needs, in persecutions, in distresses, for Christ's sake. For when I am weak, then I am strong (2 Corinthians 12:9–10).*

9. Paul was an ambassador for God who worked tirelessly to spread the message of Christ to the world. So why did God not immediately heal Paul of his "thorn" so he could better spread the gospel? What was God revealing to Paul through his trial (10)?

_____
_____
_____
_____

10. What is your longest-running prayer request? What makes you think God hasn't answered it like He answered Paul's request to remove his "thorn"?

Continue earnestly in prayer, being vigilant in it with thanksgiving (Colossians 4:2).

_____

_____

_____

_____

> *Paul understood that the reason for adversity was to keep him humble. The Lord was revealing astounding truth to him, and he could not afford to become prideful.*

Day 21: Into the Light

There are three main principles you can learn when you face adversity. First, *adversity is God's choice tool for building godly, spiritual character into your life.* Until you experience heartache, disappointment, and pain, you are not properly equipped for service (see 2 Corinthians 1:3–7). God uses adversity to mold and shape you. He does not bring it into your life without purpose.

Adversity builds godly character in your life.

Second, *adversity usually comes in the areas where you feel the most confident.* God wants to break you of the idea that you are sufficient on your own. He made you for a loving, intimate relationship with Himself, and at times He will use adversity to remind you of the fact that you are dependent on Him. "I am the vine, you are the branches. He who abides in Me, and I in him, bears much fruit; for without Me you can do nothing" (John 15:5).

Adversity comes in areas you feel most confident.

Third, *God's ultimate purpose is to conform you into the likeness of Jesus.* Through adversity, God develops love, joy, peace, longsuffering, kindness, goodness, faithfulness, gentleness, and self-control in you (see Galatians 5:22–23). He uses difficulties to get your attention, reveal weaknesses, remove pride and self-centeredness, increase your aversion to sin, demonstrate His faithfulness, prepare you for future service, and enable you to comfort others who are also facing adversity.

God's purpose is to make you like Christ.

When you face dark times, keep your focus on God. Remember that He understands what you are going through and that He cares about you. Allow Him to do the work He needs to do in your life and don't resist Him. Be confident that He will see you through and bring you into the light. When He does and you look back on the situation, it will all be worth it.

Allow God to do the work He needs to do in your life and don't resist Him.

James, a bondservant of God and of the Lord Jesus Christ, to the twelve tribes which are scattered abroad: greetings. My brethren, count it all joy when you fall into various trials, knowing that the testing of your faith produces patience. But let patience have its perfect work, that you may be perfect and complete, lacking nothing. If any of you lacks wisdom, let him ask of God, who gives to all liberally and without reproach, and it will be given to him. But let him ask in faith, with no doubting, for he who doubts is like a wave of the sea driven and tossed by the wind. For let not that man suppose that he will receive anything from the Lord; he is a double-minded man, unstable in all his ways (James 1:2–8).

11. Read James 1:1–8. Why does James say you can "count it all joy" when you face adversity (2–3)?

_____

_____

_____

_____

_____

12. How do trials lead to developing patience and endurance (4)? How does going through adversity lead to greater wisdom (5)?

_____

_____

_____

_____

13. What condition does James say you need to have to receive wisdom from God (6)? How does this lead to "profiting" from your trial?

_____

_____

_____

_____

_____

_____

14. As you look back on a trial you have faced, where do you now see evidence of God's joy, peace, love, and provision in the experience?

_____

_____

_____

_____

_____

You have need of endurance, so that after you have done the will of God, you may receive the promise (Hebrews 10:36).

15. How can you help a hurting friend or loved one experience the kind of joy James is talking about in this passage?

_____

_____

_____

_____

_____

The key to finding joy in adversity is where you place your focus. If you concentrate on your circumstances, you will become disheartened and discouraged. But when you fix your eyes on Jesus, you learn to rejoice in your difficulties.

Living the Principle

When you go through trials, you may wonder, *Why does it have to be so painful?* Unfortunately, there is no simple answer to this question because God's discipline and instruction are unique to each individual. God will work uniquely in your unique situation—and usually that will require touching an area deep within your soul.

One thing you can know for sure when you are facing trials is that God is doing something immensely important in and through you. He would never allow you to suffer without a significant reason, nor would He permit your trouble to continue a minute more than is necessary. Once again, the key to getting through adversity is to not run from the problems. Face them with faith in God, knowing He will not give you more than you can bear.

How will you live out Life Principle 7 this week? Carve out some chunks of time for prayer. First, pray for others who are facing dark times. Ask the Lord to intervene where He sees fit and to help those who are hurting find joy in the midst of their pain. Ask Him to use you as an instrument of His comfort and care. Second, pray about your own dark times. Thank God for His presence and the ways He makes His love known. Thank Him for His promise to limit your adversity. Ask Him for wisdom to help you survive and thrive in your season of struggle.

> When facing trials, know that God is doing something important in you.

Life Lessons to Remember

❖ God has put a limit on all adversity (see Lamentations 3:31–33).
❖ Adversity is God's tool for building godly character in you (see Romans 5:3–4).
❖ Adversity usually comes in the areas where you feel the most confident (see 2 Corinthians 12:7–9).

Notes AND Prayer Requests

USE THIS SPACE TO WRITE ANY KEY POINTS, QUESTIONS,
OR PRAYER REQUESTS FROM THIS WEEK'S STUDY.

*F*ight All Your Battles on Your Knees and You Win Every Time

Then someone told David, saying, "Ahithophel is among the conspirators with Absalom." And David said, "O Lord, I pray, turn the counsel of Ahithophel into foolishness!"

2 SAMUEL 15:31

Life's Questions

Have you ever been wrongly accused by someone you know? Have you ever endured the wrath and rejection of a coworker or loved one? Perhaps some of the most hurtful situations you've experienced came through the condemnation of a loved one. Whether or not you merited that person's criticism, the pain he or she inflicted was no doubt devastating and likely took a long time to overcome. You might even still be feeling the effects of the betrayal today.

What is your first instinct when your heart is broken by another? Perhaps it is to immediately confront the person, accuse him or her of wrongdoing, and then do everything in your power to make that person's life miserable. When faced with ongoing personal attacks, you may be tempted to "fight fire with fire," seek vengeance where you can find it, and give your attacker a taste of his or her own medicine. After all, this is just basic human nature.

But the Bible urges you to resist such gut reactions. As a child of God, you have a *responsibility* to respond in a godly manner when someone challenges you to combat—and that begins with going to God *first*. In this, you can see that Life Principle 8 holds the key to turning your circumstances around: *Fight all your battles on your knees and you win every time.*

PRINCIPLE IN ACTION
Jacob (Genesis 32:24–32)
Elisha (2 Kings 6:8–23)
David (Psalm 32:1–11)
Jesus (Matthew 26:36–38)
Rhoda (Acts 12:12–17)

We are capable of submitting, and therefore we are capable of resisting the devil. When we do, he must flee.

—CHARLES F. STANLEY

Day 22: Positive Resistance

During the days of World War II, a number of *resistance movements* sprang up in countries that had been occupied by Nazi Germany. These movements (sometimes referred to as "the Underground") sought to free the occupied country through acts of non-cooperation, disinformation, hiding downed pilots, and even outright warfare. The resistance fighters took the stance that they were not going to stand idly by and allow Hitler's evil to continue. They would choose to resist the wrongs, whatever the cost to them personally.

As a Christian, you are part of God's resistance movement against evil.

As a believer in Christ, you are also part of a *resistance movement* against evil. But your resistance to your enemy, the devil, is accomplished through prayer. Peter wrote, "Your adversary the devil walks about like a roaring lion, seeking whom he may devour . . . resist him, [standing] steadfast in the faith" (1 Peter 5:8–9). James echoed this teaching: "Submit to God. Resist the devil and he will flee from you. Draw near to God and He will draw near to you" (James 4:7–8). You are to actively resist evil through your persevering prayers.

Prayer is an active stance against the enemy.

On the surface, this type of resistance may seem passive. But in practice, it is anything but. Prayer is an *active* stance that is both *intentional* and *powerful*. What's different is that you are not relying on your own strength to fight the battle. Rather, you are leaning into the strength and authority of almighty God to handle the situation. You are agreeing to join the struggle by praying rather than turning away, backing off, or retreating. You are also agreeing to fight the battle God's way instead of your own.

Such resistance takes strength and courage in the heat of the moment. It also takes patience and perseverance. It requires you to "not lose heart" (Luke 18:1).

Then Jesus came with them to a place called Gethsemane, and said to the disciples, "Sit here while I go and pray over there." And He took with Him Peter and the two sons of Zebedee, and He began to be sorrowful and deeply distressed. Then He said to them, "My soul is exceedingly sorrowful, even to death. Stay here and watch with Me" (Matthew 26:36–38).

1. Read Matthew 26:36–46. What battle was Jesus facing in this passage? How would you describe His state of mind?

   _____

   _____

   _____

   _____

   _____

2. Notice that Jesus asked three of His closest friends to accompany Him (36–37). Why is there power in numbers when it comes to prayer?

   _____

   _____

   _____

   _____

3. What did Jesus ask of God in His prayer (39, 42)? How did He demonstrate His dependence on the Father, even in this moment of adversity?

_____

_____

_____

4. What does Jesus' example tell you about how to battle the enemy in prayer?

_____

_____

_____

5. What did Jesus' prayer time in Gethsemane ultimately accomplish?

_____

_____

_____

_____

Almost one thousand years after David went to the Mount of Olives to seek God, his descendant, Jesus, went there, too. At the foot of the Mount of Olives is the Garden of Gethsemane, where Jesus accepted the Father's will and prepared to do battle with our sin.

He went a little farther and fell on His face, and prayed, saying, "O My Father, if it is possible, let this cup pass from Me; nevertheless, not as I will, but as You will." Then He came to the disciples and found them sleeping, and said to Peter, "What! Could you not watch with Me one hour? Watch and pray, lest you enter into temptation. The spirit indeed is willing, but the flesh is weak." Again, a second time, He went away and prayed, saying, "O My Father, if this cup cannot pass away from Me unless I drink it, Your will be done. And He came and found them asleep again, for their eyes were heavy. So He left them, went away again, and prayed the third time, saying the same words. Then He came to His disciples and said to them, "Are you still sleeping and resting? Behold, the hour is at hand" (Matthew 26:39–45).

Day 23: Faithfully Submitted

In 1 Peter 5:8–9 and James 4:7–8, both authors highlight two key words that are at the heart of your ability to resist the devil: *submission* to God and *faith*. *Submission* to God is saying, "I can't, but You can." In your battlefield prayer, you might say, "Lord, I can't defeat the devil on my own. But with You, I can." This is the position Paul took when he wrote, "I can do all things through Christ who strengthens me" (Philippians 4:13).

James taught that *submission* occurs when you seek to develop a closer relationship with God. As you spend time with Him, you get to know Him better and discover how *He* wants you to overcome evil. You can draw near to God by praying and spending time in His Word, by setting aside time to listen to Him and to wait on Him for guidance,

Submission is acknowledging you need God's strength to fight your battles.

and by periodically closing off all other influences that might distract you from knowing Him better.

The better you know God, the more you will witness His awesome power, experience His vast love, learn from His immense wisdom, and grow in your faith. In time, this will lead you to realize, "Yes, God *can* defeat the devil on my behalf. Yes, God *will* win in any conflict with the enemy. Yes, God *does* want me to be able to overcome my adversary and to live in victory in Christ Jesus."

Submission leads you to conclude you need God to fight the battles on your behalf.

LORD, how they have increased who trouble me! Many are they who rise up against me. Many are they who say of me, "There is no help for him in God." But You, O LORD, are a shield for me, my glory and the One who lifts up my head. I cried to the LORD with my voice, and He heard me from His holy hill (Psalm 3:1–4).

6. Read Psalm 3. King David wrote this psalm when he was a fugitive, on the run from his son Absalom, who had just led a rebellion against him. How would you describe David's tone in the psalm? What emotions was he feeling?

   _____

   _____

   _____

   _____

7. How does David use adoration and praise in this psalm of prayer (3–4)?

   _____

   _____

   _____

   _____

I lay down and slept; I awoke, for the LORD sustained me. I will not be afraid of ten thousands of people who have set themselves against me all around. Arise, O LORD; save me, O my God! For You have struck all my enemies on the cheekbone; you have broken the teeth of the ungodly. Salvation belongs to the LORD. Your blessing is upon Your people (Psalm 3:5–8).

8. How does David show that even in the midst of this crisis, he was still faithfully submitted to God (5–6)?

   _____

   _____

   _____

   _____

9. David's prayer is not passive, for he asks God to arise and save him from his enemies (7). What confidence does David show in God's ability to provide for him (6, 8)?

   _____

   _____

   _____

   _____

10. If you were to write a similar psalm of prayer about people "who rise up against" you (1), what specifically would you say?

   _____

   _____

   _____

   _____

Many people believed David's reign was over and that not even God could help him. Yet they were wrong. Doubters and skeptics are everywhere, which is why to succeed in the Christian life, you need the church. You must surround yourself with strong, godly believers who love and encourage you and show you how to stay faithful to the Lord.

Day 24: A Measure of Faith

Faith is saying to God, "I believe You will." Faith views your battle to overcome the enemy as being already *done* with God gaining the victory. When David said, "I trust in You" in Psalm 25:2, he meant, "It is done. Lord, You are perfect in nature. You do all things well. And You have victory over all my enemies." He had absolute faith in God's ability. There was no hint David merely *hoped* God would come through because he knew it was as good as done.

You grow in faith by exercising it—by trusting God in situation after situation, circumstance after circumstance, and relationship after relationship. You grow in faith by developing a personal history in which you obey God, and He remains faithful in His loving care for you. But you can only remain firm in your faith if you completely submit to God—in *all areas of your life*. When you refuse to submit to the Lord, you are saying, "I can handle this. I don't need Your help." That's precisely what Satan wants you to do: trust your ability and not in the all-powerful God. It is also the place where he will level his greatest attack against you!

In Romans 12:3, Paul writes, "God has dealt to each one a measure of faith." God has given you a standard by which you can correctly appraise yourself—and know if pride is getting in the way of you submitting your entire life to God. Like David, you can know that God will fight the battle for you and will secure the victory. But He wants you to exercise your faith by depending completely on Him and submitting everything to Him.

11. Read 2 Kings 5:1–11. How is Naaman described (1)? What idea did his servant have for him to be healed of his affliction (3)?

_____

_____

_____

_____

Faith is acknowledging God has already won the victory.

You can only remain firm in your faith if you submit completely to God.

Naaman . . . was a great and honorable man . . . [His servant] said to her mistress, "If only my master were with the prophet who is in Samaria! For he would heal him of his leprosy" (2 Kings 5:1–3).

Naaman went with his horses and chariot, and he stood at the door of Elisha's house. And Elisha sent a messenger to him, saying, "Go and wash in the Jordan seven times, and your flesh shall be restored to you, and you shall be clean." But Naaman became furious, and went away and said, "Indeed, I said to myself, 'He will surely come out to me, and stand and call on the name of the LORD his God, and wave his hand over the place, and heal the leprosy.' Are not the Abanah and the Pharpar, the rivers of Damascus, better than all the waters of Israel? Could I not wash in them and be clean?" So he turned and went away in a rage. And his servants came near and spoke to him, and said, "My father, if the prophet had told you to do something great, would you not have done it? How much more then, when he says to you, 'Wash, and be clean'?" So he went down and dipped seven times in the Jordan, according to the saying of the man of God; and his flesh was restored like the flesh of a little child, and he was clean (2 Kings 5:9–14).

12. Naaman was an important person in the Syrian army. When he left his country, he carried with him a vast quantity of gold and a letter from the king of Syria himself. But how did Elisha respond when Naaman appeared at the door of his house (9–10)?

_____

_____

_____

_____

13. Why did Naaman become furious at the request (11–13)? What was God seeking to do by setting these conditions for his healing?

_____

_____

_____

_____

14. What did Naaman's servants say to him that convinced him of the need to submit completely to God's instructions (13–14)?

_____

_____

_____

_____

15. What does this story tell you about having pride in your heart when you come to God in prayer? How have you seen God bring you into submission to Him in your life?

_____

_____

_____

_____

God could have healed Naaman immediately without him dipping in the Jordan's waters. However, in order for Naaman to recognize God as Lord, he first had to submit to His authority.

Living the Principle

When David fled from his son Absalom, the situation seemed dire for him. Absalom had gained popularity among the people, and it appeared that the nation was with him. But it wasn't long after that God delivered

Absalom stole the hearts of the men of Israel (2 Samuel 15:6).

the kingdom of Israel back into David's hands. And though David did everything he could to protect his son, Absalom still lost his life (see 2 Samuel 18). That is what always happens when a person harbors unforgiveness and revenge in his heart. He hurts the people around him unnecessarily and eventually destroys himself.

When people attack you, don't react to them out of fear and rage. Be like David and have a *battle plan*. Your combat strategy must begin and end with getting on your knees and acknowledging that God is in control of your situation. He will handle everything for you if you will humble yourself and obey Him. However, you must stop being distracted by your own feelings and the details of your circumstances. Put your focus on Him and what He can teach you. Whenever you surrender yourself completely to God and trust Him with your struggles, you will find He is faithful to lead you to victory.

How will you live out Life Principle 8 this week? Spend some time evaluating your relationships with the most difficult people in your life. How did your enemies become your enemies? What incidents, encounters, and confrontations fueled your animosity? What strategies for dealing with those people have failed in the past? Take these people to God in prayer and ask for His strategy on how to deal with the situation. Reach out to those you need to forgive and seek forgiveness for any wrong you've done that the Lord reveals to you.

Have a battle plan for when people attack you.

Life Lessons to Remember

❖ Prayer and obedience to God are the biblical approach to overcoming all your troubles (see 2 Chronicles 7:14; Philippians 4:6–7).
❖ You can remain firm in your faith only when you completely submit all areas of your life to God (see James 4:7–10).
❖ Having a prayer-centered battle plan in place will help you respond effectively when troubling circumstances arise (see Luke 18:1–8).

> *What we do know with certainty is that any time the devil is confronted with Jesus, Jesus wins. When we place our faith and hope in Christ and resist the devil, the devil cannot score a victory over our lives.*

Notes AND Prayer Requests

USE THIS SPACE TO WRITE ANY KEY POINTS, QUESTIONS,
OR PRAYER REQUESTS FROM THIS WEEK'S STUDY.

_____

_____

_____

_____

_____

_____

_____

_____

_____

_____

_____

_____

_____

_____

Trusting God Means Looking Beyond What You Can See to What God Sees

*And Elisha prayed, and said, "L*ORD*, I pray, open his eyes that he may see." Then the L*ORD *opened the eyes of the young man, and he saw. And behold, the mountain was full of horses and chariots of fire all around Elisha.*

2 KINGS 6:17

Life's Questions

What is it about the future that causes you to be afraid? Is it a conflict that you dread? Are you doubtful about ever receiving your heart's desire? Are you caught in a bad situation that you fear will never change? You may have some suspicions, fears, or hopes about your future, but the truth is that you don't *know* what tomorrow will bring. This may cause you some anxiety, but when your faith is in God, it should bring you hope.

The Bible is clear that you are not to give in to fear and anxiety. Jesus commanded, "Let not your heart be troubled, neither let it be afraid" (John 14:27). But when you are facing the uncertainties of life, this can be extremely difficult to do. Yet it is those times when God's command is the most pertinent: Do *not* be afraid! The Lord provides you with all the resources you need to overcome fear. Your part is to trust that God sees more than your limited perspective and be confident that He is working in ways you cannot see.

This is at the heart of Life Principle 9: *Trusting God means looking beyond what you can see to what God sees.* The circumstances and obstacles you observe today may be truly overwhelming, but God's resources are even greater and more powerful than you can imagine. God sees your tomorrow—and *all of*

PRINCIPLE IN ACTION
Caleb (Joshua 14:6–12)
David (1 Samuel 17:33–37)
Nehemiah (Nehemiah 4:7–21)
Thomas (John 20:24–29)
Silas (Acts 16:24–34)

The more we learn to trust God, the more we learn that He is utterly trustworthy. He never fails us or forsakes us.
—CHARLES F. STANLEY

your tomorrows—and He is ready to deal with them. Therefore, you can put your faith in Him and obey whatever He tells you to do.

Day 25: Putting Giants into Proper Perspective

As young David stared across the Elah Valley into the eyes of his enemy, he recalled the times God had delivered him from the brink of disaster. God had always given him the ability he needed to triumph. But now he faced one of the greatest challenges of his life—a trained and well-armed warrior named Goliath. His enemy was a literal giant of a man who had put fear into the Israelite army's heart for the past forty days. What could he hope to accomplish?

At some point, you will also face what seems to be a mammoth trial. That is why you must know how to respond to every threat by laying hold of the kind of victorious faith that looks beyond what you can see to what God sees. This was the secret of David's success. Had he looked merely at the giant facing him, he would have turned around and run away. But through faith, David could see what his countrymen could not.

The Lord had developed David's trust in Him until it had become an unshakable force. This is why David could say to his people, "Who is this uncircumcised Philistine, that he should defy the armies of the living God?" (2 Samuel 17:26). The Israelites only saw a giant who could not be overcome in battle. But David saw an opportunity for the Lord to show up on His people's behalf. And he was willing to step into the fray to make that happen.

1. Read 1 Samuel 17. How does the Bible describe Goliath (4–7)? Why was no one willing to fight him in single combat (11)?

_____

_____

_____

_____

2. What did David say to King Saul when he was summoned (32)? What does Saul's response reveal about his perspective of the situation (33)?

_____

_____

_____

_____

_____

I will praise You, O LORD, with my whole heart; I will tell of all Your marvelous works (Psalm 9:1).

God can develop your trust in Him until it becomes an unshakable force.

The Philistine said, "I defy the armies of Israel this day; give me a man, that we may fight together." When Saul and all Israel heard these words of the Philistine, they were dismayed and greatly afraid (1 Samuel 17:10–11).

David said to Saul, "Let no man's heart fail because of him; your servant will go and fight with this Philistine." And Saul said to David, "You are not able to go against this Philistine to fight with him; for you are a youth" (1 Samuel 17:32–33).

3. What evidence did David provide that God would fight for him (34–36)? How had these past victories shaped his perspective on God?

_____

_____

_____

_____

4. What is a "giant problem" that you are facing today? Is your perspective more like David's or King Saul's? Explain.

_____

_____

_____

_____

So David prevailed over the Philistine with a sling and a stone, and struck the Philistine and killed him (1 Samuel 17:50).

5. What hope does this story give you as it relates to your situation? What would it take for you to see all your battles from God's perspective?

_____

_____

_____

_____

David chose five smooth stones and a slingshot as his weapons instead of the bulky armor of Saul. He faced Goliath clothed in the strong faith of the living God. And mere men cannot penetrate or defeat God-centered faith!

Day 26: Recall and Reject

Every challenge presents you with the opportunity to see the Lord display His faithfulness to you. Every difficulty gives you the chance to trust God, even when you cannot see how He will possibly work on your behalf. The secret is to train your heart and mind to look beyond what you can see and ask God to reveal what He sees.

David founded his faith in the sovereignty of God, which is why he knew he would not fail in his quest to defeat the Philistine giant. Other people doubted him, including his own brothers. They accused him of pride and excessive self-confidence. They reminded him of what he was up against. They doubted him and urged him to reconsider his plan. But David's confidence in God would not be shaken.

Every challenge gives you the chance to trust God and see what He will do.

You build faith in God by recalling past victories.

You build faith in God by rejecting discouraging words.

How can you gain that kind of faith? One way is by *recalling past victories*. David was a shepherd who had defended his sheep from attacks by wild animals. He had witnessed God deliver him from both the paw of the lion and the grasp of the bear (see 1 Samuel 17:32–37). David first won the spiritual victory in his mind. In the same way, you need to overcome feelings of fear and doubt by focusing on the truth of God's Word.

David also *rejected discouraging words*. No one in the Israelite camp—from his brothers to the king—encouraged David in his quest to defeat Goliath. If David had listened to their disparaging comments, he would have given up. However, he instead turned his heart toward the Lord . . . and there he found the encouragement he needed to succeed.

David was not the only one in the Bible who faced overwhelming situations. In 2 Kings 6, a story is told of the prophet Elisha who also faced a daunting enemy. And, like David, he also needed to view the battle from God's perspective.

[The king of Syria] sent horses and chariots and a great army [to Dothan], and they came by night and surrounded the city. And when the servant of the man of God arose early and went out, there was an army, surrounding the city with horses and chariots. And his servant said to him, "Alas, my master! What shall we do?" So he answered, "Do not fear, for those who are with us are more than those who are with them." And Elisha prayed, and said, "LORD, I pray, open his eyes that he may see." Then the LORD opened the eyes of the young man, and he saw. And behold, the mountain was full of horses and chariots of fire all around Elisha (2 Kings 6:14–17).

6. Read 2 Kings 6:8–23. Elisha knew the Syrian forces had come for *him* (12–13). Why would he have had good reason to panic (14–15)?

_____

_____

_____

7. Why didn't Elisha panic as his servant did (16–17)?

_____

_____

_____

8. What stands out the most to you in the description of what Elisha's servant saw (17)? How do you think this affected his perspective thereafter?

_____

_____

_____

9. Think of a problem you're facing that's causing you concern. If you could get a glimpse of God's involvement in that situation, as Elisha's servant did, what might you see?

_____

_____

_____

Elisha did not pray that his servant would stop seeing the enemy. He prayed that he would start seeing the goodness and provision of the Lord.

10. How can you develop the kind of "supernatural vision" that Elisha had? How can you learn to look at a situation that seems hopeless and see God's forces at work there?

_____

_____

_____

Day 27: Recognize, Respond, Rely, and Reckon

Another way to develop the kind of faith that men like David and Elisha possessed is to *recognize the true nature of the battle*. When David entered the conflict against Goliath, he clearly understood the battle was the Lord's and that God would give him the victory (see 1 Samuel 17:47). Elisha understood the spiritual nature of the battle as well and that God was fighting on the Israelites' behalf.

David and Elisha *responded to the challenge with a positive confession.* David said to Goliath, "I come to you in the name of the Lord of hosts, the God of the armies of Israel" (1 Samuel 17:45). David firmly declared his belief that he could not lose because God was with him. Elisha likewise declared, "Do not fear, for those who are with us are more than those who are with them" (2 Kings 6:16). Both declared that God had given the victory.

The two men clearly *relied on the power of God,* which is the next step in developing a strong faith. David did not need a spear or a javelin to defeat Goliath, but only a homemade slingshot—and, of course, the power of God. Elisha did not need a weapon at all, for God answered his prayer to strike the Syrians with blindness (see 2 Kings 6:18). God provided the victory in both cases, and He received the glory.

A final way to develop a faith that sees beyond human perspective is to *reckon the victory.* As discussed, even before David stepped onto the battlefield, he knew he would not lose. He knew it wasn't his reputation on the line, but God's. Elisha was also convinced of victory before the battle began, for he could see the heavenly armies surrounding his enemy. In the end, he simply led the Syrians out of his country (see 2 Kings 6:19–20).

11. Read Isaiah 55:8–9. What does this passage say about *recognizing* how God works in this world? What does this say about your perspective versus God's?

_____

_____

_____

You build faith in God by recognizing the true nature of the battle.

You build faith in God by responding to the trial with a positive confession.

You build faith in God by relying on His power.

You build faith in God by reckoning the victory.

You are a chosen generation, a royal priesthood, a holy nation, His own special people, that you may proclaim the praises of Him who called you out of darkness (1 Peter 2:9).

12. Turn to 1 Peter 2:9. What allows you to *respond* to the challenges you face and proclaim your victory in Christ?

_____

_____

_____

_____

The LORD, the Creator of the ends of the earth, neither faints nor is weary. His understanding is unsearchable. He gives power to the weak, and to those who have no might He increases strength (Isaiah 40:28–29).

13. Read Isaiah 40:28–29. What promise are you given in this passage about *relying* on God's power?

_____

_____

_____

_____

In Him also we have obtained an inheritance, being predestined according to the purpose of Him who works all things according to the counsel of His will, that we who first trusted in Christ should be to the praise of His glory (Ephesians 1:11–12).

14. Now turn to Ephesians 1:11–12. What inheritance have you been given? How does this allow you to *reckon* the victory and be convinced that God will prevail?

_____

_____

_____

_____

15. What current challenge do you need to see from God's perspective? How will you go to battle today for that need in prayer?

_____

_____

_____

_____

"Call to Me, and I will answer you, and show you great and mighty things, which you do not know" (Jeremiah 33:3).

Living the Principle

God can reveal how He is protecting you if you have spiritual eyes to see.

How did David and Elisha know that God was protecting them? They listened to the Spirit of God. You may think it is difficult to pay attention to God when you face overwhelming troubles, especially those that seem impossible. Like Elisha's servant, your mind searches for a way to deal with what you're seeing. In despair you cry out, "What can I do?"

The first thing to do is close your physical eyes because they're not helping. Stop measuring your problems against your ability to handle them because the enemy will use your senses to magnify what you're going through. Then you must open your spiritual eyes—the ones fixed on God. Worship Him. Read His Word. Pray. Remember how He has helped others in the past, and thank Him that the mighty wisdom and power that was available to them has been provided to you as well. God is ready, willing, and able to rescue you from the jaws of defeat, and He will do whatever is necessary to lead you to triumph when you obey Him.

How will you live out Life Principle 9 this week? Begin by creating a list of personal experiences in which God helped you overcome an obstacle you considered insurmountable, answered a prayer in an unexpected way, or gave you peace of mind in the midst of frightening circumstances. Spend time in prayer, thanking God for all the ways He has helped you overcome these obstacles in the past and given you peace of mind. Commit to seeking Him first when you face a challenge in the future and ask for His perspective.

Close your physical eyes in times of trouble and open your spiritual eyes.

Life Lessons to Remember

❖ Recall past victories (see Psalm 145:5–7) and reject discouraging words (see Psalm 40:14–16).
❖ Recognize the true nature of the battle (see Psalm 20:6–8) and respond to the challenge with a positive confession (see Psalm 118:6–9).
❖ Rely on the power of God (see Psalm 66:3–5) and reckon the victory (see Psalm 98:1).

When something threatens our lives, we naturally feel great fear.
There is no sin in this. It's how we respond to that fear—
with a courageous trust in God or a desire for self-preservation—
that makes the difference.

Notes AND Prayer Requests

USE THIS SPACE TO WRITE ANY KEY POINTS, QUESTIONS,
OR PRAYER REQUESTS FROM THIS WEEK'S STUDY.

If Necessary, God Will Move Heaven and Earth to Show You His Will

*O our God, will You not judge them? For we have no power
against this great multitude that is coming against us;
nor do we know what to do, but our eyes are upon You.*

2 CHRONICLES 20:12

Life's Questions

What is God's will for your life? Do you have an answer, or do you think, *Good question! If God tells you what He wants me to do, please let me know.* Perhaps you know how God is leading you in certain areas of your life, and you're committed to following Him, but there are other areas in which you have no idea what to do. You might wonder, *Why does God's will seem hidden from me? Can I truly know what God has planned for my life?*

Yes you can! God does not hide His will from you. In Ephesians 1:8, Paul writes that the riches of God's grace abound toward you "in all wisdom and prudence." He adds that God has made known to you "the mystery of His will" and given you "the spirit of wisdom and revelation in the knowledge of Him" (9, 17). Just as a child grows in his ability to use all the brain cells he was given at birth, you grow in your ability to understand the deeper things of God as you grow in your relationship with Christ.

When this occurs, you will discover—as Life Principle 10 states—that *if necessary, God will move heaven and earth to show you His will.* In the midst of the bordering-on-chaos busyness you find in your world today, God will take the lead in making His will known. What you must do is *recognize* how He is moving so you can act on His direction.

PRINCIPLE IN ACTION
Noah (Genesis 7:1–4)
David (1 Samuel 23:13)
Joseph (Matthew 1:20)
John the Baptist (Mark 1:1–11)
Martha and Mary (John 40–44)

When our hearts are clean and submissive, He reveals His will and protects us. He also keeps our attention where it belongs— on Him.

—CHARLES F. STANLEY

Day 28: Attention Getters

God is committed to showing you how to follow the plan He has designed for your life. He wants you to listen for His voice to hear what He wants you to do and how He wants you to do it (see Isaiah 30:19–21). When you begin to wander from the course God has set, you will find that He takes all kinds of measures to recapture your attention and protect you from harm. There are several means he uses to help you to take notice.

First, He will give you *a restless spirit*. Sometimes, God will get your attention by making you unsettled in certain areas of your life. If you experience such restlessness deep within—something you cannot quite identify—it is time to stop and pray, "Lord, are You trying to say something to me?" Then wait for His direction.

God may also use *a spoken word* to break into your world and reveal Himself to you. He will get your attention by using the words of others. If several people within a short span of time begin telling you the same thing, you need to ask the Lord if He is trying to speak to you through them. "Where there is no counsel, the people fall; but in the multitude of counselors there is safety" (Proverbs 11:14).

God may also use *an unusual blessing* to gain your attention. A check may arrive in the mail for just the amount you need to fund a mission trip you are considering. Or maybe an opportunity suddenly opens up for a ministry you are contemplating. God will often open doors that He wants you to step through. Of course, if you are an overly self-sufficient person, the Lord may use some other method to get your focus on Him. But remember that no matter which method He uses, it expresses His love.

God is committed to showing you how to follow His plan for your life.

God will get your attention through a restless spirit.

God will get your attention through a spoken word.

God will get your attention through an unusual blessing.

1. Read Joshua 10:1–14. What situation were Joshua and the Israelites facing (1–7)?

_____

_____

_____

The five kings . . . gathered together and went up, they and all their armies (Joshua 10:5).

2. How did God miraculously reveal His will in this story (11–13)?

_____

_____

_____

And it happened, as they fled before Israel and were on the descent of Beth Horon, that the Lord cast down large hailstones from heaven on them as far as Azekah, and they died. There were more who died from the hailstones than the children of Israel killed with the sword (Joshua 10:11).

3. When was the last time you—like Joshua and the Israelites—knew *exactly* what God wanted you to do in a situation? What happened? How do you feel about it now?

_____

_____

_____

4. Extraordinary circumstances call for extraordinary requests (12, 14). What's the most extreme thing you can imagine asking the Lord to do in order to accomplish His will?

_____

_____

_____

Then Joshua spoke to the LORD . . . and he said in the sight of Israel: "Sun, stand still over Gibeon" (Joshua 10:12).

5. What comfort or inspiration do you take from the fact that God intervened in the movement of the solar system in order to accomplish His purposes (13)?

_____

_____

_____

So the sun stood still, and the moon stopped, till the people had revenge upon their enemies (Joshua 10:13).

God invites you to partner with Him in the work of His kingdom, but you must never forget that you are very much dependent on Him in every way.

Day 29: Other Attention Grabbers

God answered Joshua's prayer by literally causing the sun and moon to stand still. The miracle definitely got the Israelites' attention, for the author of Joshua noted, "There has been no day like that, before it or after it, that the LORD heeded the voice of a man" (10:14). Yet sometimes, God will reveal His will to you not through answered prayer but *unanswered* prayer.

Most prayers are offered with the expectation—or at least the hope—of a *yes* response. But the Bible is clear that this is not always how God chooses to work. Often, he will answer a prayer with *no*. You can see this in the story of David after he committed adultery with Bathsheba and a child was born to them. David prayed for God to save his infant son's life, but the boy died (see 2 Samuel 12:15–18). The Lord may remain silent to your prayers as a way of prompting you to examine yourself.

God also uses *disappointment* to direct your life. When the nation of Israel refused God's instruction to take possession of the Promised Land, God judged them for their unbelief. They quickly changed their mind and said they desired to enter the land, but the Lord said no—it was too late (see Numbers 14). God got their attention through a sense of disappointment. In a similar way, the Lord may allow setbacks to keep you from charting your own course.

God may reveal His will through unanswered prayer.

God also uses disappointment to direct your life.

God may use other extraordinary measures to guide you on His path.

The Lord may use other *extraordinary circumstances* to point you along the path He wants you to take. He used a donkey to let Balaam know what He wanted him to do (see Numbers 22:28–30). He used a bush that didn't burn up to communicate His will to Moses (see Exodus 3). He used a whirlwind to set Job straight (see Job 38:1) and a great fish to compel Jonah to do what He had asked (see Jonah 1:17).

You must learn to look for the presence of God in every circumstance of life, for He leaves His footprints and handiwork all around you.

[Saul] fell to the ground, and heard a voice saying to him, "Saul, Saul, why are you persecuting Me?" And he said, "Who are You, Lord?" Then the Lord said, "I am Jesus, whom you are persecuting. It is hard for you to kick against the goads." So he, trembling and astonished, said, "Lord, what do You want me to do?" (Acts 9:3–6).

6. Read Acts 9:1–19. Paul, a devout Jew, was in the act of putting followers of Jesus to death when the Lord met him on the road to Damascus. How did God use both *disappointment* and *extraordinary measures* to get his attention (3–4)?

_____

_____

_____

_____

_____

7. How did God reveal His will to Paul (5–6)?

_____

_____

_____

Ananias answered, "Lord, I have heard from many about this man, how much harm he has done to Your saints in Jerusalem. And here he has authority from the chief priests to bind all who call on your name." But the Lord said to him, "Go, for he is a chosen vessel of Mine to bear My name before Gentiles, kings, and the children of Israel. For I will show him how many things he must suffer for My name's sake." And Ananias went his way and entered the house (Acts 9:13–14).

8. What means did God use to communicate the next part of His plan to Ananias (10)? What was Ananias's response (13–14)?

_____

_____

_____

_____

9. The way God spoke with Ananias seems extraordinary, but it doesn't seem to have fazed him at all. How might a person prepare for a situation such as this?

_____

_____

_____

_____

10. In what ways has God used *unanswered prayer*, *disappointments*, and even *extraordinary measures* to communicate His will to you?

_____

_____

_____

> *The Lord got Saul's full attention on the Damascus Road,*
> *and He used the temporary blindness and humiliation to transform*
> *the zealous Pharisee named Saul into the powerful apostle*
> *and missionary named Paul.*

Day 30: Whatever It Takes

Paul's encounter with the risen Christ stopped him in his tracks. The Lord used temporary blindness to halt his persecution of the Christians, show him that Jesus was truly the Messiah, and transform his life so he would bear His name "before Gentiles, kings, and the children of Israel" (Acts 9:15). Paul had to go through defeat before this occurred.

God also used *defeat* to show the Israelites they were not following His will. After the peoples' stunning victory over Jericho (see Joshua 6), they were filled with confidence. But God got their attention by allowing them to suffer an embarrassing defeat to the small town of Ai. One of the men, named Achan, had neglected to do everything the Lord had commanded in their battle at Jericho. The defeat caused Joshua to ask, "Lord God, why have You brought this people over the Jordan at all—to deliver us into the hand of the Amorites?" (7:7). Suffering the loss caused the people to discern where they had taken a wrong turn.

God may use defeat to show you when you are not following His will.

Later, during the time of the judges, when "everyone did what was right in his own eyes" (Judges 17:6), the nation of Israel fell into a cycle of idolatry and disobedience. At one point, God responded by bringing judgment through the Midianites, who devastated the land. "They would encamp against them and destroy the produce of the earth as far as Gaza, and leave no sustenance for Israel, neither sheep nor ox nor donkey" (6:4). Only when God *took away every material belonging* did the Israelites cry out to Him and repent.

God may take away material belongings to reveal His will.

God also uses *tragedy*, *sickness*, and *affliction* to reveal His will. When King Hezekiah of Judah became prideful, God used an illness to alert him to the problem (see 2 Chronicles 32:24–25). When King Nebuchadnezzar took credit for the splendor of His kingdom, God afflicted him with madness (see Daniel 4:28–33). And God certainly used Paul's temporary affliction of blindness to get his attention. While not every tragedy has such a direct cause, it is a good idea to examine your life when going through afflictions and ask if God is using them to guide you.

God may use tragedy, sickness, and affliction to reveal His will.

God knows exactly where you are in your journey of faith and precisely what it will take to get your attention. So stay alert. If any of these divine methods are occurring—or recurring—ask God what He wants to tell you. And then listen . . . not simply to hear, but also to obey.

May the God of peace who brought up our Lord Jesus from the dead, that great Shepherd of the sheep, through the blood of the everlasting covenant, make you complete in every good work to do His will, working in you what is well pleasing in His sight, through Jesus Christ, to whom be glory forever and ever. Amen (Hebrews 13:20–21).

11. Read Hebrews 13:20–21. Why is your heavenly Father called the "God of peace" (20)? What kind of peace does He bring?

_____

_____

_____

_____

12. How complete is your commitment to God's will at this point in your life? Which areas are easiest for you to turn over to Him? Which areas are most difficult?

_____

_____

_____

_____

_____

13. What are some of the specific "good works" that are part of God's will for your life (21)?

_____

_____

_____

_____

14. What are the most effective strategies for you to determine whether something is "pleasing" in God's sight (21)?

_____

_____

_____

_____

You are a chosen generation, a royal priesthood, a holy nation, His own special people, that you may proclaim the praises of Him who called you out of darkness into His marvelous light (1 Peter 2:9).

15. Why is it important to give Jesus the glory when you make wise choices to follow God's will (21)?

_____

_____

_____

_____

It is God working in you that enables you to do anything worthwhile for His kingdom. You obey the Lord, submit to His will and purpose, rely on His Holy Spirit who dwells within you for your every need, and please Him by giving Him all the honor and glory.

Living the Principle

God's will is *His* to communicate and fulfill. No matter what God reveals to be His plan, He will make sure everything is in place for it to come to pass. Your responsibility is simply to obey Him right now. It is God's right to exclude or include you from the process as He so desires.

If you feel that God's will remains a mystery to you, perhaps it is because He is revealing it to you one step at a time. God knows every detail of your circumstances and how they will unfold, but He does not always reveal them at once. Instead, He uses the situation as an opportunity to teach you to trust Him. Unfortunately, if you are unwilling to wait for His timing, you are going to prolong your struggle and miss out on maturing in your faith.

Another reason you may feel that God's will is hidden from you could be because you've failed to obey Him in some area. Maybe God has shown you what to do, but His command seems unreasonable or unimportant to you. Understand that you will not be able to move forward until you submit to Him in *every* area that He has called you to obey. You must surrender yourself to God completely, whether it means engaging in the battle under God's leadership or watching what He is doing from the sidelines.

How will you live out Life Principle 10 this week? Are you having trouble discerning God's will for your life? If so, spend time in prayer, meditate on God's Word, and ask the Holy Spirit to reveal what God may be communicating to you. If you are still unclear, consider talking with a trusted friend about how God may be trying to get your attention—whether it is through a restless spirit, the words of others, an unusual blessing, an unanswered prayer, a disappointment, extraordinary circumstances, a defeat, financial trouble, or an affliction. Spend time in prayer and ask God to speak to you through His Word so you can attentively listen to what He may be communicating to you.

> God will ensure everything is in place in your life for His will to come to pass.

Life Lessons to Remember

❖ God always knows exactly where you are in your journey of faith (see Romans 8:29–30).

❖ God is committed to helping you live out the specific plan that He has designed for you (see Jeremiah 29:11–13).

❖ The key to understanding God's will is to listen to Him (see Isaiah 30:19–21).

Notes AND Prayer Requests

USE THIS SPACE TO WRITE ANY KEY POINTS, QUESTIONS,
OR PRAYER REQUESTS FROM THIS WEEK'S STUDY.

_____

_____

_____

_____

_____

_____

_____

_____

_____

_____

_____

_____

_____

_____

*G*od Assumes Full Responsibility for Your Needs When You Obey Him

My God shall supply all your need according to
His riches in glory by Christ Jesus.

PHILIPPIANS 4:19

Life's Questions

In times of great loss or trial, you may be tempted to question whether God really cares about you. If certain things have gone terribly wrong, and you find there are needs in your life that continue to go unmet, it can strike an unpleasant chord deep inside you. You may find yourself wrestling with thoughts of doubt or uncertainty.

After all, this is God we're talking about—the all-powerful Creator and Sustainer of the universe. Everything you know about Him confirms He is fully capable of providing for you. You've seen Him provide for countless others. You've read passages of Scripture that teach He helps those in need: "The righteous cry out, and the LORD hears, and delivers them out of all their troubles" (Psalm 34:17); "Call upon Me in the day of trouble; I will deliver you, and you shall glorify Me" (Psalm 50:15). And so the questions arise: "Why isn't God delivering me? Why has He allowed these bad things to happen? Haven't I been faithful? Does He want to help me?"

Yes, He does. In fact, God takes great joy in meeting your needs and supplying the desires of your heart. Yet there is a condition. As Life Principle 11 explains, *God assumes full responsibility for your needs when*

PRINCIPLE IN ACTION
Sarah (Genesis 18:9–12)
Joshua (Joshua 6:20–21)
Naomi (Ruth 1:17–22)
The Preacher (Ecclesiastes 2:1–11)
Isaiah (Isaiah 30:21)

God is faithful and does not change. In this one truth, we find our reason for hope and unwavering confidence.

—CHARLES F. STANLEY

you obey Him. Is obeying God the top priority in your life? Are you submitting yourself fully to Him? Are you trusting in Him despite your circumstances? These questions deserve your attention.

Day 31: Ready, Willing, and Able

Do you really believe God is able and eager to meet all of your needs? Most people would say yes. But when difficulty comes, problems arise, and sorrow strikes, it is easy to wonder where God is and how you can trust Him. Yet you must remember the Lord is not only capable of meeting all of your needs, but He is also able to satisfy the deepest desires of your heart.

Some may say, "I know God is capable of meeting my needs, but will He? Doesn't He know I'm struggling?" The Lord knows the battle that is ensuing around your life. And while questions like these are inevitable at some point, there is a deeper principle to learn: how to focus on your faith when you are under trial. God is committed to meeting your needs, but first He wants to know you are committed to living your life for Him.

Jesus taught His disciples not to worry but to "seek first the kingdom of God and His righteousness, and all these things shall be added to you" (Matthew 6:33). This was a promise, a commitment, and a pledge of action that you can also claim. God knows you have emotional and material needs—food, shelter, and clothing. But Jesus said the focus of your life should not be set on material products or "feel good" experiences, but on God and His kingdom. When your will is aligned with His, you find that He meets your needs and desires.

Do you believe God is able and eager to meet your needs?

Make the focus of your life God and His kingdom.

The LORD said to Moses, "Behold, I will rain bread from heaven for you.... 'At twilight you shall eat meat, and in the morning you will be filled with bread'" (Exodus 16:4, 12).

1. Read Exodus 16:1–16. Which needs of the Israelites had God assumed the responsibility to meet after delivering them from Egypt (4, 12)?

_____

_____

_____

_____

The LORD said to Moses, "Go on before the people, and take with you some of the elders of Israel. Also take in your hand your rod with which you struck the river, and go" (Exodus 17:5).

2. Read Exodus 17:1–7. How did God show the Israelites that He would meet their needs while they were in the wilderness (5)?

_____

_____

_____

_____

3. By this time, the Israelites had seen God miraculously provide them with water at Marah (see Exodus 15) and had feasted on quail and manna. What *should* have been their attitude toward God by now? What was their response instead (3, 7)?

_____

_____

_____

_____

_____

4. In what ways do these stories show the Israelites were not focusing on God or trusting Him to meet their needs? What does it say about God that He didn't punish the people for their first couple of doubt-fueled panic attacks?

_____

_____

_____

_____

5. In what ways are you aligning your will with God's and focusing your life on Him?

_____

_____

_____

_____

The people thirsted there for water, and the people complained against Moses, and said, "Why is it you have brought us up out of Egypt, to kill us and our children and our livestock with thirst?" So Moses cried out to the LORD, saying, "What shall I do with this people? They are almost ready to stone me!" . . . So he called the name of the place Massah and Meribah, because of the contention of the children of Israel, and because they tempted the LORD, saying, "Is the LORD among us or not?" (Exodus 17:3–4, 7).

Therefore do not be unwise, but understand what the will of the Lord is (Ephesians 5:17).

The Lord provides regular tests to see if you will obey Him, even when you don't fully understand the reasons for His commandments. Your obedience always brings blessing; and when you submit to Him, He assumes full responsibility for your needs.

Day 32: Promise Keeper

The value of any commitment is based on three things: (1) the ability of the promise maker to fulfill the promise, (2) the integrity of the promise maker, and (3) whether he or she has the character to follow through on the promise. God certainly qualifies on all accounts. He has all the wisdom, power, and ability necessary to fulfill His promises. He also

God has all the wisdom, power, and ability necessary to fulfill His promises.

has proven His integrity. He is utterly faithful to His Word. He is holy and immutable. He is unchanging.

When you have an unmet need, the first thing you need to do is pray and tell the Lord what you are facing. This is not to "inform" God of the problem (He already knows) but to declare your trust in Him and His ability to meet the need. Many times, God will allow a need to come into your life so He can teach you to trust Him in a greater way. As you walk in the Spirit, alert to God, you will begin to hear what He is saying to you. As you obey His commandments, you will develop a pattern of trusting in Him and seeing the results.

When you are walking in step with God, He assumes full responsibility for the answer to your needs, problems, challenges, and circumstances. But again, remember this is according to *His* will, *His* purpose, *His* plan, and in *His* timing. God may choose to answer your prayers quickly, or He may wait for a season—and "meeting your needs" does not necessarily mean He will meet every desire you have. He will provide for you in the right way, at the right time, and in just the right amount you need to keep depending on Him.

6. Read Luke 10:1–12. What was Jesus doing in this passage? Why did He say, "The laborers are few" (2)?

_____

_____

_____

_____

_____

7. What instructions did Jesus give these seventy-two followers (3–4)? In what ways would this have made them completely dependent on God to meet their needs?

_____

_____

_____

_____

_____

8. If you had been among the seventy-two disciples that Jesus sent out, what would have been the hardest part of following His instructions? Explain.

_____

_____

_____

_____

_____

> **When you have an unmet need, pray and tell the Lord what you are facing.**

> **When you walk in step with God, He assumes the responsibility to meet your needs.**

> *The Lord appointed seventy others also, and sent them two by two before His face into every city and place where He Himself was about to go. Then He said to them, "The harvest truly is great, but the laborers are few; therefore pray the Lord of the harvest to send out laborers in His harvest. Go your way; behold, I send you out as lambs among wolves. Carry neither money bag, knapsack, nor sandals; and greet no one along the road. But whatever house you enter, first say, 'Peace to this house'" (Luke 10:1–5).*

9. Some might say Jesus was sending His disciples out as "freeloaders" (7). How would you respond to that charge? What was their "work" He had sent them to do (9)?

_____

_____

_____

_____

10. Consider a situation in your life when you obeyed God in a radical way and gave Him complete control of the consequences. What happened as a result?

_____

_____

_____

_____

_____

For you remember, brethren, our labor and toil; for laboring night and day, that we might not be a burden to any of you, we preached to you the gospel of God (1 Thessalonians 2:9).

Day 33: The Deeper Lesson

One of God's greatest desires is for you to learn to trust His wisdom and timing. Anytime you *expect* God to move a certain way, you have missed the deeper lesson He wants you to learn. God's desire for your life is rooted in the relationship He wants to have with You. It begins within you the moment you say, "God, it's not what I want that matters, but it's who You want me to be. It's not what I want to do, but what you want me to do."

Making such statements requires *faith*. It demands complete trust in God, even when you do not understand why He has allowed circumstances to unfold a certain way. Think of all the people in the Bible who trusted the Lord and gained a wondrous victory: Moses, David, Esther, Jeremiah, Elijah, the disciples, and Mary, to name just a few. God wants you to have the victory as well. He knows your heart. When you are completely surrendered to Him, He sees your devotion and goes to work on your behalf.

"And if a son of peace is there, your peace will rest on it; if not, it will return to you. And remain in the same house, eating and drinking such things as they give, for the laborer is worthy of his wages. Do not go from house to house. Whatever city you enter, and they receive you, eat such things as are set before you. And heal the sick there, and say to them, 'The kingdom of God has come near to you'" (Luke 10:6–9).

Learn to trust in God's wisdom and timing.

When you surrender to God, He sees your devotion and goes to work on your behalf.

God calls you to make Him your sole source of supply.

He said to His disciples, "Therefore I say to you, do not worry about your life, what you will eat; nor about the body, what you will put on. Life is more than food, and the body is more than clothing. Consider the ravens, for they neither sow nor reap, which have neither storehouse nor barn; and God feeds them. Of how much more value are you than the birds? And which of you by worrying can add one cubit to his stature?

If you then are not able to do the least, why are you anxious for the rest? Consider the lilies, how they grow: they neither toil nor spin; and yet I say to you, even Solomon in all his glory was not arrayed like one of these. If then God so clothes the grass, which today is in the field and tomorrow is thrown into the oven, how much more will He clothe you, O you of little faith? And do not seek what you should eat or what you should drink, nor have an anxious mind. For all these things the nations of the world seek after, and your Father knows that you need these things. But seek the kingdom of God, and all these things shall be added to you"
(Luke 12:22–31).

God calls you to trust Him—and Him alone—to be your total source of supply. As you do, you will discover a hunger in your heart to be more like Christ, draw nearer to the heart of God, and know more about the truth He presents in His Word. You will discover a thirst for the things of God and a desire to experience His goodness on a new level. You will come to realize you can always count on God's love, wisdom, power, and grace—He will never fail you. He is the God who cares, and He will provide what you need at just the right time.

11. Read Luke 12:22–34. What does Jesus mean when He says, "Life is more than food, and the body is more than clothing" (23)?

_____

_____

_____

_____

12. What point was Jesus making by asking His disciples to consider how God feeds the ravens (24) and adorns the lilies (27)?

_____

_____

_____

_____

_____

13. What does Jesus say the disciples should pursue (31–32)? How does such a mind-set foster a spirit of generosity (33)?

_____

_____

_____

14. If someone were to ask the people closest to you where your treasure is, what would they say? What does that tell you?

_____

_____

_____

_____

15. How would you describe your level of faith in God to meet your needs? What encouragement do you receive from this passage?

_____

_____

_____

_____

True satisfaction in life flows out of fulfilling the purpose for which we were created—to enjoy an intimate relationship with God.

Living the Principle

Trusting in God requires you to settle two questions in your heart. The first question is whether you think God *can* help you. Do you believe God is completely *able* to intervene in your situation? Do you have confidence that the One who laid the foundations of the earth (see Genesis 1), delivered the children of Israel out of Egypt (see Exodus 14:13–31), and defeated death to save you from your sins (see 1 Corinthians 15) has the power to help you?

The second question you must ask yourself is whether you believe God *will* help you. Will God respond to you when you cry out to Him in prayer? Will He intervene in your situation? Does He even care about what you are facing? Paul answered that question for you in Romans 8:32 when he wrote, "He who did not spare His own Son, but delivered Him up for us all, how shall He not with Him also freely give us all things?"

God is both able and willing to supply everything you need. Therefore, if there are still areas in your life where you are lacking, you need to spend time in prayer this week asking God to reveal what He is trying to teach you. Maybe there is something in your life that shouldn't be there . . . or perhaps He is filling a deeper need in you.

How will you live out Life Principle 11 this week? Is there a need you have that you need to take to God in prayer? Or do you feel God calling you to meet the need of another person? Look for ways this week to not only identify your own needs but also look for how God may be calling you to provide for others. Is there a ministry He wants you to support? Is there an act of service He wants you to do? Take your needs to God in prayer, and thank Him for the opportunity He provides to participate in His kingdom work in this world.

> **Do you truly believe God *can* help you?**
>
> **Do you truly believe God *will* help you?**

Life Lessons to Remember

❖ God is able to provide for you (see Psalm 65:4–6), and His timing is perfect (see Luke 12:30–31).

❖ God's integrity and love ensure He will carry out His promises to you (see Psalm 37:25–28).

❖ God will use you as part of His plan to meet needs in this world (see Hebrews 13:16).

Notes and Prayer Requests

USE THIS SPACE TO WRITE ANY KEY POINTS, QUESTIONS,
OR PRAYER REQUESTS FROM THIS WEEK'S STUDY.

_____

_____

_____

_____

_____

_____

_____

_____

_____

_____

_____

_____

_____

_____

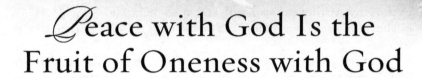

Peace with God Is the Fruit of Oneness with God

I will both lie down in peace, and sleep;
for You alone, O LORD, make me dwell in safety.

PSALM 4:8

Life's Questions

At night when everything is quiet, uneasy thoughts can bombard you. You want to sleep and get the rest you need, but your responsibilities and problems fill your mind. You try to focus on other things—counting sheep or the tick-tocks of your clock—but you can't stop the anxieties from tormenting you and keeping you awake. In those moments, you would give *anything* for some genuine, soul-calming peace.

Have you experienced sleepless nights alone with your troubled thoughts? Have you replayed scenarios over and over in your mind that you wish you could forget? Have you struggled through those stressful moments, wondering why your mental faculties could not let go and rest? Maybe you even felt like Asaph the psalmist, who wrote, "My hand was stretched out in the night without ceasing; my soul refused to be comforted . . . I complained, and my spirit was overwhelmed . . . I am so troubled that I cannot speak" (Psalm 77:2–4).

On the night Jesus was betrayed, He said to His disciples, "My peace I give to you; not as the world gives do I give to you. Let not your heart be troubled, neither let it be afraid" (John 14:27). Jesus promised to give His peace—but why is that peace so elusive and hard to grasp? In truth, peace is God's gift to you. But you cannot have it apart from an intimate relationship with Him. As Life Principle 12 states, *Peace with God is the fruit of oneness with God.*

PRINCIPLE IN ACTION
Adam and Eve (Genesis 2:25)
Wise Men (Matthew 2:1–12)
Jesus (Matthew 26:39)
Nicodemus (John 3:1–21)
Paul (Romans 5:1)

God's peace is an inner sense of contentment and quietness, regardless of life's circumstances. It is steadfast confidence in our ever-faithful, immutable heavenly Father.

—CHARLES F. STANLEY

Day 34: The Right Response

You maintain peace and balance by abiding in Christ.

How do you maintain a sense of peace and spiritual balance when trials strike? The answer is found in an *abiding* relationship with Jesus Christ. As He said on that same night to His disciples, "Abide in Me, and I in you. As the branch cannot bear fruit of itself, unless it abides in the vine, neither can you, unless you abide in Me" (John 15:4). An unshakable peace is available to all who turn the eyes of their hearts to Jesus.

Chances are that when adversity strikes, one of the first things you do is wonder why it is happening to you. You may ask what you have done wrong. You may look at others who seem more "deserving" of adversity—people who openly defy God and His Word—and wonder why their lives seem so trouble free. Your next thought may be to question what kind of impact the adversity will have on your life. You may start to despair about how it will affect your relationships, your work, and your future.

No one outside of God is equipped to handle your problems.

While reactions such as these are normal, you also need to remember another response: to turn to the One who holds all comfort and security firmly within His grasp. No one outside of God is equipped to handle your problems, and He never meant for you to be strong on your own. Regardless of how many exhortations you may hear to the contrary, you were never meant to be a self-sufficient army of one. You were created with a healthy need for God. He wants you to find courage, hope, and strength in Him and His Word.

All things are lawful for me, but all things are not helpful. All things are lawful for me, but I will not be brought under the power of any. Foods for the stomach and the stomach for foods, but God will destroy both it and them. Now the body is not for sexual immorality but for the Lord, and the Lord for the body. And God both raised up the Lord and will also raise us up by His power (1 Corinthians 6:12–14).

1. Read 1 Corinthians 6:12–20. In this passage, Paul is responding to believers in Corinth who believed they had the right to do as they pleased. How might these Corinthian Christians have come to this conclusion (12)?

   _____

   _____

   _____

   _____

2. How was this attitude affecting their oneness with God? How was it affecting their relationship with the Lord (15–17)?

   _____

   _____

   _____

   _____

   _____

3. How is your body connected to the body of Christ (15)?

_____

_____

_____

_____

4. How might being "one spirit with [God]" affect the decisions you make every day (17)?

_____

_____

_____

_____

5. What might the apostle Paul say to someone who argued, "It's my body, and I can do what I want with it" (18–20)?

_____

_____

_____

_____

_____

Paul had no interest in allowing the sinful patterns from which he had escaped through God's grace to enslave him again. He didn't ask, "What's wrong with it?" as much as, "Is this the Lord's will for me? Will it honor and glorify Him?"

Day 35: An Unshakable Peace

Life is filled with uncertainties. Every day, you see news reports on the latest natural disaster in the nation or crisis in your community. In such an unsure world, what can you do to confront the feelings of anxiety that naturally come over you? The first step is to recognize anxiety for what it is: _the opposite of peace_. Anxiety is the fan that flames the fires of doubt and confusion. When you cave in to thoughts of anxiety, you lose your spiritual focus and mind-set.

The key to overcoming anxiety is found in the presence of God. When you choose to keep your mind focused on God and trust in Him completely, He fills you with His "perfect peace" (Isaiah 26:3). When

Do you not know that your bodies are members of Christ? Shall I then take the members of Christ and make them members of a harlot? Certainly not! Or do you not know that he who is joined to a harlot is one body with her? For "the two," He says, "shall become one flesh." But he who is joined to the Lord is one spirit with Him. Flee sexual immorality. Every sin that a man does is outside the body, but he who commits sexual immorality sins against his own body. Or do you not know that your body is the temple of the Holy Spirit who is in you, whom you have from God, and you are not your own? For you were bought at a price; therefore glorify God in your body and in your spirit, which are God's (1 Corinthians 6:15–20).

Recognize that anxiety is the opposite of peace.

You will keep him in perfect peace, whose mind is stayed on You (Isaiah 26:3).

91

*Turn your eyes upon Jesus,
look full in His wonderful face,
and the things of earth will grow
strangely dim, in the light of
His glory and grace.*

—HELEN LEMMEL

you accept His timetable and limitations in a given situation, He will begin to remove the anxieties you experience. As the hymn states, when you "turn your eyes upon Jesus" and "look full in His wonderful face," you will find His mercy and grace, forgiveness and hope, peace and everlasting security.

What would you give to experience the unshakable peace of God? Are you willing to give control of your future to Him and follow His plan? Are you willing to trust He will take care of you and meet your needs? Will you trust Him in quietness, knowing He will never forget you? Will you believe in your heart that His peace and presence are sure and immovable?

*Moses went and spoke these
words to all Israel. And he said
to them: "I am one hundred
and twenty years old today.
I can no longer go out and
come in. Also the LORD has
said to me, 'You shall not cross
over this Jordan.' The LORD
your God Himself crosses over
before you; He will destroy
these nations from before
you, and you shall dispossess
them. Joshua himself crosses
over before you, just as the
LORD has said. And the LORD
will do to them as He did to
Sihon and Og, the kings of
the Amorites and their land,
when He destroyed them.
The LORD will give them
over to you, that you may do
to them according to every
commandment which I have
commanded you. Be strong
and of good courage, do not
fear nor be afraid of them; for
the LORD your God, He is the
one who goes with you. He will
not leave you nor forsake you"*
(Deuteronomy 31:1–6).

6. Read Deuteronomy 31:1–8. The Israelites had been wandering in the desert for forty years, and the time had come for them to finally take the Promised Land. But now the people were losing Moses, their leader (2). What fears would the people have had about the future as they listened to Moses's words?

_____

_____

_____

_____

7. What did Moses promise the Lord would do on their behalf (3–5)?

_____

_____

_____

_____

8. Why did Moses say they did not need to give in to fear and anxiety (6–8)?

_____

_____

_____

_____

9. Moses instructed the Israelites to look to God for peace during this stressful time in their history. What stressful situation do you need to give to God today?

_____

_____

_____

_____

10. How does it make you feel to know the Lord goes before you—that He already knows your future and will never forsake you (8)?

_____

_____

_____

_____

_____

_____

The word peace *in Hebrew,* shalom, *means "the completion, fulfillment, unity, and harmony that come as a result of God's presence."*

Day 36: A Peace That Passes Understanding

David lived in a world that was anything but certain and secure. At one point, he found himself on the run from King Saul (who wanted to end David's life) so he could never take the throne. Yet during this tense time, David found the strength to write, "In the shadow of Your wings I will make my refuge, until these calamities have passed by. I will cry out to God Most High, to God who performs all things for me. He shall send from heaven and save me" (Psalm 57:1–3).

How could David write such confident words as he was hiding in a cave from a man who wanted to end his life? The answer is found in the way David led his life up to this point. He was a man who sought God's presence in everything he did, whether he was confronting a lion, a bear, or a giant named Goliath. David had learned to give every situation to God, and he had unshakable peace that God would protect him and fulfill His promises.

The safest place for you to run when trials come your way is into the everlasting arms of Jesus. He is the "Prince of Peace" (Isaiah 9:6) who secured your eternal future through His death on the cross. So if a conflict, sorrow, or crisis is filling you with anxiety, allow God's peace to invade your heart. Tell Him all you are feeling. He understands and knows that life can be difficult—but He has a solution. Your peace resides in your Savior, who loves you unconditionally. He has promised to keep you safe and deliver you into the Father's arms.

Then Moses called Joshua and said to him in the sight of all Israel, "Be strong and of good courage, for you must go with this people to the land which the LORD has sworn to their fathers to give them, and you shall cause them to inherit it. And the LORD, He is the one who goes before you. He will be with you, He will not leave you nor forsake you; do not fear nor be dismayed" (Deuteronomy 31:7–8).

David fled from Naioth in Ramah, and went and said to Jonathan, "What have I done? What is my iniquity, and what is my sin before your father, that he seeks my life?" (1 Samuel 20:1).

The safest place for you to run when trials come is into the arms of Jesus.

Be anxious for nothing, but in everything by prayer and supplication, with thanksgiving, let your requests be made known to God; and the peace of God, which surpasses all understanding, will guard your hearts and minds through Christ Jesus (Philippians 4:6–8).

11. Read Philippians 4:6–8. What does it mean to "be anxious"? Why is anxiety a counterproductive state of mind?

_____

_____

_____

_____

12. Why is thanksgiving an essential part of making your requests known to God (6)?

_____

_____

_____

_____

13. What does Paul say you need to put into your mind when you are feeling anxious (8)? Why is it so important to continually "meditate on these things"?

_____

_____

_____

_____

_____

14. Why is the peace of God so easily disrupted? Why is it so easy for anxiety to gain a foothold in your life?

_____

_____

_____

_____

*These things I have spoken to you, that in Me you may have peace. In the world you will have tribulation; but be of good cheer, I have overcome the world"
(John 16:33).*

15. How do you keep God's peace as a fixture in your life? How do you use it to continually guard your heart and mind?

_____

_____

_____

_____

_____

As you fill your mind with the holy and acceptable things of God, you begin to see and respond to the world as He does—in truth, righteousness, and in accordance with His will.

Living the Principle

Do you long for deep and abiding peace? Does your soul need rest from the worries that surround you? Your anxiety can be a telltale sign that your focus isn't where it should be. Instead of rejoicing in the strength, wisdom, and love of God, you may have allowed your attention to be consumed by the details of your circumstances. You may be so busy trying to figure out how to fix your situation that you've forgotten the only effective solution is to submit yourself to God. As Jesus said, "I have spoken to you, that in Me you may have peace. In the world you will have tribulation; but be of good cheer, I have overcome the world" (John 16:33).

It is time to start thinking differently about your situation. As Paul instructs in Romans 12:2, it is time to "be transformed by the renewing of your mind." You do this by continually filling your mind with the things of God—by beginning each day connecting with Him through prayer and reading His Word. Your time with God will give you the direction, strength, and focus you need and will fill you with the peace for which your heart yearns.

How will you live out Life Principle 12 this week? Begin by taking some time to examine your heart. Are you at peace? If not, what is causing your unrest or worry? What areas of your life have you not fully turned over to God? What promises does God provide to you in His Word that He will care for you? As you seek the Lord in prayer, ask Him to shine a light on anything that is preventing you from forming a greater oneness with Him.

> Anxiety can be a sign your focus isn't where it should be.

Life Lessons to Remember

- ❖ Only God is equipped to handle your problems (see Psalm 62:5–7).
- ❖ Accepting God's timetable and instruction will help you dispel rising anxiety (see Habakkuk 2:1–3).
- ❖ The safest place for you to turn when trials come your way is into the everlasting arms of Jesus (see Deuteronomy 33:27).

A person who has genuine, godly peace can endure an avalanche of hardship and difficulty and still enjoy an inner peace that surpasses all human understanding. Why? Because it does not come from pleasant circumstances, nice events, or good things others may do for us. Instead, it is based on the fact that the Spirit of our holy, omnipotent, and never- changing God lives within us.

Notes AND Prayer Requests

USE THIS SPACE TO WRITE ANY KEY POINTS, QUESTIONS,
OR PRAYER REQUESTS FROM THIS WEEK'S STUDY.

LIFE PRINCIPLE 13

Listening to God Is Essential to Walking with God

Hear, O My people, and I will admonish you!
O Israel, if you will listen to Me!

PSALM 81:8

Life's Questions

Have you ever been in a situation in which people simply refused to listen to you, even though you had something important to say? Perhaps the solution to a problem seemed obvious to you, but others were so busy voicing their opinions that you couldn't get a word in edgewise. You tried to reason with them, but they refused to yield the floor.

Frustrating, isn't it? Now imagine what it must be like to be God in heaven, who possesses the most profound and complete knowledge about every topic in the universe. He has the wisdom His people need to solve even their deepest problems. He is willing and available to help with all the resources that only He can provide. But unfortunately, whenever His people bow their heads to communicate with Him, they do all the talking!

Have your conversations with God been one-sided? Have you tended to relay your list of needs and requests to Him without pausing to listen for His instruction? If so, you've been a bit like that person unwilling to yield the floor. As Life Principle 13 states, *Listening to God is essential to walking with God.* If you want to have a relationship with Him, you have to listen to Him. If you want Him to transform your life, you need to hear what He's saying.

PRINCIPLE IN ACTION
Samuel (1 Samuel 3:1–10)
Elijah (1 Kings 19:10–13)
David (Psalm 31:3–5)
Solomon (Proverbs 3:5–6)
Philip (Acts 8:26–40)

We can never know the mind of God fully because we are finite creatures, but we can grow in our understanding about who God is, how He operates in our world, and why He does the things He does.

—CHARLES F. STANLEY

Day 37: Learning to Listen

Nothing is more urgent, necessary, or rewarding than listening to God.

One of the most important lessons you can learn is how to listen to God. In your complex and hectic life, nothing is more urgent, more necessary, or more rewarding than hearing what God has to say to you in the moment and responding to it with an obedient spirit. As in any relationship, both *talking and listening* must take place for growth to occur.

Unfortunately, listening to God is a skill that doesn't come naturally for most people. Everyday distractions might account for some of the difficulties. But often your ability to listen will be determined in part by the attitude you carry into your conversations with Him. Your mind-set can be affected by your prior relationship with God, your understanding about God, and your feelings toward Him. The result is that you might be predisposed to hearing certain things from Him and not hearing other things.

The extent to which you identify with Christ will determine what you hear God say to you.

The extent to which you identify with Christ will determine, in part, what you hear God say to you. If you are truly seeking to become more like Him, and striving to make Him the Lord of your life, you are going to hear God's counsel. But if you are merely content with the fact you are saved, you probably won't hear God's voice. And that is a great danger for believers, for if you fail to hear from God, it will lead you to make some unwise and costly mistakes.

Samuel ministered to the LORD before Eli. And the word of the LORD was rare in those days; there was no widespread revelation (1 Samuel 3:1).

1. Read 1 Samuel 3:1–8. What does it mean that "the word of the LORD was rare in those days" (1)? Why do you suppose that was the case?

_____

_____

_____

_____

The LORD called Samuel. And he answered, "Here I am!" (1 Samuel 3:4–5).

2. How did Samuel hear God speak to Him (4)? How did he respond (5)?

_____

_____

_____

_____

So he arose and went to Eli, and said, "Here I am, for you did call me." Then Eli perceived that the LORD had called the boy (1 Samuel 3:8).

3. Eli was the chief priest of the tabernacle, the highest religious authority in Israel. Why did it take him so long to realize God was speaking to Samuel (8)?

_____

_____

_____

_____

4. What does this passage reveal about God's methods of speaking to His servants?

_____

_____

_____

5. God audibly spoke to Samuel three times to get His attention. What methods do you feel He is using to get your attention?

_____

_____

_____

God, who at various times and in various ways spoke in time past to the fathers by the prophets, has in these last days spoken to us by His Son (Hebrews 12:1–2).

When God first spoke to Samuel, the boy didn't yet know His voice—but he learned to hear it. The Lord desires for you to enjoy a close relationship with Him, and He has done everything necessary to make it possible.

Day 38: Message Received

Samuel was one of the mightiest prophets in the Old Testament, but even he had to learn how to hear God's voice. In Samuel's case, he heard God speak to him through his physical ears. God used this same form of *direct revelation* to communicate His will to Abraham (see Genesis 12:1), Moses (see Exodus 3:4), Job (see Job 38), and others. But God also uses other ways to get His message to people and make sure it is received.

The Bible is clear that God *does* speak to His people today. The author of Hebrews opens his letter this way: "God, who at various times and in various ways spoke in time past to the fathers by the prophets, has in these last days spoken to us by His Son" (1:1–2). God is not silent but alive and active. He speaks to you individually and in a way that you can hear Him, receive His message, and obey Him. Don't doubt He is fully capable of communicating to you right where you are—in the midst of your circumstances—in a personal way.

One clear way God speaks to you personally is through His written Word, for it contains His truth and inspiration. As Paul wrote, "All Scripture is given by inspiration of God, and is profitable for doctrine, for reproof, for correction, for instruction in righteousness" (2 Timothy 3:16). When you allow the Holy Spirit to open your heart, He will give

God uses many means to communicate His will.

God speaks to you personally through His Word.

Now an angel of the Lord spoke to Philip, saying, "Arise and go toward the south along the road which goes down from Jerusalem to Gaza." This is desert. So he arose and went. And behold, a man of Ethiopia, a eunuch of great authority under Candace the queen of the Ethiopians, who had charge of all her treasury, and had come to Jerusalem to worship, was returning. And sitting in his chariot, he was reading Isaiah the prophet. Then the Spirit said to Philip, "Go near and overtake this chariot." So Philip ran to him, and heard him reading the prophet Isaiah, and said, "Do you understand what you are reading?" And he said, "How can I, unless someone guides me?" And he asked Philip to come up and sit with him. The place in the Scripture which he read was this: "He was led as a sheep to the slaughter; and as a lamb before its shearer is silent, so He opened not His mouth. In His humiliation His justice was taken away, and who will declare His generation? For His life is taken from the earth." So the eunuch answered Philip and said, "I ask you, of whom does the prophet say this, of himself or of some other man?" (Acts 8:26–34).

you a deeper understanding of Scripture. You will begin to claim His promises for your life and gain a deeper understanding of His provision, care, and love.

6. Read Acts 8:26–40. How did God communicate His message to Philip (26)?

_____

_____

_____

_____

_____

7. Notice that God didn't state the exact reason for Philip's journey before he left. When did Philip receive further instructions? How did those instructions come to him (29)?

_____

_____

_____

_____

_____

_____

8. What problem did the Ethiopian express to Philip (31, 34)?

_____

_____

_____

_____

9. How did God use His Word to communicate His message to the Ethiopian? How did God use Philip as part of this process?

_____

_____

_____

_____

_____

10. What does this passage tell you about how God speaks through His Word? How is He using you in the process to communicate His message to others?

_____

_____

_____

_____

_____

Day 39: The Proper Response

God is serious about His relationship with you. He speaks for your benefit, so it is important for you to not only listen to Him, but also *respond in obedience*. Sometimes He will challenge you to change your thinking or release certain unhealthy feelings and opinions. Sometimes He will command you to change aspects of your behavior. Yet with every instruction He gives, you can be certain that it is always intended for your good.

As a believer in Christ, you have an enemy who is intent on filling the airwaves with lies and miscommunication. He will try to get you to doubt God's instructions—and even that God is speaking to you in the first place! The good news is that you have the strong, active, and constant support of Jesus as your defender against Satan's lies. He is praying continually that you will be strengthened and kept safe from the enemy of your soul (see John 17:14–17).

However, the choice is still yours when it comes to obeying God's voice or obeying the lies of the enemy. Here again the Bible can help you, for it is an extremely practical book with truth that can be applied directly to daily situations and circumstances. The Bible is not merely a book of "do's" and "don't's" but a book of "how to's." It tells you not only to avoid listening to the enemy's falsehoods but also how you can recognize the voice of the Lord. It also reveals the blessing you will receive for obedience and the consequences of disobedience.

11. Read Genesis 19:12–29. Lot was a righteous man, but he was living in one of the most evil cities on earth. So God sent two angels to take Lot and his family from the city of Sodom before He destroyed it. What were God's instructions to Lot (12)?

_____

_____

_____

_____

_____

_____

God is serious about His relationship with you.

You can choose to obey God's voice or the lies of the enemy.

Then the men said to Lot, "Have you anyone else here? Son-in-law, your sons, your daughters, and whomever you have in the city—take them out of this place! (Genesis 19:12).

101

"For we will destroy this place, because the outcry against them has grown great before the face of the LORD, and the LORD has sent us to destroy it." So Lot went out and spoke to his sons-in-law, who had married his daughters, and said, "Get up, get out of this place; for the LORD will destroy this city!" But to his sons-in-law he seemed to be joking (Genesis 19:13–14).

12. What were the consequences of disobedience (13)?

_____

_____

_____

_____

13. How did Lot's family respond to the command (14–15)? Why do you think Lot "lingered" instead of immediately departing the condemned city (16)?

_____

_____

_____

_____

And while he lingered, the men took hold of his hand, his wife's hand, and the hands of his two daughters, the LORD being merciful to him, and they brought him out and set him outside the city. So it came to pass, when they had brought them outside, that he said, "Escape for your life! Do not look behind you nor stay anywhere in the plain." . . . But his wife looked back behind him, and she became a pillar of salt (Genesis 19:16–17, 26).

14. How did God show His mercy to Lot and his family (17–22)? What were the consequences for Lot's wife when she disobeyed God's direct command (26)?

_____

_____

_____

_____

15. Is there any area in your life where you are "lingering" when it comes to obeying God? What will you do to move forward into God's will?

_____

_____

_____

_____

I thought about my ways, and turned my feet to Your testimonies. I made haste, and did not delay to keep Your commandments (Psalm 119:59–60).

Living the Principle

You have the freedom to approach the God of creation at any moment.

Do you realize the amazing privilege you have in being able to go to God in prayer? You have the freedom to approach the God of all creation at any moment to ask for His wisdom, comfort, and power. As the author of Hebrews affirms, "We do not have a High Priest who cannot sympathize with our weaknesses, but was in all points tempted as we are, yet without sin. Let us therefore come boldly to the throne of grace, that we may obtain mercy and find grace to help in time of need" (4:15–16).

Jesus understands everything you're going through and all with which you struggle in this life, and His desire is to guide you through your troubles in a way that glorifies God and makes you into a mature believer. You also have the Holy Spirit living within you to help you hear God's instruction and give you power over sin. However, the Lord cannot guide you if you choose not to walk with Him, and you cannot walk with Him if you refuse to allow Him to lead. And, of course, He cannot lead you if you refuse to listen to Him and obey.

How will you live out Life Principle 13 this week? Are you willing to be quiet before God and hear what He has to say? Are you willing to look for the ways that He might be speaking to you? This week, create an action plan for how you will intentionally listen to God and commit to obey Him, regardless of what He tells you to do. Recruit a small group of trusted Christian friends to hold you accountable to your plans.

> Jesus understands everything you are going through.

Life Lessons to Remember

❖ God is speaking to you in many ways, but you have to be willing to listen (see Hebrews 1:1–3).
❖ God always gives instruction to you for your benefit (see Isaiah 51:1–16).
❖ The choice is yours when it comes to obeying God's voice or the lies of the enemy (see Joshua 24:15).

Many references in Scripture mention the "fullness of time." God isn't in a hurry. He deals in eternal consequences, and He continually seeks the fulfillment of the full scope of His plan and purpose. . . . It isn't always easy to wait patiently before the LORD until you are sure that you have the fullness of His message. But how much more satisfying the results are when you know that you have heard God's entire message!

Notes AND Prayer Requests

USE THIS SPACE TO WRITE ANY KEY POINTS, QUESTIONS,
OR PRAYER REQUESTS FROM THIS WEEK'S STUDY.

_____

_____

_____

_____

_____

_____

_____

_____

_____

_____

_____

_____

_____

_____

God Acts on Behalf of Those Who Wait for Him

Since the beginning of the world men have not heard
nor perceived by the ear, nor has the eye seen any God besides You,
who acts for the one who waits for Him.

ISAIAH 64:4

Life's Questions

You live in an instant-gratification culture. You are conditioned to expect to get what you want, on demand, with the touch of a keystroke. Waiting is practically outdated. It's also extremely frustrating, especially when you're hoping for good news or relief from your troubles. No wonder Proverbs 13:12 states, "Hope deferred makes the heart sick." The longer you wait to see your desire fulfilled—whatever it may be—the more discouraged your heart grows. That is, of course, unless your hope and trust are centered exclusively on Christ.

In Micah 7:7, the prophet writes, "I will look to the LORD; I will wait for the God of my salvation; my God will hear me." While no one likes waiting, it is actually a big part of your walk of faith. God will use times of delay to refocus your attitude, remove hindrances that keep His will from being enacted, and prepare the way for you to take the next step in His plan. When you demonstrate your faith and trust in His ability to accomplish all things at the right time, you acknowledge that He is Lord of your life.

It is not always easy to be patient when God asks you to wait on Him, but it is the only way to be sure that you are operating in His timing. As Life Principle 14 explains, *God acts on behalf of those who wait for Him.*

PRINCIPLE IN ACTION
Abraham (Genesis 21:1–3)
David (2 Samuel 3:1)
Job (Job 42:10–17)
Israelites (Ezekiel 39:21–29)
Daniel (Daniel 10:12–14)

God doesn't always meet our needs immediately. Why not? Because often He is preparing us for something new.

—CHARLES F. STANLEY

So, if you want God's best for your life, you must trust Him to provide it in His time. His knowledge of you and your situation is absolutely perfect, and He is going to make sure you are completely prepared for the blessings He has in store for you.

Day 40: Wait for It

Waiting rooms can be hard classrooms, but God promises you vast rewards if you choose not to rush ahead of Him. One of these rewards is that you *discover His will.* God always has a purpose for allowing delays; and even as you wait, He is working all things together for your good and His glory (see Romans 8:28). As you eagerly await His provision, you must keep your eyes on Him and listen for His voice and direction. In doing so, you will learn to do His will, and your relationship with Him will grow deeper.

One reward of waiting on God is that you discover His will.

Another reward for waiting on God is that you receive His *supernatural energy and strength.* God invites you to claim His promise in Isaiah 40:31: "Those who wait on the LORD shall renew *their* strength; they shall mount up with wings like eagles, they shall run and not be weary, they shall walk and not faint." God uses times of delay to increase your energy, faith, endurance, and strength. You grow in the likeness of Christ and all His attributes—including love, joy, peace, patience, kindness, goodness, faithfulness, gentleness, and self-control (see Galatians 5:22–23). Waiting on God is never wasted time!

A second reward is that you receive His strength.

The LORD had said to Abram: "Get out of your country, from your family and from your father's house, to a land that I will show you. I will make you a great nation; I will bless you and make your name great; and you shall be a blessing. I will bless those who bless you, and I will curse him who curses you; and in you all the families of the earth shall be blessed" (Genesis 12:1–3).

1. Read Genesis 11:27–12:9. One of the greatest examples of waiting in the Bible is found in the story of Abraham and Sarah. In their day, the culture placed great emphasis on a woman's ability to bear children—especially male heirs. What impact might have Sarah's barrenness had on her social standing? What impact might it have had on her feelings of self-worth?

   _____

   _____

   _____

   _____

2. What was God's promise to Abraham (12:2)? When did God say this would occur?

   _____

   _____

   _____

3. How old was Abraham when God made this promise (4)? Why do you think Abraham was quick to follow God's instructions, even when he knew it would be almost physically impossible for this promise to be fulfilled through him and his wife?

_____

_____

_____

_____

4. What else did God promise to Abraham (7)? What stood in the way of this particular promise being fulfilled (6)?

_____

_____

_____

_____

5. How would you describe Abraham and Sarah's faith in this story? In what ways is it similar or different from your own?

_____

_____

_____

_____

_____

*When you wait for the Lord, you should look forward to what
He will do with joyful expectation and confident hope,
because He is providing His very best for you.*

Day 41: The Purpose of Patience

It took a great deal of faith for Abraham and Sarah to follow the call of a God they did not know, leave their homeland in Ur, and travel to the unknown land of Canaan. It took even more faith for them to believe God would do the impossible and give them an heir. Even though at times their trust in God's plan wavered—and they tried to take matters into their own hands—in the end they learned that God always fulfills His promises in His own time. You will discover the same to be true in your life when you operate according to God's schedule.

In addition to discovering God's will and receiving supernatural strength, you will also receive *victory in battles* when you wait on the Lord. Proverbs 20:22 states, "Wait for the LORD, and He will save you." When

---

So Abram departed as the LORD had spoken to him, and Lot went with him. And Abram was seventy-five years old when he departed from Haran. Then Abram took Sarai his wife and Lot his brother's son, and all their possessions that they had gathered, and the people whom they had acquired in Haran, and they departed to go to the land of Canaan. So they came to the land of Canaan. Abram passed through the land to the place of Shechem, as far as the terebinth tree of Moreh. And the Canaanites were then in the land. Then the LORD appeared to Abram and said, "To your descendants I will give this land." And there he built an altar to the LORD, who had appeared to him (Genesis 12:4–7).

The promise that he would be the heir of the world was not to Abraham or to his seed through the law, but through the righteousness of faith (Romans 4:13).

A third reward of waiting on God is that you receive victory in battles.

you try to do things your way, in your own hurried time, you end up defeated because you lack the experience, wisdom, vision, and power to fight your battles effectively. But when you are patient and obey God's commands, He ensures your victory and keeps you from acting foolishly or precipitously.

Waiting on God also brings *the fulfillment of your faith*. In Isaiah 49:23, God states, "They shall not be ashamed who wait for Me." You will never regret operating in God's timing, even if it feels that you are standing still while everyone else around you is going on to bigger and better things. Every person's timetable is unique, and you will only lose perspective if you try to compare your progress to someone else's. When you trust God and obey Him, you can be certain you will see the fulfillment of every hope you've entrusted to Him—at the right time.

> A fourth reward is that waiting on God brings fulfillment of your faith.

6. Read Genesis 16:1–16. As the years passed, Abraham and Sarah began to grow impatient with God's timing and decided to take matters into their own hands. What was Sarah's plan to get an heir (2)?

_____

_____

_____

_____

_____

> *Then Sarai, Abram's wife, took Hagar her maid, the Egyptian, and gave her to her husband Abram to be his wife, after Abram had dwelt ten years in the land of Canaan. So he sent in to Hagar, and she conceived. And when she saw that she had conceived, her mistress became despised in her eyes. Then Sarai said to Abram, "My wrong be upon you! I gave my maid into your embrace; and when she saw that she had conceived, I became despised in her eyes. The LORD judge between you and me." So Abram said to Sarai, "Indeed your maid is in your hand; do to her as you please." And when Sarai dealt harshly with her, she fled from her presence (Genesis 16:3–6).*

7. The plan worked, and Hagar gave birth to a baby boy. Why didn't this lead to the blessings Abraham and Sarah expected (4–5)?

_____

_____

_____

_____

8. What were the consequences for Hagar and her child (6)?

_____

_____

_____

_____

> *"He shall be a wild man; his hand shall be against every man, and every man's hand against him. And he shall dwell in the presence of all his brethren"* (Genesis 16:12).

9. How did God describe what this child would be like (12)? What problems could you see this creating for Abraham and Sarah?

_____

_____

_____

_____

10. When in your life did you try to rush God's plan? What did you learn from the experience?

Wait on the LORD; be of good courage, and He shall strengthen your heart (Psalm 27:14).

_____

_____

_____

_____

_____

*Sarah found out the hard way that whatever we acquire
outside of God's will often turns to ashes. Her plan to raise
a family through Hagar misfired badly.*

Day 42: At Work While You Wait

Think of waiting on God as something like planting a garden. You put a seed under the soil and water it. And then you wait . . . and wait . . . and wait. Nothing seems to be happening. But after the sun and rain nourish the earth, the seeds begin to grow. Finally, you begin to see evidence of what you've planted. If you had grown impatient and dug up your seeds because nothing seemed to be happening, you would have ruined your garden.

Some fruit takes a long time to mature—and the One who wants to bring it forth in your life knows exactly how long you need to wait. Sometimes, the wait will be short, while at other times it will be much longer. Regardless, you can know God *is always working on your behalf.* Isaiah spoke of the God "who acts for the one who waits for Him" (64:4). Every day, you have the greatest Mediator working on your behalf. Even when things seem to go wrong, He is making sure everything works according to His purpose.

The One who wants to bring forth fruit in your life knows how long you need to wait.

Although waiting is difficult, it is not wasted time. God gives you instructions through periods of actively waiting. He may change your circumstances. He keeps you in step with Himself and prepares you for His answers. He uses the time to sift your motives and strengthen your faith. When you choose to wait, God rewards you with blessings both large and unexpected. So trust Him and be patient—He is producing the most wonderful and precious fruit in your life that you could ever imagine.

God uses time to sift your motives and strengthen your faith.

Sarah said, "God has made me laugh, and all who hear will laugh with me." She also said, "Who would have said to Abraham that Sarah would nurse children? For I have borne him a son in his old age" (Genesis 21:6–7).

11. Read Genesis 21:1–7. Abraham and Sarah waited decades for God to fulfill His promise to them. Why do you think God paused so long before doing what He said He would do?

_____

_____

_____

_____

12. What reflections did Sarah have on the fulfillment of God's promise and her time of waiting (6–7)?

_____

_____

_____

_____

The Angel of the LORD called to Abraham a second time out of heaven, and said: "By Myself I have sworn, says the LORD, because you have done this thing, and have not withheld your son, your only son—blessing I will bless you, and multiplying I will multiply your descendants as the stars of the heaven and as the sand which is on the seashore; and your descendants shall possess the gate of their enemies. In your seed all the nations of the earth shall be blessed, because you have obeyed My voice." So Abraham returned to his young men, and they rose and went together to Beersheba (Genesis 22:15–19).

13. Read Genesis 22:15–19. How did Abraham's seed bless "all the nations of the earth" (18)? What does this say about waiting on God's timing?

_____

_____

_____

_____

14. What advice might Abraham and Sarah offer today for those who struggle with patience and waiting on God?

_____

_____

_____

15. What are you waiting for God to deliver in your life today? What encouragement do you gain from Abraham and Sarah's story?

_____

_____

_____

_____

God always blesses obedience, and obedience always follows genuine faith. If you do not obey, it is because you do not truly believe (see Hebrews 3:18–19).

Living the Principle

You could call Abraham not only a man of faith (see Galatians 3:9), but also a man of endurance. Despite a stumble along the way, he ran a faithful race. For *twenty-five years* he kept in step with God, until (at age 100) he and his wife (age ninety) had a son. Why the long wait? Apparently, God wanted Abraham to learn the connection between waiting, trust, and hope. That hope, Paul says, prompts you to wait on God "with perseverance" (Romans 8:25).

During your season of waiting, you may feel lost, discouraged, and unmotivated. You may feel as if God has forgotten you. But know He has not. God is always at work, and at this very moment He is engineering your situation to provide His very best for you. However, you must be patient until His plan comes together. Do not run ahead of God! The delays may be challenging, but they are growing your faith in Him. After all, "Faith is the substance of things hoped for, the evidence of things not seen" (Hebrews 11:1). So look to Him, strengthen yourself in His Word and love, and remain confident He is working on your behalf.

How will you live out Life Principle 14 this week? If you are wondering what God wants you to do during a time of waiting, you should continue in your present course until He gives you further instructions. As long as you are obeying Him, you will continue on the correct path. Also, talk to a trusted Christian friend or mentor about times you've waited for God to work. Share the frustrations and anxiety you felt, and then describe how God acted on your behalf. Spend time in prayer with the person, thanking God for His past work in your life and asking Him to help you align yourself to His timetable.

> God wants you to learn the connection between waiting, trust, and hope.

Life Lessons to Remember

- ❖ When you wait, you discover God's will in the areas that most concern you (see Isaiah 30:18).
- ❖ When you wait, you receive supernatural physical energy and strength (see Psalm 27:13–14).
- ❖ When you wait, you see God working on your behalf (see Psalm 40:1–3).

Notes AND Prayer Requests

USE THIS SPACE TO WRITE ANY KEY POINTS, QUESTIONS,
OR PRAYER REQUESTS FROM THIS WEEK'S STUDY.

_____

_____

_____

_____

_____

_____

_____

_____

_____

_____

_____

_____

_____

_____

_____

LIFE PRINCIPLE 15

Brokenness Is God's Requirement for Maximum Usefulness

Therefore thus says the LORD "If you return, then I will bring you back; you shall stand before Me; if you take out the precious from the vile, you shall be as My mouth. Let them return to you, but you must not return to them."

JEREMIAH 15:19

Life's Questions

Sometimes life just doesn't make sense. You seek God and try to be obedient to Him, but trouble and heartbreak confront you at every turn. Perhaps you thought your situation would get easier once you accepted Christ as your Savior, but you've found just the opposite to be true. Now you not only have to deal with all the troubles the world throws at you, but you also feel responsible to honor God in how you respond to them.

Somewhere inside you, you've come to the realization you're just not strong enough to live the holy life that Christ has called you to. Good! God never meant you to live the Christian life in your own strength and by your own resources. The trials you've been experiencing are part of the breaking process in which God is freeing you from your self-sufficiency so you'll allow Christ to live in and through you. He is using your trials as a teacher. He wants to use the adversity you are facing as part of His miracle-working plan to mold you into the person He wants you to be.

As Life Principle 15 teaches: *Brokenness is God's requirement for maximum usefulness.* It's through brokenness that God helps you stop depending on yourself and start looking to Him for your strength, wisdom, and power. It's through brokenness that you discover what God has planned for you. It's through brokenness that you become whole.

PRINCIPLE IN ACTION
Moses (Exodus 2:11–15)
David (2 Samuel 12:1–14)
Isaiah (Isaiah 6:1–8)
Paul (2 Corinthians 12:7–10)
John Mark (Colossians 4:10)

As a Christian, you must focus your heart on Jesus and obey Him implicitly, which often means giving up what you think you want.
—CHARLES F. STANLEY

113

Day 43: Depending on God Alone

||||||||||||||||||||||||||||||||||||||||||||||||||||||||||||||||||||||||||||||||||||||||||||||||||||||||||||||||||||||||||||||||||||||||||||

All too often, Christians struggle to get to what they perceive as "the top." They forge their long list of accomplishments, perhaps with the hope they will one day be able to hand it to God and say, "See what I've done for You?" They look at what they've done and conclude that God *must* be compelled to reward and prosper them for all their good deeds.

The truth is, God will never accept you on the basis of what *you've done*. Rather, He will receive you because of what *Christ has done* on the cross (see Ephesians 2:8–9). This is why He instructs you to stop depending on what you can accomplish and instead rely on Him (see Proverbs 3:5–6)—not only for your salvation, but also for every aspect of life. He calls you to repent of your sinful habits, self-reliance, and prideful desires until you can truly say, "All that I am and all that I have is God's. He is in me and I am in Him, and that's all that matters."

What is God stripping away from your life? What do you trust in more than the Lord? God will break your dependence on anything other than Himself . . . no matter how long it takes or how difficult it may be. The sooner and more wholeheartedly you embrace the process, the easier it will be for you. God is committed to bringing you to a place of spiritual maturity—conforming you to the likeness of Christ (see Romans 8:29)—so He can work through you and bring others to spiritual maturity through your testimony (see 2 Corinthians 1:3–7).

God does not accept you on the basis of what you've done but on what Christ did for you.

God will break any dependence you have that is not on Him.

Jesus said to them, "All of you will be made to stumble because of Me this night." . . . Peter answered and said to Him, "Even if all are made to stumble because of You, I will never be made to stumble" (Matthew 26:31, 33).

Jesus answered, "I have told you that I am He. Therefore, if you seek Me, let these go their way," that the saying might be fulfilled which He spoke, "Of those whom You gave Me I have lost none." Then Simon Peter, having a sword, drew it and struck the high priest's servant, and cut off his right ear (John 18:8–10).

1. Read Matthew 26:31–35. What did Jesus say would happen when He was arrested (31)? What bold statements did Peter make in response (33, 35)?

_____

_____

_____

_____

_____

_____

2. Turn to John 18:1–27. What request did Jesus make of the soldiers who came to arrest him (8–9)? How did Peter react when Jesus said these words (10)?

_____

_____

_____

_____

_____

_____

3. Peter had vowed to stay with Jesus to the end and backed it up by striking the high priest's servant with a sword. But what happened once Peter was inside the courtyard of that same high priest, warming himself by the fire (15–17, 25–27)?

_____

_____

_____

_____

_____

4. How do you think Peter could make such a shift—from his bold stance to never deny Christ to his absolute refusal to even acknowledge that he knew Jesus?

_____

_____

_____

_____

_____

5. What does this story tell you about relying on your own strength during times of crisis? What work was God doing in Peter's heart through this failure?

_____

_____

_____

_____

_____

When Peter denied Jesus three times, the enemy was invisibly working behind the scenes to encourage his spiritual failure. Always remain on the alert to detect the activity of your adversary so you can resist him and stand firm in the faith (1 Peter 5:8–11).

Day 44: Responding to Brokenness

Maybe you are facing a time of brokenness, and it feels as though the emotional pain is more than you can bear. Or perhaps you are dealing with a series of disappointments that have completely undermined your sense of security. The way you react to these crucibles—these "dark nights of the soul"—will have a seismic impact on your relationship with

Then the servant girl who kept the door said to Peter, "You are not also one of this Man's disciples, are you?" He said, "I am not."... Now Simon Peter stood and warmed himself. Therefore they said to him, "You are not also one of His disciples, are you?" He denied it and said, "I am not!" One of the servants of the high priest, a relative of him whose ear Peter cut off, said, "Did I not see you in the garden with Him?" Peter then denied again; and immediately a rooster crowed (John 18:17, 25–27).

The way you respond to brokenness has an impact on your relationship with God.

God and your outlook on life. Instead of giving in to certain natural instincts and becoming fearful or bitter, ask the Lord to reveal what He is teaching you.

The apostle Paul faced such a time of suffering and "pleaded with the Lord three times" that it might depart from him (2 Corinthians 12:8). Three times this faithful servant asked God to remove a source of suffering, and three times God said no. Yet while God did not remove Paul's "thorn," He did help Paul to understand it was given to keep him from exalting himself and from relying on anything other than Christ (2 Corinthians 12:7–11). The Lord also taught Paul that His grace would always be sufficient for all of his weaknesses.

The same is true for you. Whenever you experience brokenness, God's grace can sustain you. He will show you how to relinquish your reliance on earthly forms of security and teach you how to rest in His wonderful provision and love. In this way, you will grow in the likeness of Christ and be prepared for future service.

> *When you experience brokenness, know that God's grace can sustain you.*

6. Read Matthew 26:69–75. What details does Matthew add about how strongly Peter denied knowing Christ (72, 74)?

_____

_____

_____

> *But again he denied with an oath, "I do not know the Man!" . . . Then he began to curse and swear, saying, "I do not know the Man!" Immediately a rooster crowed. And Peter remembered the word of Jesus* (Matthew 26:72, 74–75).

7. How would you describe the kind of brokenness Peter experienced when he heard the rooster crow and realized what he had done (74–75)?

_____

_____

_____

> *He said to him the third time, "Simon, son of Jonah, do you love Me?" Peter was grieved because He said to him the third time, "Do you love Me?" And he said to Him, "Lord, You know all things; You know that I love You." Jesus said to him, "Feed My sheep"* (John 21:17).

8. Read John 21:15–25. The events in this passage take place after Jesus had risen from the dead and been reunited with the disciple who had abandoned Him. What is the significance of Jesus asking Peter *three times* if he loved Him (15–17)?

_____

_____

_____

9. What did Jesus tell Peter to do if He truly loved Him (17)? In what ways was Jesus using Peter's brokenness to further God's plan?

_____

_____

_____

10. How do you sense Jesus working through your brokenness to move you into the next part of God's plan for your life?

A man's heart plans his way, but the Lord directs his steps (Proverbs 16:9).

_____

_____

_____

_____

_____

Jesus told Peter the type of death that awaited him (see John 21:18–19). And yet Peter still loved the Savior who forgave him with such a passion that he never shrank from fulfilling his purpose, even to the very end.

Day 45: Embracing God's Plan

God was stripping away self-reliance from Peter's life so that the disciple would operate in the Lord's strength rather than his own. It was a difficult lesson to learn, but it was one God needed to take Peter through to equip him to lead the early church. Perhaps Peter had this in mind when he later wrote, "Do not think it strange concerning the fiery trial which is to try you . . . but rejoice to the extent that you partake of Christ's sufferings, that when His glory is revealed, you may also be glad with exceeding joy" (1 Peter 4:12–13).

God will strip away your self-reliance so you can operate in His strength.

It's a tall order, to be sure. When everything goes wrong and the unthinkable happens, your first instinct is likely to ask, "Why me?" It's as though you feel you are being picked on or singled out for abuse. Your second instinct is likely to try to rid or distance yourself from the situation as quickly as possible. A better approach is to look for God's hand in it. He is using your brokenness to give you a new perspective of His mercy and provision, help you develop a more realistic comprehension of yourself, and give you compassion and understanding for the suffering of others when they also go through trials.

Are you facing a season of trials and brokenness? Then embrace the promise of Jeremiah 15:19: "If you take out the precious from the vile, you shall be as My mouth." If you trust in God and learn from Him through your trial, He will reveal Himself and work through you in wonderful ways. The Lord has one goal in mind for your brokenness: spiritual victory. So be confident that Jesus can take your weakness and turn it into strength, hope, and honor.

God will reveal Himself through your season of brokenness.

Then Peter, filled with the Holy Spirit, said to them, "Rulers of the people and elders of Israel . . . Let it be known to you all, and to all the people of Israel, that by the name of Jesus Christ of Nazareth, whom you crucified, whom God raised from the dead, by Him this man stands here before you whole" (Acts 4:8, 10).

11. Read Acts 4:1–22. In this passage, Peter experiences the very consequences he feared that night in the courtyard (3). Yet here he seems unfazed by it. What had changed (8)?

_____

_____

_____

_____

_____

12. How would you summarize Peter's response when asked "by what power" he was healing people and teaching about Jesus (7–12)?

_____

_____

_____

_____

_____

Now when they saw the boldness of Peter and John, and perceived that they were uneducated and untrained men, they marveled. . . . And seeing the man who had been healed standing with them, they could say nothing against it (Acts 4:13–14).

13. What was the proof that Peter was operating in God's power and not his own (13–17)?

_____

_____

_____

_____

_____

Peter and John answered and said to them, "Whether it is right in the sight of God to listen to you more than to God, you judge. For we cannot but speak the things which we have seen and heard" (Acts 4:19–20).

14. How did Peter reveal He had embraced God's plan for his life (18–22)?

_____

_____

_____

_____

15. How did Peter's season of brokenness make this triumph possible? What hope does this give you if you are going through your own season of brokenness?

_____

_____

_____

_____

_____

Real success is never about your own intelligence, education, beauty, or talent. Rather, it is about the Lord Jesus Christ shining through you.

Living the Principle

In Romans 8:20–21, Paul states, "The creation was subjected to futility, not willingly, but because of Him who subjected it in hope; because the creation itself also will be delivered from the bondage of corruption into the glorious liberty of the children of God." In other words, you experience frustrating trials so that you can be free of the sin nature that is left within you. While it is true you are forgiven of all your sin when you accept Christ as your Lord and Savior, the tendency to want to sin remains within you—and God must break you of it.

As the story of Peter illustrates, God uses trials for two reasons: (1) to transform you into the image of Christ (see Romans 8:29; Ephesians 5:1), and (2) to develop your potential as His representative in the world (see Philippians 3:9–10; Colossians 1:24). God used Peter's denial to *break* him of his pride and *shape* him into His representative to the world. As Peter himself would later remark, "Therefore let those who suffer according to the will of God commit their souls to Him in doing good, as to a faithful Creator" (1 Peter 4:19).

How will you live out Life Principle 15 this week? Identify a specific trial or difficult situation you are currently facing. In a journal, write down your initial reaction to the situation on one side of the page. Were (or are) you scared? Devastated? Angry? Insecure? On the other side, write down the best possible scenarios as to what God might be accomplishing in your life (or in the lives of others) as a result of the situation. Spend some time in prayer, asking God to change your focus from the worst to the best possible scenario. Then, take this a step further and *thank* Him for what He is teaching you through the trial.

> You experience trials so you can be free of the sin nature left within you.

Life Lessons to Remember

❖ Through brokenness, you gain a new perspective of God's mercy and provision in your life (see Psalm 73:25–26).
❖ Through brokenness, you develop a more complete and accurate comprehension of yourself (see Psalm 73:21–23).
❖ Through brokenness, your compassion and understanding for the suffering of others grows (see Hebrews 5:2).

Jesus chose Peter. Why? For the same reason that He chooses us: Jesus sees all that we can be. For us to become all that we can be, however, we must experience a "breaking"—a sanding, a sifting, a chiseling of our souls so that we truly begin to be conformed to the likeness of Jesus Christ. That's what happened to Peter, and it's what happens to each one of us.

Notes AND Prayer Requests

USE THIS SPACE TO WRITE ANY KEY POINTS, QUESTIONS,
OR PRAYER REQUESTS FROM THIS WEEK'S STUDY.

_____

_____

_____

_____

_____

_____

_____

_____

_____

_____

_____

_____

_____

_____

Whatever You Acquire Outside of God's Will Eventually Turns to Ashes

Because you clapped your hands, stamped your feet, and rejoiced in heart with all your disdain for the land of Israel, indeed, therefore, I will stretch out My hand against you, and give you as plunder to the nations.

EZEKIEL 25:6–7

Life's Questions

The temptation sits before you, beckoning you to come take it. It looks so much like the desire of your heart that you can't stop thinking about it. An alarm goes off within your spirit. Something just isn't right about what you want to do. Still, the opportunity is so enticing, you're tempted to shake off the warning. You say to yourself (in your most convincing voice), *Why shouldn't I have this? After all, other people have so much more. In the grand scheme of the universe, why would God care about this?*

The alarm in your spirit goes off again. God's Word makes it clear that He *does* care. You also know that you are up against a skilled opponent when it comes to deceit. He has a plan that he has tested and perfected, and his schemes worked against men such as Abraham, Jacob, Samson, David, and Peter. But then you look again at that thing you want, and like Eve in the Garden, it seems to you "pleasant to the eyes" (Genesis 3:6). So the argument continues. *What if this is my only chance to be happy? God wouldn't deny me that, would He? What if God never gives me what I really want?*

When thoughts like these enter your mind and you find yourself wrestling with temptation, you need to remember the words of Life

PRINCIPLE IN ACTION
Pharaoh (Exodus 3:19–20)
Rich Fool (Luke 12:16–21)
Prodigal Son (Luke 15:11–32)
Rich Man (Luke 16:19–30)
Ananias and Sapphira
  (Acts 5:1–11)

How do we become content? We do this by asking God to teach us how to have gratitude for what we have, rather than complain about what we're missing.

—CHARLES F. STANLEY

Principle 16: *Whatever you acquire outside of God's will eventually turns to ashes.* The source of your temptation—the object that seems like the desire of your heart—will never satisfy you. However, you will find that it leads you into dangerous territory outside of God's will.

Day 46: Accumulate More or Desire Less

Some people think God's refusal to grant them some cherished wish is the worst thing that can happen to them. They believe they will be truly disappointed and devastated if that deep desire continues unmet. So they pursue their desire, either in opposition to God's will or in disregard of it—and end up *truly* disappointed, even if they get what they thought they wanted.

In many ways, these people are like the Israelites in Moses's day who, in spite of God's deliverance and continual provision in the wilderness, turned to complaining and insisting on having *more* (see Numbers 11:4, 31–34). You read in Psalm 106:15 what happened to them: "[God] gave them their request, but sent leanness into their soul." The desire became a curse.

G. K. Chesterton once said, "There are two ways to get enough: One is to accumulate more and more, the other is to desire less." While you can always collect additional possessions, relationships, successes, and anything else you believe will bring fulfillment, there will always be room for more. And when there's room for more, there's room for *wanting* more. The cycle never ends. But if you choose the second route of Chesterton's advice, "to desire less," the likelihood of living a fulfilling life increases.

How do you develop a lifestyle of wanting less? By going back to the deepest desire present in every human heart—the one thing everyone is truly longing for—to know God. Once you satisfy yourself with His presence, you require far less of what the world has to offer.

1. Read Exodus 16:16–36. In a previous study, you looked at how God had miraculously provided for His people by giving them manna. What were His instructions for gathering it (16)? Why do you think He was so specific with these directions?

_____

_____

_____

_____

Pursuing our own goals above God's purposes only leads to disappointment.

When there's room for more, there's room for *wanting* more.

"Let every man gather it according to each one's need, one omer for each person, according to the number of persons; let every man take for those who are in his tent" (Genesis 16:16).

2. What happened to the manna when the people tried to save it for later (19–20)?

_____

_____

_____

_____

3. Why was it so important for the Hebrew people to collect only enough heaven-sent manna to get them through one day?

_____

_____

_____

_____

4. What were God's instructions about collecting manna on the Sabbath (25–26)? What happened when some of the people tried to gather it on that day (27)?

_____

_____

_____

_____

5. What conclusions can you draw from this passage on "accumulating more and more" versus "desiring less"? What does this say about operating in God's will?

_____

_____

_____

_____

Delight yourself also in the LORD, and He shall give you the desires of your heart (Psalm 37:4).

Day 47: Satisfying Yourself with What Lasts

Feelings of dissatisfaction, unfulfilled expectations, dejection, and isolation all originate from the same place: *a raging hunger for God.* Centuries ago Augustine wrote, "You made us for Yourself, and our heart is

They did not heed Moses. But some of them left part of it until morning, and it bred worms and stank. And Moses was angry with them. So they gathered it every morning, every man according to his need. And when the sun became hot, it melted. And so it was, on the sixth day, that they gathered twice as much bread, two omers for each one (Exodus 16:20–23).

Moses said, "Eat that today, for today is a Sabbath to the LORD; today you will not find it in the field. Six days you shall gather it, but on the seventh day, the Sabbath, there will be none." Now it happened that some of the people went out on the seventh day to gather, but they found none. And the LORD said to Moses, "How long do you refuse to keep My commandments and My laws? See! For the LORD has given you the Sabbath; therefore He gives you on the sixth day bread for two days. Let every man remain in his place; let no man go out of his place on the seventh day." So the people rested on the seventh day (Exodus 16:25–30).

Feelings of dissatisfaction originate from a raging hunger for God.

restless until it rests in You." There is always more you can learn about God, and you will never fully know Him while you live on earth (see 1 Corinthians 13:12).

However, once you enter into a relationship with the Lord, He promises to reveal more of Himself to you as you fellowship with Him. As God said to the prophet Hosea, "I will betroth you to Me forever; yes, I will betroth you to Me in righteousness and justice, in lovingkindness and mercy; I will betroth you to Me in faithfulness, and you shall know the LORD" (2:19–20). To fellowship with God—to talk to Him and listen to Him as you study the Bible, pray, and worship Him—is to get to know Him better. He has *betrothed* (or engaged) His people to Himself for one reason: to let Himself be known.

When you develop your relationship with God and discover more about His holy character, He illuminates your heart and mind, gives you a greater desire to know Him more intimately, and enables you to leave your fleshly desires behind in the process. You find that your worldly desires simply cannot compare to the deep comfort, joy, and fulfillment the Lord offers you. Rather, you see the things you acquire outside of His will turning to ashes, while the blessings He gives you endure and satisfy your soul.

6. Read Joshua 7. In the past, God had allowed the children of Israel to plunder the cities they had conquered (see Numbers 31:11), but He required the spoils from Jericho to be dedicated to Him. Why do you think Achan chose to violate this command (1)?

_____

_____

_____

_____

_____

_____

7. What was the immediate consequence of Achan's action (5)? What greater impact of the defeat did Joshua fear would come to pass (7–9)?

_____

_____

_____

_____

_____

8. What reason did Achan give for sinning against God (20–22)?

_____

_____

_____

_____

Once you enter into a relationship with God, He begins to reveal more of Himself to you.

But the children of Israel committed a trespass . . . for Achan . . . took of the accursed things; so the anger of the LORD burned against the children of Israel (Joshua 7:1).

The men of Ai struck down about thirty-six men, for they chased them from before the gate as far as Shebarim, and struck them down on the descent (Joshua 7:5).

"I coveted them and took them. And there they are, hidden in the earth in the midst of my tent, with the silver under it" (Joshua 7:21).

9. How did Achan find that what he acquired outside of God's will turned to ashes? Who else suffered the consequences of his actions (24–25)?

_____

_____

_____

_____

10. What are some ways God gets His people's attention today when they place a higher priority on their desires than on His will?

_____

_____

_____

_____

If God punishes each man for his own sins, then why did Israel execute Achan's entire family? Apparently his family knew about his illicit acquisitions, but they kept quiet and so shared his guilt.

Day 48: Pursuing God

As you develop a relationship with God and discover more about His character, you begin a process in which you find yourself desiring the things of this world *less* and the things of God *more*. You move away from a mind-set of "What's in it for me?" to one of "What's in it for my relationship with Christ?" You receive many other benefits as well.

For instance, pursuing the things of God in accordance with His will deepens your *humility*. As you see God's sovereignty unveiled, you more deeply comprehend your absolute need for Him. It strengthens your *gratitude* for Him because you come to recognize God's lovingkindness motivates His forgiveness, deliverance, and guidance. Instead of coming to God with complaints about your unfulfilled desires, you come to Him with adoration and praise.

As you discover more about God's holy character, you come to understand a greater *purpose* in life. As the Holy Spirit sheds new light on verses you've read many times before, your quest for a relationship with Him becomes stronger, deeper, and more personal. Your appreciation of God's Word gives you more delight in studying and applying His truth.

Then Joshua, and all Israel with him, took Achan the son of Zerah, the silver, the garment, the wedge of gold, his sons, his daughters, his oxen, his donkeys, his sheep, his tent, and all that he had, and they brought them to the Valley of Achor. And Joshua said, "Why have you troubled us? The LORD will trouble you this day." So all Israel stoned him with stones; and they burned them with fire after they had stoned them with stones. Then they raised over him a great heap of stones, still there to this day. So the LORD turned from the fierceness of His anger. Therefore the name of that place has been called the Valley of Achor to this day (Joshua 7:24–26).

Pursuing the things of God in accordance with His will deepens your humility.

As you discover more about God's holy character, you come to understand a greater purpose in life.

125

Pursuing the things of God help you revere Him and desire to please Him more.

O God, You are my God; early will I seek You; my soul thirsts for You; my flesh longs for You in a dry and thirsty land where there is no water. So I have looked for You in the sanctuary, to see Your power and Your glory. Because Your lovingkindness is better than life, my lips shall praise You. Thus I will bless You while I live; I will lift up my hands in Your name. My soul shall be satisfied as with marrow and fatness, and my mouth shall praise You with joyful lips. When I remember You on my bed, I meditate on You in the night watches. Because You have been my help, therefore in the shadow of Your wings I will rejoice. My soul follows close behind You; Your right hand upholds me. But those who seek my life, to destroy it, shall go into the lower parts of the earth. They shall fall by the sword; they shall be a portion for jackals. But the king shall rejoice in God; everyone who swears by Him shall glory; but the mouth of those who speak lies shall be stopped (Psalm 63:1–11).

You also come to *revere* God more and *desire to please Him.* Learning something new about your Creator reminds you that you don't know *everything* about Him. As you come to terms with the depths and heights of God's love, your awe of Him grows and your desire changes from satisfying yourself to serving your God. Pleasing Him is not a chore but a joyful task done out of humility and thankfulness.

Amazingly, as you pursue your desire for God, He fulfills the other desires He has given to you. You learn afresh that acquiring anything outside of His will ultimately disappoints you. You come to realize the only true satisfaction in life comes from God.

11. Read Psalm 63. What does it mean to "thirst" for God (1)?

_____

_____

_____

_____

12. How did David reveal that his knowledge of God's character had brought him to a place of humility, gratitude, and reverence for the Lord (3–5)?

_____

_____

_____

_____

_____

13. How did David demonstrate his desire to please God and follow Him (8)?

_____

_____

_____

_____

14. Why is praise a key element of intimacy with God (11)?

_____

_____

_____

_____

15. How do you know when your soul is following "close behind" God (8)? What are some of the early warning signs of a soul that's no longer following God?

_____

_____

_____

*If God is causing you to feel restless,
ask Him what He wants you to do. He always speaks when you
make yourself available to Him.*

Living the Principle

What do you long for? Love, wealth, acceptance, stability, prominence . . . or something else? If you chase after those things apart from God's will, what you'll find will be disappointing and empty. It will burn up and turn to ashes—and it will singe you in the process as well. So don't ignore the alarm signal within you. It's God's Holy Spirit warning you that you're about to do something you will regret.

Instead, trust God and be holy as He is holy (see 1 Peter 1:15–16). Resist the temptation to go after the desire of your heart in your own strength. Remember that God will provide the absolute best for you if you trust and obey Him. Those blessings will endure, and they will be to God's glory in eternity. As David wrote, "You will show me the path of life; in Your presence is fullness of joy; at Your right hand are pleasures forevermore" (Psalm 16:11).

How will you live out Life Principle 16 this week? Do you believe God's will is truly best for you? Why or why not? These are important questions to answer in God's presence—and perhaps in the presence of some trusted Christian friends. So, this week, discuss some ways you can make sure you're seeking God's will and ways to resist temptation when it beckons to you. Ask for members in your group to help hold you accountable to pursue the things of God and let you know when they see you going for things outside His will.

Anything you chase outside of God's will eventually turns to ashes—and you will be singed in the process.

Life Lessons to Remember

❖ When you pursue your desires in opposition to God's will, you end up truly disappointed (see Psalm 106:15).
❖ As you pursue God, He will fulfill the other desires that He has given you (see Psalm 37:4–5).
❖ God's path offers pleasures and fulfillment that last forever (see Psalm 16:11).

Notes AND Prayer Requests

USE THIS SPACE TO WRITE ANY KEY POINTS, QUESTIONS,
OR PRAYER REQUESTS FROM THIS WEEK'S STUDY.

_____

_____

_____

_____

_____

_____

_____

_____

_____

_____

_____

_____

_____

_____

_____

_____

*Y*ou Stand Tallest and Strongest on Your Knees

When Daniel knew that the writing was signed he went home.
And with his windows open toward Jerusalem, he knelt down on his knees
three times that day, and prayed and gave thanks before his God,
as was his custom since early days.

DANIEL 6:10

Life's Questions

Following God isn't easy. This is as true today as it was in biblical times. The world that persecuted the prophets and crucified Christ still responds negatively to those who are committed to the Lord. Jesus explains the reason: "If they persecuted Me, they will also persecute you. . . . All these things they will do to you for My name's sake, because they do not know Him who sent Me. If I had not come and spoken to them, they would have no sin, but now they have no excuse for their sin" (John 15:20–22).

When others see God working through you, they will be convicted of their sin—and this will make them uncomfortable. As a result, they may lash out at you or try to undermine your testimony. They may do this in subtle ways by posting condescending words against you on social media. They may decide not to let their children play with your kids and exclude you from their gatherings. They may look for other ways to put you down, pull you into a verbal fight, or seek to tarnish your reputation. Persecution for your beliefs comes in many forms.

Have you encountered trouble because you're a Christian? Do you find yourself marked for scorn and derision in certain settings because you stand up for biblical truths? Have you found it difficult to get along with particular people or in certain situations because you follow

PRINCIPLE IN ACTION
Jehoshaphat
    (2 Chronicles 20:5–12)
Job (Job 26:14)
David (Psalm 142:1–2)
Daniel (Daniel 6:10)
Stephen (Acts 7:59–60)

Much of our ability to bear natural burdens is derived from developing our ability to carry spiritual burdens in prayer.

—**CHARLES F. STANLEY**

129

God? If so, you can discover the way the saints before you defended themselves. In particular, as Life Principle 17 teaches: *You stand tallest and strongest on your knees.*

Day 49: An Unsurpassed Opportunity

An older pastor got into the habit of challenging his congregation by quoting Jeremiah 33:3: "Call to Me, and I will answer you, and show you great and mighty things, which you do not know." He would then level his eyes at those gathered before him and say, "Try it. It works!"

God wants you to call to Him.

This simple thought carries a tremendous truth: *God wants you to call to Him.* He created you with a soul-deep need for intimacy with Him, and nothing else will fill it. You establish, solidify, and deepen that intimacy by an open line of communication. God makes Himself available to you 24/7—anytime you need Him and feel like talking. Often, He takes the initiative by speaking to you through His Word, His creation, or His Holy Spirit. Many times, He allows difficulties in your life so you will draw closer to Him in intimate communion.

Prayer is a powerful tool in your life.

Prayer is a powerful tool in your life as a believer. Through prayer, the Lord blesses you and frees you from bondage. In prayer, you profess your need for Christ and ask for His solutions to your problems. You learn to worship Him and grow spiritually in His loving presence. And as you spend time with God, He teaches you how to listen even more adeptly for His still, small voice. Through it all, you grow deeper in fellowship with Him.

Daniel distinguished himself above the governors and satraps, because an excellent spirit was in him. . . . So the governors and satraps sought to find some charge against Daniel concerning the kingdom; but they could find no charge or fault, because he was faithful; nor was there any error or fault found in him. Then these men said, "We shall not find any charge against this Daniel unless we find it against him concerning the law of his God" (Daniel 6:3–5).

1. Read Daniel 6:1–9. As this story opens, Daniel was living in a foreign land that was often hostile to the one true God. How do you think Daniel "distinguished himself above" his fellow governors? How might his "excellent spirit" have made itself known in the decisions he made, the way he treated others, and the way he carried himself (3)?

   _____

   _____

   _____

   _____

2. What motivated the governors and satraps to try to find a charge against him? Why were they not successful in their attempts (4–5)?

   _____

   _____

   _____

3. What do you make of the fact that Daniel's rivals viewed his devotion to God as his Achilles's heel (7–8)?

_____

_____

_____

_____

4. What connection can you draw between Daniel's "excellent spirit," his faithfulness, and his daily prayer routine?

_____

_____

_____

_____

5. What does this story tell you about people who lead godly lives?

_____

_____

_____

_____

> *"All the governors of the kingdom, the administrators and satraps, the counselors and advisors, have consulted together to establish a royal statute and to make a firm decree, that whoever petitions any god or man for thirty days, except you, O king, shall be cast into the den of lions. Now, O king, establish the decree and sign the writing, so that it cannot be changed, according to the law of the Medes and Persians, which does not alter." Therefore King Darius signed the written decree* (Daniel 6:7–9).

Submission *to God will perfect you, which means to* restore, mend, render complete, *and* equip. *It will* establish *you, which means to* make as solid as granite, make stable, place firmly, *and* render constant. *It will* strengthen *you, which means to* make strong *or* fill with strength. *And it will* settle *you, which means to* lay the foundation of your faith and your future with Christ.

Day 50: Optimizing Your Prayer Life

In its broadest definition, prayer includes both verbal and nonverbal communication. It covers our thoughts and actions toward God, as well as our words toward God. From this definition, you might conclude that you are continually in conversation with God, because everything you do in life is a message you send to or make before God. However, communication is a two-way process. It is you speaking with God and listening to what He says in return.

Entering into a regular, meaningful, and mutually satisfying dialogue with God is not an opportunity to take lightly—and it is something that will require intention on your part. After all, prayer does not happen by accident. You must actively engage in the process by

Prayer includes both verbal and nonverbal communication.

Prayer does not happen by accident.

deliberately turning your mind, heart, and voice toward God. So, what are some ways you can do this each day to establish a more powerful prayer life?

Choose a time of the day to spend with God.

First, *choose a definite time of the day to spend with the Lord in prayer.* Praying only when your schedule allows it or when your needs become urgent shows a lack of appreciation for the opportunity God offers. The time of day you choose—whether early in the morning, late in the evening, or sometime in between—is not the issue. Rather, consistency is the key. Ask God to show you the perfect time when you can be alone with Him.

Choose a place where you can be alone with God.

Second, *select a place where you can be alone with Him.* If your home and schedule are crowded, the idea of finding some privacy in order to talk to the Lord may seem like a pipe dream. However, with some creative thinking and a request for assistance from the Lord, you should be able to find a place that works ideally for you.

Commit to pray daily.

Third, *make the commitment to pray daily.* Taking the time every day to communicate with God tells Him that your heart is open to Him and that you want to learn more about Him. And as you pray, *keep a journal* that contains your requests and how God answered your prayers as a continuing testimony of His work in your life. Remember to write down the specific verses He applies to your situation and the promises He gives you from His Word.

In his upper room, with his windows open toward Jerusalem, he knelt down on his knees three times that day, and prayed and gave thanks before his God, as was his custom since early days. Then these men assembled and found Daniel praying and making supplication before his God (Daniel 6:10–11).

6. Read Daniel 6:10-17. What do we discover about Daniel's prayer life (10)?

_____

_____

_____

_____

7. Daniel's enemies gathered outside his house, as if they *expected* him to violate the king's new decree (11). What do you think they saw in Daniel that made them believe he would risk his life to pray?

_____

_____

_____

_____

The king . . . was greatly displeased with himself, and set his heart on Daniel to deliver him; and he labored till the going down of the sun to deliver him (Daniel 6:14).

8. What does it say about Daniel's faithfulness and excellence that King Darius "set his heart on Daniel to deliver him" (14)? How did Daniel's prayer routine play into this?

_____

_____

_____

_____

_____

9. How do you suppose Daniel reacted to his arrest (16)?

_____

_____

_____

_____

10. How does your approach to prayer differ from Daniel's? (For example, how many times a day do you take a break from what you're doing to talk to God? Do you kneel when you pray? Do you give thanks to God in your prayers?)

_____

_____

_____

_____

_____

Daniel's enemies could find nothing else, so they tried to use his devotion to God against him—which is never a wise decision.

Day 51: Strength in Kneeling

God honors the prayers of His people. If you go to Him—seeking Him earnestly and obeying His commands—He will provide all you need. If you don't know what to say, the Holy Spirit will show you. At times, tears are just as effective as words. Just as God understands the hurt you feel, so He knows how to deal with and guide you through any trial you must endure.

Whenever a trial strikes, turn to Him immediately in prayer. His presence will fill you with hope, and He will give you the strength and wisdom you need to face the situation with confidence. Throughout your life, you will face many difficult situations. Some will be exciting, while others may feel as though they will break your heart. However, no matter what challenges come, you can be sure God is in the difficulty with you. He enjoys seeing you rejoice over His blessings, but He also mourns with you when tragedy strikes.

Always remember that God is bigger than any problem you face—and that the distance between victory and defeat is the distance between your knees and the floor as you kneel before your wondrous Lord and Savior. You are never taller or stronger than when you are on your knees! God knows the way before you, and He can guide you through

So the king gave the command, and they brought Daniel and cast him into the den of lions. But the king spoke, saying to Daniel, "Your God, whom you serve continually, He will deliver you." Then a stone was brought and laid on the mouth of the den, and the king sealed it with his own signet ring and with the signets of his lords, that the purpose concerning Daniel might not be changed (Daniel 6:16–17).

God honors the prayers of His people.

God is bigger than any problem you face in life.

And when he came to the den, he cried out with a lamenting voice to Daniel. The king spoke, saying to Daniel, "Daniel, servant of the living God, has your God, whom you serve continually, been able to deliver you from the lions?" Then Daniel said to the king, "O king, live forever! My God sent His angel and shut the lions' mouths, so that they have not hurt me, because I was found innocent before Him; and also, O king, I have done no wrong before you." Now the king was exceedingly glad for him, and commanded that they should take Daniel up out of the den. So Daniel was taken up out of the den, and no injury whatever was found on him, because he believed in his God. And the king gave the command, and they brought those men who had accused Daniel, and they cast them into the den of lions—them, their children, and their wives; and the lions overpowered them, and broke all their bones in pieces before they ever came to the bottom of the den (Daniel 6:20–24).

the difficulty if you will trust Him. And when you submit to Him in obedience, He applies His unlimited resources, wisdom, and power to help you.

11. Read Daniel 6:18–28. King Darius spent a sleepless night worrying about Daniel, whom he had been forced to throw into a pit with starving lions. What does Darius acknowledge about Daniel's God (20)? How confident is he that God will deliver Daniel?

_____

_____

_____

_____

12. How does a person get recognized as a "servant of the living God" (20)?

_____

_____

_____

13. God sent His angel to close the lions' mouths and protect Daniel (22). What's the most obvious, irrefutable answer to prayer you've ever experienced?

_____

_____

_____

14. What key truths about God and the way He works are revealed in Daniel's story?

_____

_____

_____

15. What is the end result for the jealous satraps and governors (24)? What does this story tell you about both God's mercy and His justice?

_____

_____

_____

Love does no harm to a neighbor; therefore love is the fulfillment of the law (Romans 13:10).

Living the Principle

Being on your knees before God is not only a physical stance but also an attitude of the heart. When you fall to your knees in prayer, you are seeking God and demonstrating your willingness to submit to His plan. As you do, you begin to feel His power in your life and start to trust His hand in every situation. Instead of worrying about the obstacles in your path, you focus on Him and how He is working in you. This gives you the assurance and boldness to face your troubles because you're confident that God's plan for your life will be accomplished.

Praying is the most powerful thing you can do, for God has granted you the privilege to come before Him with authority. You can do this because of your position in Christ. As Hebrews 4:15–16 explains, "We do not have a High Priest who cannot sympathize with our weaknesses, but was in all points tempted as we are, yet without sin. Let us therefore come boldly to the throne of grace, that we may obtain mercy and find grace to help in time of need."

How will you live out Life Principle 17? This week, the enemy may try to convince you to "tone down" or keep your walk with God a secret. He may tell you that you don't have any authority or power in Christ. He may remind you of past mistakes to keep you feeling defeated. Don't let him succeed! Instead, put the steps outlined in this lesson into practice so you will have a more effective prayer life and see through his lies. *Choose a definite time of the day to spend with the Lord in prayer. Select a place where you can be alone with Him. Make the commitment to pray daily.* As you follow these steps, be sure to talk with Christian friends about their prayer habits. Find out what works for them and exchange some tips and ideas.

> Being on your knees before God represents an attitude of the heart.

Life Lessons to Remember

❖ God is greater than any problem you will ever face (see 1 John 4:4).
❖ Whatever you face, you must trust God with it (see 2 Samuel 22:2–4).
❖ God invites you to test the power of prayer (see Jeremiah 33:3).

Those who spend time alone with the Lord find comfort, hope, and joy in His presence. They find themselves being built up, from the inside out, and they generally emerge from a time with the Lord feeling refreshed and more courageous as they face their needs or tackle their problems.

Notes AND Prayer Requests

USE THIS SPACE TO WRITE ANY KEY POINTS, QUESTIONS,
OR PRAYER REQUESTS FROM THIS WEEK'S STUDY.

_____

_____

_____

_____

_____

_____

_____

_____

_____

_____

_____

_____

_____

_____

As a Child of a Sovereign God, You Are Never a Victim of Your Circumstances

For the children of Israel shall abide many days without king or prince, without sacrifice or sacred pillar, without ephod or teraphim. Afterward the children of Israel shall return and seek the LORD their God and David their king.

HOSEA 3:4-5

Life's Questions

Large-scale tragedies, such as natural disasters or terrorist attacks, often inspire heated debate about God's presence. "Where is God in all this suffering?" people ask. "How could He allow something like this to happen? Doesn't He care about our world?" Such questions are as inevitable when global crises come as they are challenging.

Yet their impact pales in comparison to the questions and emotions that arise within *you* when a tragedy hits close to home. When an unexpected trial strikes you with a force that (literally or figuratively) knocks you off your feet, the pain and loss can be far more intense than you ever thought possible. In your darkest moments, you may question your ability to survive. Your stunned and overwhelmed mind will likely look for some explanation to which you can cling. You may wonder, *What did I do to deserve this? Why would God allow this?*

During these times of heartbreak, it is extremely important for you to remember Life Principle 18: *As a child of a sovereign God, you are never*

PRINCIPLE IN ACTION
Sarah (Genesis 18:13–15)
Moses (Numbers 11:10–15)
Job's Friends (Job 42:7–9)
Cyrus (Ezra 1:1–4)
Jonah (Jonah 1:1–3)

God can work through every situation in your life to bring you closer to Himself.

—CHARLES F. STANLEY

a victim of your circumstances. You may not know why this adversity has come into your life, but you can trust that God is with you and loves you. You can place your hope in His sovereignty and know He is always in control.

Day 52: Hope in a Sovereign God

You are guaranteed to face unexpected turns in life as you seek to follow God.

Life does not run on a smooth or straight course. You are *guaranteed* to face treacherous bumps and unexpected turns along the way—in the form of trials, difficulties, mistakes, and tragedies. Some of these you will be able to see approaching from miles away, while others will hit you with little warning. Some will be easily navigable, while others will send you into a tailspin if you're not careful. But you never have to be a victim of your circumstances.

Your particular situation need not define who you are or how you react. As a believer, your identity has already been clearly defined in Christ. Your decisions and behaviors in every situation should thus honor the Lord Jesus. Your identity should always be based on the salvation He has provided for you.

The Bible reveals that you *can* endure in spite of adverse circumstances.

Hebrews 11 is populated with men and women in the Bible who endured in spite of adverse circumstances. These are individuals who became known for their faith because they *refused* to allow their present circumstances to dictate their future. Now, you may say, "Of course they persevered—God worked powerfully in their situations. Just look how their stories turned out!" However, you must understand that each of these people, like you, did not know how their story would end. They did not know whether or not God would keep His promises to them. It took going through their difficult experiences to learn "there has not failed one word of all His good promise" (1 Kings 8:56) that the Lord made to His people.

So, how did these men and women demonstrate such strong faith in God? By trusting in the fact that the Lord was able to help them and work everything out for their good (see Romans 8:28). Even when nothing else made sense to them, they placed their hope in their sovereign Lord—and He rewarded them for their confidence.

By faith we understand that the worlds were framed by the word of God, so that the things which are seen were not made of things which are visible (Hebrews 11:3).

1. Read Hebrews 11. What do these Bible "Hall of Famers" have in common? What are some areas of common ground they shared?

_____

_____

_____

_____

_____

2. Why is it impossible to please God without faith (6)?

_____

_____

_____

Without faith it is impossible to please Him, for he who comes to God must believe that He is, and that He is a rewarder of those who diligently seek Him (Hebrews 11:6).

3. What are some trials that Moses endured that could have left him with a victim mentality (23–29)?

_____

_____

_____

By faith he forsook Egypt, not fearing the wrath of the king; for he endured as seeing Him who is invisible (Hebrews 11:27).

4. What do you take away from the fact that Rahab—a woman who lived most of her life among God's enemies and whose reputation was tainted—is included in this list (31)?

_____

_____

_____

By faith the harlot Rahab did not perish with those who did not believe, when she had received the spies with peace (Hebrews 11:31).

5. What does it mean that "the world was not worthy" of these faithful people (38)? What does their example say about never being a victim of your circumstances?

_____

_____

_____

They were stoned, they were sawn in two, were tempted, were slain with the sword. They wandered about in sheepskins and goatskins, being destitute, afflicted, tormented—of whom the world was not worthy (Hebrews 11:37–38).

Why is faith necessary to please God? Because you cannot serve Him unless you are convinced that He not only exists but also that His plans for you are "good and acceptable and perfect" (Romans 12:2).

Day 53: The Confidence to Endure

A story is told of a fifth-grade boy who had to memorize the entire list of godly people in Hebrews 11. It proved to be one of the most transformative lessons of his life. When he later became a pastor and went through a rough time, the Lord reminded him of these great people of faith and gave him the confidence to endure as they did.

God's Word will give you the confidence to endure.

Just consider some of the names on this list. Noah, who was told to build an ark for a cataclysmic flood that would cover the earth. Joseph, who endured one betrayal after another yet persevered in his faith. Moses, who "endured as seeing Him who is invisible" (Hebrews 11:27) and led God's people out of bondage in Egypt. Or David, who obeyed God even though, at times, everything seemed to work against him becoming king of Israel.

Had any of these individuals considered themselves victims of their circumstances, they would have begun their journey with God in defeat and discouragement. But instead, they focused on the almighty hand of the Lord and triumphed with Him. In the same way, you can say, "God, if they endured so can I, because You are sovereign just as You were then, and You love me as You loved them. Therefore, I will not consider myself a victim of my circumstances. Rather, I will view every situation as an opportunity for Your glory to shine forth in victory."

View your difficulties as opportunities for God to reveal His victory and glory.

O LORD my God, I cried out to You, and You healed me. O LORD, You brought my soul up from the grave; You have kept me alive, that I should not go down to the pit. Sing praise to the LORD, you saints of His, and give thanks at the remembrance of His holy name. For His anger is but for a moment, His favor is for life; weeping may endure for a night, but joy comes in the morning (Psalm 30:2–5).

6. Read Psalm 30. What are some of the trials that David endured (1–3)?

_____

_____

_____

_____

7. What had David learned about God's character through his trials (4–5)? How had that understanding served to build his faith?

_____

_____

_____

_____

I cried out to You, O LORD; and to the LORD I made supplication: "What profit is there in my blood, when I go down to the pit? Will the dust praise You? Will it declare Your truth? Hear, O LORD, and have mercy on me; LORD, be my helper!" You have turned for me my mourning into dancing; You have put off my sackcloth and clothed me with gladness (Psalm 30:8–11).

8. How had David seen God come through for him when he cried out for help (8–11)?

_____

_____

_____

_____

9. Sometimes God gives you the strength to *endure* your circumstances rather than *overcome* them. (Remember that some people mentioned in Hebrews 11 died for their faith.) Why is that distinction important to remember when the way gets rough?

_____

_____

_____

_____

10. Practically speaking, how does David's instruction to "sing praise to [God] and not be silent" (12) apply to you today—regardless of what you are facing?

_____

_____

_____

To the end that my glory may sing praise to You and not be silent. O LORD my God, I will give thanks to You forever (Psalm 30:12).

When darkness covers your heart, you may think you have no hope. But just as the sun disperses the nighttime at daybreak, your circumstances will change at the Lord's command.

Day 54: Running Your Course

The Lord has mapped out all the detours, hills, and valleys of your life. He knows all the difficulties you will face. He understands you will continually clash with the world, the flesh, and the devil until you are home with Him. Yet He didn't just set you on the path and hope you would find the way. He sent the Holy Spirit to dwell in you, guide you, and encourage you.

This is the power you have to stand strong when the going gets rough and not run away. Endurance requires something that doesn't come easily—trust in the unseen, sovereign God. But with the Holy Spirit to remind you of His faithfulness, you *can* remain committed to Him. And the longer you faithfully obey the Lord, regardless of the circumstances, the stronger your faith becomes. You become prepared for greater service and expanded ministry. You become strong, stalwart, and steadfast.

You aren't alone as you run this race of life. The One who endured the cross lives in you, equipping you to do anything He calls you to do. If you stumble, He is there to pick you up. All you need to do is call on Him to infuse you with His wisdom and power, and then obey what He tells you to do. Remember that you are *never* a victim of your circumstances, for your sovereign God can use everything that happens to you for your blessing and His glory.

The Lord has mapped out all the difficulties you will face in this life.

The One who endured the cross lives in you.

11. Read Hebrews 12:1–2. Who are the "cloud of witnesses"? (Look again at Hebrews 11.)

_____

_____

_____

Therefore we also, since we are surrounded by so great a cloud of witnesses . . . (Hebrews 12:1).

Let us lay aside every weight, and the sin which so easily ensnares us, and let us run with endurance the race that is set before us . . . (Hebrews 12:1).

12. What is the "weight" the author of Hebrews encourages you to lay aside (1)?

_____

_____

_____

_____

_____

_____

Looking unto Jesus, the author and finisher of our faith, who for the joy that was set before Him endured the cross, despising the shame, and has sat down at the right hand of the throne of God (Hebrews 12:2).

13. What is the key to running your race with endurance (2)? How does looking to Christ enable you to persevere in the midst of difficulties?

_____

_____

_____

_____

_____

_____

14. As far as you can tell right now, what kind of race has been set before you?

_____

_____

_____

_____

_____

Do you not know that those who run in a race all run, but one receives the prize? Run in such a way that you may obtain it (1 Corinthians 9:24).

15. How has endurance proved necessary in that race? In what ways have you built up your spiritual endurance?

_____

_____

_____

_____

_____

_____

Jesus endured the pain, scorn, sorrow, rejection, and betrayal of the cross for the joy set before Him. It was enough to keep Him focused and stop Him from answering His accusers. He looked forward to fulfilling the purpose for which He came, which was to restore your relationship with the Father.

Living the Principle

God is sovereign, which means everything that touches your life serves some purpose. Nothing that happens to you is ever meaningless or useless, and you are never merely a victim of an unfair world. God has an important purpose for refining you, which is to conform you to the image of His Son and glorify Himself through you. The more jolting the hardship, the greater the ministry God is preparing for you. The deeper the cut, the more profoundly God will use you to do His work in the world if you will trust and obey Him.

Are you in the middle of a trial? Do you wonder why God has allowed such a painful experience in your life? If so, ask Him—in a humble and respectful manner—to help you understand why He permitted the adversity and what He wants you to learn from it. Then, take the necessary steps to avoid becoming bitter and resentful. Remember that God is in control, and His love for you never changes. "As many as received Him, to them He gave the right to become children of God, to those who believe in His name" (John 1:12). You are not a victim. You are God's beloved child. So have faith in Him.

How will you live out Life Principle 18 this week? Set aside some time for a heart-to-heart talk with God about any difficult circumstances you're facing. Ask the questions that are bothering you—and then listen for His response. Share your situation with fellow believers in Christ and get their perspective on the situation. Have they encountered similar trials that left them asking the same questions? How did they endure? How did it build their faith? Spend time reading the stories of the heroes of the faith in Hebrews 11. Let God's Word set your mind at ease and reassure you that He has a purpose in all your circumstances.

> Nothing that happens to you is ever meaningless.

Life Lessons to Remember

❖ Your sovereign God has determined to use everything that happens to you for your blessing and His glory (see Romans 8:28).
❖ You can find comfort and encouragement in the lives of saints who trusted God in the face of adversity (see Hebrews 11).
❖ To endure, you must keep your eyes on Jesus (see Hebrews 12:1–3).

Courage is required to face and endure times of adversity, and also to make the changes in our lives that adversity compels us to make.

Notes AND Prayer Requests

USE THIS SPACE TO WRITE ANY KEY POINTS, QUESTIONS,
OR PRAYER REQUESTS FROM THIS WEEK'S STUDY.

LIFE PRINCIPLE 19

*A*nything You Hold Too Tightly, You Will Lose

[Woe to you] who drink wine from bowls, and anoint yourselves
with the best ointments, but are not grieved for the affliction of Joseph.
Therefore they shall now go captive as the first of the captives,
and those who recline at banquets shall be removed.

AMOS 6:6–7

Life's Questions

What do you consider to be an absolute necessity in your life? What could you not live without? What would utterly devastate you if you lost it? Is it a relationship, a possession, a position, or something else in your life? Is it more important to you than God? If so, you need to consider how tight a hold it actually has on you, because it could become counterproductive and even dangerous. What would you do if God asked you to give it up? Could you obey Him? Does the thought of letting it go cause you to feel anxious, insecure, or out of control?

For some people, money is central. They *worship* wealth—which means they devote most of their time, energy, and attention to gaining it and keeping it. They regard wealth as the key to power and prestige, and the thought of losing it keeps them up at night. Perhaps you feel you don't fall into this camp, but consider these questions: *How much time do you spend each day thinking about your finances as compared to meditating on God's Word? How much time do you spend shopping as compared to serving the Lord in outreach? Are you likely to spend more time discussing an upcoming expense or the way the Holy Spirit helped you that day?*

The Bible has a name for those things in your life that keep you from trusting and honoring God: an *idol.* God has strong feelings when it comes to idols in your life, and He is not going to allow you to keep those things in your grasp. As Life Principle 19 teaches, *Anything you hold too tightly, you will lose.* If you are looking to anything other than God for your sense of acceptance, accomplishment, and security, then you are

PRINCIPLE IN ACTION
People of Shinar (Genesis 11:1–9)
Sarah (Genesis 16:5)
Saul (1 Samuel 18:8)
Uzziah (2 Chronicles 26:16–23)
Gomer (Hosea 2:14)

When you leave God out of your financial life, you are in grave danger of making money your idol.

—CHARLES F. STANLEY

God will assert His
rightful role as the only
Lord of your life.

headed for serious trouble, because it will not last. Sooner or later, God will assert His rightful role as the only Lord of your life.

Day 55: The One Who Blesses

François Fénelon was an archbishop who lived during the seventeenth century in the village of Cambrai in France. In 1697, the episcopal palace in which he lived burned to the ground, taking with it his library and his writings. But when informed of the tragedy, he said, "I had rather that the fire had seized my house than a poor man's cottage." Fénelon's ability to depend on God in his trials allowed him to write letters of encouragement to believers who needed the right spiritual perspective on their trials. In one such letter, he wrote:

> Do not worry about the future. It makes no sense to worry if God loves you and has taken care of you. However, when God blesses you, remember to keep your eyes on Him and not the blessing. Enjoy your blessings day by day, just as the Israelites enjoyed their manna; but do not try to store the blessings for the future. . . .
>
> Sometimes in this life of faith, God will remove His blessings from you. But remember that He knows how and when to replace them, either through the ministry of others or by Himself. He can raise up children from the very stones.
>
> Eat then your daily bread without worrying about tomorrow. There is time enough tomorrow to think about the things tomorrow will bring. The same God who feeds you today is the very God who will feed you tomorrow. God will see to it that manna falls again from Heaven in the midst of the desert, before His children lack any good thing.

Trouble and perplexity drive me to prayer, and prayer drives away perplexity and trouble.
—FRANÇOIS FÉNELON

How difficult would it be for you to adopt this attitude? If you lived with faith of this kind—if you made a concerted effort to focus on the One who blesses instead of the blessings themselves—how would it affect your stress level and anxiety? Can you, like Fénelon, humbly "eat then your daily bread without worry about tomorrow"?

"Do not lay up for yourselves treasures on earth, where moth and rust destroy and where thieves break in and steal" (Matthew 6:19).

1. Read Matthew 6:19–24. What does Jesus say about acquiring possessions in this world (19)? What is the problem with storing up earthly treasures?

_____

_____

_____

146

2. What kind of treasures does a person lay up in heaven (20)?

_____

_____

_____

3. What does Jesus mean when He says, "For where your treasure is, there your heart will be also" (21)? How does this relate to the idols you set up in your life?

_____

_____

_____

_____

4. How does focusing on the things of God enable you to let go of earthly possessions? How does it free you from anxiety about your future?

_____

_____

_____

5. Which of the two masters that Jesus mentions do you tend to serve (24)? What are the consequences of serving *mammon* (riches and wealth) above God?

_____

_____

_____

> "Lay up for yourselves treasures in heaven, where neither moth nor rust destroys and where thieves do not break in and steal. For where your treasure is, there your heart will be also. The lamp of the body is the eye. If therefore your eye is good, your whole body will be full of light. But if your eye is bad, your whole body will be full of darkness. If therefore the light that is in you is darkness, how great is that darkness! No one can serve two masters; for either he will hate the one and love the other, or else he will be loyal to the one and despise the other. You cannot serve God and mammon" (Matthew 6:20–24).

Whatever has your attention is your treasure,
but only God is truly worthy of your heart.

Day 56: Who's the Boss?

Admit it. In a tough situation, your first response is to take charge and try to make things right. As a member of the human race, you want to live with the confidence that everything will be okay, and the things that aren't right can be fixed with concentrated effort. You tell yourself, *If I plan carefully and work hard enough, I can overcome any difficulty.* The problem comes when the challenge is greater than your resources or lies outside your scope of influence. God allows such trials into your life for a reason: He wants you to recognize *He is in control.*

God allows some trials into your life so you can recognize He is in control.

God wants to be your all-sufficient Lord, Master, Savior, and Friend.

Yet God doesn't want to be merely the resource you call on when you're in trouble. He wants to be your all-sufficient Lord, Master, Savior, and Friend. He knows you intimately because He formed your very cells and fibers (see Psalm 139:13–16). He has a good plan for every day of your life (see Ephesians 2:10). He knows how to fulfill His purpose for you (see Psalm 138:8). To allow anyone other than Him—even yourself—to assume control of your life would only prove to be self-defeating.

When you face circumstances that rapidly deplete your spiritual, emotional, and physical reserves, the natural instinct is to cling to something strong out of fear. The question you must consider is whether your worries drive you to the arms of God or to your own resources. In the Bible, we read of a man who had good reason to worry, for he had just assumed leadership of God's people and had been charged to lead them into battle.

"Now therefore, arise, go over this Jordan, you and all this people, to the land which I am giving to them—the children of Israel. Every place that the sole of your foot will tread upon I have given you" (Joshua 1:2–3).

6. Read Joshua 1:1–9. In this passage, God commissioned Joshua to succeed Moses as leader of the Israelites. In one sentence, how would you summarize His message to Joshua?

_____

_____

_____

_____

7. When the Israelites arrived at the Promised Land, they found it occupied by some formidable enemies. Why was it important for them to be reminded that God had already given the land to them (6)?

_____

_____

_____

"Be strong and of good courage, for to this people you shall divide as an inheritance the land which I swore to their fathers to give them. Only be strong and very courageous, that you may observe to do according to all the law which Moses My servant commanded you; do not turn from it to the right hand or to the left, that you may prosper wherever you go. This Book of the Law shall not depart from your mouth, but you shall meditate in it day and night, that you may observe to do according to all that is written in it" (Joshua 1:6–8).

8. Why do you have reason to "be strong and of good courage" (6)?

_____

_____

_____

_____

9. How is it possible to meditate on God's Word "day and night" (8)? Why is it critical to know God's Word when situations come that could cause worry?

_____

_____

_____

_____

10. If you were to fully embrace the strength God offers and give Him complete control of your life, how would your outlook on life be different? What could you accomplish?

_____

_____

_____

Joshua didn't waver in his mission because he was assured that the true leader of Israel—the Lord God—would never fail or forsake them. You can have the same assurance as long as you remember that listening to God is essential to walking with Him and receiving His blessings.

"Have I not commanded you? Be strong and of good courage; do not be afraid, nor be dismayed, for the LORD your God is with you wherever you go" (Joshua 1:9).

Day 57: Loosening Your Grip

Are you hanging on to something other than the Lord? Are you gripping some form of earthly security instead of trusting Him to help you? Remember, whatever you hold too tightly you will lose. God will not allow you to keep whatever you are clutching—whether it is your wealth, your giftedness, your relationships, or your religious rituals—as your source of confidence, for that role belongs only to Him. He will allow your security in those things to fail so you can see that He is your sovereign Lord.

A British general stationed in India during the 1800s reported how the residents of a small village would capture a monkey. The villagers would take a coconut, cut a hole in it, fill the hole with grain, and leave the coconut near the mango trees where the monkeys played. The hole was only large enough to admit the monkey's open hand, and when the creature reached inside the coconut to grasp the grain, it would become stuck. The monkey was unwilling to let the grain go and free its hand, and so it was captured easily.

When you grab hold of things too tightly and refuse to let go, you are in many ways acting like this monkey—and you will get caught. God longs for you to release yourself into *His* control. He longs for you to say the words that David once prayed long ago: "Whenever I am afraid, I will trust in You. In God (I will praise His word), in God I have put my trust; I will not fear. What can flesh do to me?" (Psalm 56:3–4). When you look to God as the source of your sufficiency, you will find that you also never have to give in to fear.

Whatever you hold too tightly outside of God you will ultimately lose.

God longs for you to release yourself into *His* control.

Then one from the crowd said to Him, "Teacher, tell my brother to divide the inheritance with me." But He said to him, "Man, who made Me a judge or an arbitrator over you?" And He said to them, "Take heed and beware of covetousness, for one's life does not consist in the abundance of the things he possesses." Then He spoke a parable to them, saying: "The ground of a certain rich man yielded plentifully. And he thought within himself, saying, 'What shall I do, since I have no room to store my crops?' So he said, 'I will do this: I will pull down my barns and build greater, and there I will store all my crops and my goods. And I will say to my soul, "Soul, you have many goods laid up for many years; take your ease; eat, drink, and be merry."' But God said to him, 'Fool! This night your soul will be required of you; then whose will those things be which you have provided?' "So is he who lays up treasure for himself, and is not rich toward God" (Luke 12:13–21).

11. Read Luke 12:13–21. What did the man who approached Jesus want from Him (13)?

_____

_____

_____

_____

12. Why did Jesus use a rich person as a cautionary figure in this parable (16)?

_____

_____

_____

_____

13. What clues do you get from the parable that the rich man believed he was self-sufficient? What were his plans (17–19)?

_____

_____

_____

_____

_____

14. What was it about the man's attitude that so offended God (20)?

_____

_____

_____

_____

15. If the man who approached Jesus took the lessons of the parable to heart, what do you think would have been his next move?

_____

_____

_____

_____

_____

Wealth can never substitute for a relationship with God, and it will ultimately only make the heart feel hollow (see Ecclesiastes 6:2).

Living the Principle

As we discussed in Life Principle 10, God will move heaven and earth to show you His will. He wants you to know what's going on and what His plan is for you. However, no matter what the circumstances may be, your most important responsibility is always to trust and obey Him. If there is something you are honoring above God, He will let you know that it displeases Him. He will call you to lay that person, possession, or situation down on your own.

God will not share the control of your life with something or someone else. Paul wrote, "The love of money is a root of all kinds of evil, for which some have strayed from the faith in their greediness, and pierced themselves through with many sorrows" (1 Timothy 6:10). You neither honor God nor help yourself by having a divided heart, so make a decision about what will rule your life once and for all. Surrender whatever is coming between you and the Lord.

The good news is that no matter what God requires you to give up, your life will be better without it in the long run. God is not punishing you by taking this precious thing from you. He is preparing to give you something even better: *Himself.* So, *how will you live out Life Principle 19 this week?* Make a list of the things that are consuming your time and attention and you are having trouble giving up. If necessary, ask a trusted Christian friend or mentor to help you. Turn it over to God in prayer. Release your grip and give it to Him. Ask Him to take control.

> **Your most important responsibility is always to obey and trust God.**

Life Lessons to Remember

❖ God loves you too much to allow you to be sufficient or dependent on anything other than Himself (see 2 Corinthians 12:7–10).

❖ Only God has the credentials to assume control of your life (see Psalm 139:13–16).

❖ Trusting God is the ideal antidote to fear and insecurity (see Psalm 56:3–4).

We live in a fallen world—all of us will face times of suffering and heartache. Sometimes God keeps us from certain tests and trials, but at other times He allows them, knowing that the testing strengthens and perfects our faith in Him.

Notes AND Prayer Requests

USE THIS SPACE TO WRITE ANY KEY POINTS, QUESTIONS,
OR PRAYER REQUESTS FROM THIS WEEK'S STUDY.

Disappointments Are Inevitable; Discouragement Is a Choice

Though the fig tree may not blossom, nor fruit be on the vines;
though the labor of the olive may fail, and the fields yield no food;
though the flock may be cut off from the fold, and there be no
herd in the stalls—yet I will rejoice in the LORD

HABAKKUK 3:17-18

Life's Questions

Life doesn't always turn out the way you think it should. In fact, it rarely does. If you're like most people, your hopes and expectations almost always exceed your reality. Opportunities that you're counting on happening don't turn out the way you thought they would. People you believed you could depend on end up letting you down. The plans you design for yourself go awry in ways you never anticipated. The result is disappointment . . . one of the biggest challenges of the human experience.

What hopes do you have for your life? What opportunities, relationships, or situations are you constantly reaching for? What are you asking God to make a reality for you? There's nothing wrong with having such hopes and dreams. They often serve as excellent motivators that inspire you to strive for the best. Of course, the harder you strive to fulfill your hopes and dreams, the greater your potential for disappointment if those things don't come to pass.

PRINCIPLE IN ACTION
Israelites (Exodus 6:9)
Joshua (Joshua 3:1–17)
Job (Job 19:25–26)
Daniel (Daniel 6:21)
Paul and Silas (Acts 16:25–30)

Fear and discouragement are subject to your will, especially when you are walking in step with God. Through faith in Him, you can rule over them, not them over you.

—CHARLES F. STANLEY

During those times of disillusionment, the most important thing for you to remember is Life Principle 20: *Disappointments are inevitable; discouragement is a choice.* Will you allow your disappointments to dishearten you? Will you allow them to impede you from becoming everything that God created you to be? Or will you rise up, learn from them, and move on? The decision is yours, so make sure you choose wisely.

Will you rise up from your disappointments and move on?

Day 58: Unanticipated Directions

Everyone has known the ache of sadness that comes when life moves in an unanticipated and undesired direction. Consider the case of Joseph in the Bible, a Nazarene carpenter betrothed to a godly young woman named Mary. Like any Jewish man, he looked forward to the day when he would take a wife and start a family. Then came the news.

Mary was *pregnant*. What a devastating blow to the young carpenter's hopes and plans. Not only would he have no bride, but also, according to Jewish law, his betrothed was eligible for the death penalty (see Deuteronomy 22:23–24). His disappointment must have been overwhelming. Yet his first instinct was to protect Mary. "Joseph . . . being a just man, and not wanting to make her a public example, was minded to put her away secretly" (Matthew 1:19).

If a young woman who is a virgin is betrothed to a husband, and a man finds her in the city and lies with her, then you shall bring them both out to the gate of that city, and you shall stone them to death with stones (Deuteronomy 22:23–24).

What Joseph didn't know is that Mary hadn't violated the law. In fact, God had special plans for her pregnancy. The Lord's angel had told her, "You will conceive in your womb and bring forth a Son, and shall call His name JESUS. He will be great, and will be called the Son of the Highest" (Luke 1:31–32). The Lord also sent an angel to confirm His plan to Joseph. He said, "Joseph, son of David, do not be afraid to take to you Mary your wife, for that which is conceived in her is of the Holy Spirit" (Matthew 1:20).

Joseph did not allow his initial disappointment to give way to discouragement. Rather, he accepted God's will, obeyed the Lord, and brought Mary home to live with him, as a virgin, until the birth of the child. "And he called His name JESUS" (Matthew 1:25).

1. Read Psalm 34. David experienced his share of disappointment in life. After being anointed king of Israel (see 1 Samuel 16), he had been forced by the jealous King Saul to run for his life. When David wrote this psalm, he was hiding out in enemy territory. In spite of his setbacks, what could he still say about God's goodness (1–3)?

I will bless the LORD at all times; His praise shall continually be in my mouth. My soul shall make its boast in the LORD; the humble shall hear of it and be glad. Oh, magnify the LORD with me, and let us exalt His name together (Psalm 34:1–3).

_____

_____

_____

_____

2. How did David reveal that he was not discouraged and still trusted in the Lord (4)?

_____

_____

_____

_____

_____

I sought the LORD, and He heard me, and delivered me from all my fears. They looked to Him and were radiant, and their faces were not ashamed (Psalm 34:4–5).

3. How could someone who is struggling with disappointment "taste and see that the LORD is good" (8)? What would this look like in a person's life?

_____

_____

_____

_____

_____

_____

Oh, taste and see that the LORD is good; blessed is the man who trusts in Him! Oh, fear the LORD, you His saints! There is no want to those who fear Him (Psalm 34:8–9).

4. How might someone who's struggling with disappointment respond to David's claim "there is no want to those who fear [God]" (9)?

_____

_____

_____

_____

_____

_____

5. How do you respond to David's words that "many are the afflictions of the righteous, but the LORD delivers him out of them all" (19)? How does David's story give you hope in the midst of your disappointments?

_____

_____

_____

_____

_____

Many are the afflictions of the righteous, but the LORD delivers him out of them all. He guards all his bones; not one of them is broken. Evil shall slay the wicked, and those who hate the righteous shall be condemned. The LORD redeems the soul of His servants, and none of those who trust in Him shall be condemned (Psalm 34:19–22).

"The LORD, He is the One who goes before you.
He will be with you, He will not leave you nor forsake you;
do not fear nor be dismayed" (Deuteronomy 31:8).

155

Day 59: Letting Go of Disappointment

God has a unique plan for your life that cannot be changed by circumstances.

The Lord has a unique plan for your life—one that cannot be changed by unexpected circumstances. He has worked out the who, what, when, where, why, and how of your time on this earth. For this reason, when you confront a situation that does not line up with your understanding of how God wants your life to proceed, you need to stop and look to Him for direction. Sometimes He allows disappointments to teach you to "walk by faith, not by sight" (2 Corinthians 5:7). So you can't allow challenges to steal your enthusiasm or confidence in Him.

You don't have to be the victim of your feelings. In the daily disappointments that threaten to consume your emotional resources and deflect your attention from the Lord, you can grasp hold of the hope that being a beloved child of God brings to you. As a believer in Christ, you have been chosen by God. In choosing you, God is saying, "I want to be in a close relationship with you. I want you to take your disappointments to me. I want to lift you up and show you the incredible things I have in store for you."

God has blessings for you—more than you can imagine.

As you choose to look to God, listen, learn, and move ahead, the wounded places in your heart and the scars of old disappointments melt away in the light of God's restoring love. He does have blessings for you—more than you can imagine. So let go of disappointments and the fear of hoping and trusting again. Know that God holds your future in His hands, and you will never lose by looking forward to what He has in store.

Therefore, having been justified by faith, we have peace with God through our Lord Jesus Christ, through whom also we have access by faith into this grace in which we stand, and rejoice in hope of the glory of God (Romans 5:1–2).

6. Read Romans 5:1–5. What does it mean to "have peace with God" (1)?

_____

_____

_____

7. What is the connection between the tribulations you experience in life and your ability to persevere (3)?

_____

_____

_____

_____

8. What does it mean to have good *character*? What role does perseverance play in building a godly character within you (4)?

_____

_____

_____

9. Why does hope come from character (4)? How has having hope enabled you personally to overcome past defeats and embrace the future?

_____

_____

_____

10. Why does Paul say that hope does not disappoint (5)? In what area of your life do you need God's love and hope right now?

_____

_____

_____

Not only that, but we also glory in tribulations, knowing that tribulation produces perseverance; and perseverance, character; and character, hope. Now hope does not disappoint, because the love of God has been poured out in our hearts by the Holy Spirit who was given to us (Romans 5:3–5).

Trials, difficulties, and adversities are often God's way of developing a Christlike character in you. No one likes trials, but the Lord can use them for your good, if you will trust Him.

Day 60: Trusting God in the Dark

As a believer in Christ, you trust God to accomplish what He promises in His Word. But the real battle of faith comes when God responds in a way you don't expect or in a way you perceive as negative. What should you do when you don't understand God's plan—or when it involves your suffering? Will you continue to rely on Him in spite of the disappointment? Or will you turn away from Him in discouragement?

The prophet Habakkuk experienced such a decision. He cried out for the Lord to judge the wickedness of Judah but was horrified when he learned that God would do so through the "bitter and hasty" Babylonians (see Habakkuk 1:1–6). The prophet cried out, "O LORD, You have appointed them for judgment. . . . Why do You look on those who deal treacherously, and hold your tongue when the wicked devours a person more righteous than he?" (1:12–13).

Habakkuk could not understand why God chose to work the way He did. However, in spite of these feelings, he demonstrated the essence of true faith. Habakkuk continued to trust the Lord's wisdom and faithfulness, regardless of what happened. Do you have confidence in God in spite of the circumstances? Do you cling to God and His Word, even when it means you must suffer hardship? Can you say, along with Habakkuk, that though your resources and reserves vanish, you will still "rejoice in the LORD" (3:18)?

The real battle of faith comes when God responds in a way you don't expect.

Do you have confidence in the Lord in spite of the circumstances?

What then shall we say to these things? If God is for us, who can be against us? He who did not spare His own Son, but delivered Him up for us all, how shall He not with Him also freely give us all things? (Romans 8:31–32).

11. Read Romans 8:31–39. In Paul's day—just as today—there were many people who conspired against followers of Christ. Many Christians were enduring at least some form of persecution for their beliefs. Given this, how can Paul say, "If God is for us, who can be against us" (31)? What are some "opponents" you encounter today?

_____

_____

_____

_____

_____

12. What example does Paul provide to show that God has held nothing back from you when it comes to your salvation and eternal life with Him (32)? How should this shape your perspective on the disappointments you encounter in life?

_____

_____

_____

_____

_____

Who shall separate us from the love of Christ? Shall tribulation, or distress, or persecution, or famine, or nakedness, or peril, or sword? (Romans 8:35).

13. God does not require you to understand His will, just obey it—and sometimes you may question why He is leading you in a certain direction. What hope can you have that God still loves you and is working for you in that situation (35)?

_____

_____

_____

_____

For I am persuaded that neither death nor life, nor angels nor principalities nor powers, nor things present nor things to come, nor height nor depth, nor any other created thing, shall be able to separate us from the love of God which is in Christ Jesus our Lord (Romans 8:38–39).

14. Disappointments in life will come, but what does Paul say that you should always remember in the midst of your difficulties (38–39)?

_____

_____

_____

_____

15. How have you been persuaded that nothing in this life will separate you from God's love?

_____

_____

_____

Living the Principle

How do you respond when disappointments come your way? Do you become angry, frustrated, and disheartened? Or do you say, "Lord, I may not know why You allowed this, but I trust You, knowing that Your best for my life is still ahead"? If you respond with discouragement and resentment, you will begin a downhill slide away from God's purpose. But if you respond with trust and praise, it will build your faith and bring you closer to the Lord.

Whenever you face disappointments, remember that your situation is in God's hands and under His sovereign control. Meditate on the fact that He loves you unconditionally and is providing His very best for you. Recall the blessings He has already given you. No matter what disappointments come, use them as stepping-stones to greater faith. Instead of becoming discouraged, you'll be filled with His courage—and there's nothing more encouraging than that.

How will you live out Life Principle 20 this week? Spend some quiet time in God's presence. Talk to Him about any disappointments you've experienced. What were the circumstances that caused you to set your expectations so high? What caused your disappointment? How did you react? How do you feel about your reaction now? Get it off your chest, give it to God, and thank Him for the opportunity to build your faith and trust in Him. Also, reach out to someone you know who feels as if he or she has hit a dead end. Share the promises you have learned this week and encourage that person to persevere.

> Responding to disappointments with trust and praise will build your faith.

Life Lessons to Remember

❖ God has a unique plan for your life that will not be changed by unexpected circumstances (see Isaiah 41:9–10).

❖ Whenever a situation arises that does not line up with your understanding of God's will, stop and look to Him for direction (see Psalm 32:8).

❖ God holds your future in His hands, and you will never lose by looking forward to what He has in store for you (see Philippians 3:13–14).

Knowing the origin of a storm in your life may be an important clue as to what God desires to teach you from it, but it is never the sole lesson that God has for you. You discover the greater lesson by looking at what you do when storms strike.

Notes AND Prayer Requests

USE THIS SPACE TO WRITE ANY KEY POINTS, QUESTIONS,
OR PRAYER REQUESTS FROM THIS WEEK'S STUDY.

_____

_____

_____

_____

_____

_____

_____

_____

_____

_____

_____

_____

_____

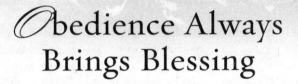

LIFE PRINCIPLE 21

Obedience Always Brings Blessing

Blessed are those who hear the word of God and keep it!

LUKE 11:28

Life's Questions

How far does God expect you to go in your obedience to Him? Perhaps you've accepted Jesus as your Lord and Savior and have submitted to Him in some important areas, but you still haven't turned *every* part of your life over to Him. Maybe you fear that God will lead you in a direction you don't want to go or give up something you want to keep. Maybe you've gotten into the habit of offering excuses for why you can't obey God. You might have fallen into a pattern of blaming conditions, situations, and other people for your lack of obedience. Or perhaps procrastination and slothfulness have hindered your efforts to submit to God completely.

It could also be that you just don't see the *need* to give God control over every part of your life. After all, didn't Paul say that "all things are lawful" for those in Christ (1 Corinthians 6:12)? If salvation comes through faith in Christ and you can't lose it, why do you need to obey God's truly difficult commands? Don't miss the rest of Paul's message: "All things are lawful . . . but I will not be brought under the power of any. . . . For you were bought at a price; therefore glorify God in your body and in your spirit, which are God's" (verses 12, 19–20).

God wants you to enjoy the freedom He gives you in every area. He wants to bless your life and meet your needs. But the only way to attain that liberty and those blessings is through obedience to Him. As James wrote to the early Christians who needed direction on how to live in an ungodly world, "He who looks into the perfect law of liberty and continues in it, *and is not a forgetful hearer but a doer of the work*, this one will

PRINCIPLE IN ACTION
Deborah (Judges 4–5)
Josiah (2 Kings 23:1–25)
Mordecai (Esther 3:1–6)
Baruch (Jeremiah 45:1–5)
Peter (Matthew 16:13–19)

We grow in faith when we hear from God, obey what He says, and then acknowledge God's faithfulness to His word in our lives.

—CHARLES F. STANLEY

be blessed in what he does" (James 1:25, emphasis added). This is why Life Principle 21 teaches, *Obedience always brings blessing.*

Day 61: A Simple Act of Obedience

Now when Jesus heard that John had been put in prison, He departed to Galilee (Matthew 4:12).

The gospel of Matthew records that shortly after Jesus was tempted in the wilderness, He came to the region of Galilee and dwelt in Capernaum, a fishing village by the sea. There He began to preach and say, "Repent, for the kingdom of heaven is at hand" (Matthew 4:17). One day as He was walking on the shore of the Sea of Galilee, He saw two brothers casting their nets. One of the men was named Simon (later renamed Peter), and the other was Andrew.

Jesus called out to them, "Follow Me, and I will make you fishers of men" (verse 19). At this point, the men had a choice. They could take the risk and follow this man—whom they may have heard about but likely didn't know personally—or they could take the safe route and stay in the fishing business. How would they respond? Would they obey Christ's call? Matthew reveals the answer: "They immediately left their nets and followed Him" (verse 20).

One simple act of obedience to God can change your life.

Shortly after, Jesus continued down the beach and saw another pair of fishermen. One was James and the other was John. Jesus made the same call to these men, and they responded in the same way: "Immediately they left the boat and their father, and followed Him" (verse 21). These four men's acts of obedience to Jesus' call would lead to the blessing of accompanying Jesus on His ministry, receiving His teaching, and seeing the miracles He performed. In so doing, they were following in the footsteps of four other men who, about 600 years before, had also taken a simple step of obedience for God.

In the third year of the reign of Jehoiakim king of Judah, Nebuchadnezzar king of Babylon came to Jerusalem and besieged it (Daniel 1:1).

1. Read Daniel 1:1–14. Daniel and his friends' story of *obedience* begins in the aftermath of the *disobedience* of their people, the Israelites. God's prophets had been warning the nation for years that their downfall was coming. How did that come to pass (1–2)?

   _____

   _____

   _____

The king appointed for them a daily provision of the king's delicacies and of the wine which he drank, and three years of training for them (Daniel 1:5).

2. What was Nebuchadnezzar's political strategy for combining the best and brightest of Judah with the best and brightest of Babylon (3–5)? What were the perks of being included in this elite group?

   _____

   _____

   _____

3. Why were the king's food and wine so offensive to Daniel and his friends (8)? What tactics did they propose for staying obedient to God (12–13)?

_____

_____

_____

_____

4. Why do you suppose the chief eunuch agreed to Daniel's proposal—especially when it involved such a risk for himself (14)?

_____

_____

_____

5. What is an area in your life where you need to take a simple step of obedience? What will you do to take that step today?

_____

_____

_____

But Daniel purposed in his heart that he would not defile himself with the portion of the king's delicacies, nor with the wine which he drank; therefore he requested of the chief of the eunuchs that he might not defile himself (Daniel 1:8).

"Please test your servants for ten days, and let them give us vegetables to eat and water to drink. Then let our appearance be examined before you, and the appearance of the young men who eat the portion of the king's delicacies; and as you see fit, so deal with your servants." So he consented with them in this matter (Daniel 1:12–14).

Godly obedience begins with a commitment to honor God above all else. When you make up your mind to put God first, temptations and challenges cannot control you.

Day 62: Long-Term Rewards

Obedience is the bottom line in the Christian life. It requires compliance to God's plan and pattern, observance of His commands, adherence to His standard, and submission to His will. Of course, if you want to obey the Lord in this manner, you first need to know what action God wants you to take, what attitude would most please Him, and what He requires of you.

Fortunately, you can begin to understand God's perspective by becoming familiar with His Word. But this alone is not enough. You must also tap into God's power by submitting to the promptings of the Holy Spirit, who helps you relate God's commands to your situation and assists you in determining the wisest course of action. Once you decide to obey, you can expect a challenge to compromise. Satan doesn't want you to follow God, so he will offer temptations to divert you and weaken your devotion. Remember, *partial* obedience is *disobedience*.

Obedience is the bottom line in the life of a Christian.

***Partial* obedience is still *disobedience*.**

It takes courage to obey God in the big and small things.

At the end of ten days their features appeared better and fatter in flesh than all the young men who ate the portion of the king's delicacies. Thus the steward took away their portion of delicacies and the wine that they were to drink, and gave them vegetables. As for these four young men, God gave them knowledge and skill in all literature and wisdom; and Daniel had understanding in all visions and dreams. Now at the end of the days, when the king had said that they should be brought in, the chief of the eunuchs brought them in before Nebuchadnezzar. Then the king interviewed them, and among them all none was found like Daniel, Hananiah, Mishael, and Azariah; therefore they served before the king. And in all matters of wisdom and understanding about which the king examined them, he found them ten times better than all the magicians and astrologers who were in all his realm (Daniel 1:15–20).

As the example of Daniel, Shadrach, Meshach, and Abed-Nego reveals, it takes courage to obey God in the big and small things in life. It takes courage to give up obvious benefits to do what the Lord asks. It takes courage to do things that may bring unwelcome results in the moment. But the long-term blessings will always outweigh the short-term losses.

6. Read Daniel 1:15–21. After ten days, how did Daniel and his obedient friends compare to the young men who had eaten the king's provisions (15)?

_____

_____

_____

_____

_____

7. How did the chief eunuch react when he saw the results (16)?

_____

_____

_____

_____

8. What specific blessings did Daniel and his friends receive for their obedience (17, 20)?

_____

_____

_____

_____

_____

9. In what ways do you suppose Daniel and his friends stood out to King Nebuchadnezzar (19)? How were they "ten times better" than the king's other advisors (20)?

_____

_____

_____

_____

_____

10. When is a time that you gave up short-term gains for long-term blessings? What did you see happen in your life and the lives of others as a result of your decision?

_____

_____

_____

_____

_____

_____

_____

_____

If we endure, we shall also reign with Him. If we deny Him, He also will deny us (2 Timothy 2:12).

> *God tells us to obey His commands—all of them—*
> *not merely the ones we like, understand, or that make us*
> *comfortable. Incomplete obedience is arrogant disobedience—*
> *and it is "evil in the sight of the LORD" (1 Samuel 15:19).*

Day 63: No Disappointments

Obeying God in every situation is an essential step in receiving His greatest blessings. So ask yourself if there is anything God has been challenging you to do that you have not yet made an effort to accomplish. Is there anything you have rationalized by saying, "It's too difficult," "I don't want to," or "I have to pray about it first"? Is there anything you are holding back?

Perhaps you have hesitated to obey God because you fear the consequences of your decision. But the Lord's command is for you to fear Him above all else. The same sovereign, omnipotent God who keeps your heart beating and the planets orbiting is more than able to handle the results of your obedience. When He tells you to do something and you know without a doubt it is His will, then you need to obey based solely on who is doing the talking.

When you choose to obey the Lord, you will *never* be disappointed. He will always bless you, because obedience *always* leads to blessing. So be encouraged if you are in a situation in which you don't understand why God is asking you to do a certain thing. God will reward you with a sense of peace and joy that compares to nothing this world has to offer if you obey Him. Therefore, set a goal to obey the Lord—and watch Him work in your life.

Obeying God in every situation is essential to receiving His greatest blessings.

Obedience *always* leads to blessing.

And Elijah the Tishbite, of the inhabitants of Gilead, said to Ahab, "As the LORD God of Israel lives, before whom I stand, there shall not be dew nor rain these years, except at my word" (1 Kings 17:1).

So he arose and went to Zarephath. And when he came to the gate of the city, indeed a widow was there gathering sticks (1 Kings 17:10).

She said, "As the LORD your God lives, I do not have bread, only a handful of flour in a bin, and a little oil in a jar; and see, I am gathering a couple of sticks that I may go in and prepare it for myself and my son, that we may eat it, and die" (1 Kings 17:12).

So she went away and did according to the word of Elijah; and she and he and her household ate for many days. The bin of flour was not used up, nor did the jar of oil run dry, according to the word of the LORD which He spoke by Elijah (1 Kings 17:15–16).

11. Read 1 Kings 17:1–16. What was the situation in Israel when this story took place (1)? How did God provide initial blessings to Elijah for his obedience (2–6)?

_____

_____

_____

_____

12. What was God's next instruction to Elijah when the brook dried up (7–9)? How did Elijah respond to this word from the Lord (10)?

_____

_____

_____

_____

13. What was the widow's response to Elijah's request? What was her situation (11–12)?

_____

_____

_____

_____

14. What happened when the widow decided to trust in the Lord and obey Him (13–16)?

_____

_____

_____

_____

15. What are you holding back from God out of fear you will lose it if you obey? What does this story tell you about God's provision?

_____

_____

_____

_____

_____

*The Lord commanded a widow to provide for Elijah,
and yet she knew nothing about it. She learned God's will
step by step as she walked with Him in faith, just as we do.*

Living the Principle

Just as Elijah's obedience benefited the widow and her son, your obedience will also often reward others—in particular, those closest to you. For instance, when a father obeys the Lord, his entire family may reap the reward of God's blessings. Likewise, a child's obedience may bless his or her parents. When you live an obedient life, those who know and love you can sense the peace and joy God has given you. Instead of conflict, there can be contentment.

God knows what is absolutely best for you, and He wants to see it accomplished in your life. So, what is hindering you from obeying God? Are you holding on to a person, goal, or activity that is less than God's best for you? It may be frightening to submit it to God, but do it anyway. God wants to bless you and give you freedom in that area, but He will only do so when you obey Him. While obedience is sometimes challenging, it will be worth it when you see God working in your life. Obey God with confidence, knowing you will be blessed when you do.

How will you live out Life Principle 21 this week? Identify the areas of obedience with which you're struggling in your life. If you're having trouble identifying them, ask the Holy Spirit to reveal them to you. Once you have gone to God in prayer, take some time to intentionally speak with Christian friends who know you well and get their input. Next, write down what you perceive to be the *costs* of obeying God in those areas, and then write down what you could see as being the potential *rewards* for obedience. When you are finished, turn those areas over to God in prayer, asking Him to show you practical ways to obey Him.

> When you live an obedient life, those who know and love you will sense the peace and joy God has given you.

Life Lessons to Remember

❖ Obeying God in the small matters is an essential step to receiving God's greatest blessings (see Mark 4:30–32).
❖ When you obey God, you will never be disappointed (see Psalm 22:5).
❖ Your obedience will always benefit others (see 2 Corinthians 4:11–15).

An effective servant is one who always submits his will to those who are in authority over him. We each are in a line of authority; no person lives without having someone in authority over him. Ultimately, that authority is Christ Jesus. It is only when we learn to submit our wills to His will and to obey those whom God has placed over us that we truly can be effective servants.

Notes AND Prayer Requests

USE THIS SPACE TO WRITE ANY KEY POINTS, QUESTIONS,
OR PRAYER REQUESTS FROM THIS WEEK'S STUDY.

To Walk in the Spirit Is to Obey the Initial Promptings of the Spirit

While Peter thought about the vision, the Spirit said to him,
"Behold, three men are seeking you."

ACTS 10:19

Life's Questions

When you accepted Jesus as your Savior, several things happened simultaneously. You received God's complete *forgiveness,* and your old sin nature was replaced with a new nature that desired God's righteousness. You received the gift of *eternal life* with God, and you likely experienced a deep and abiding sense of *peace and joy.* You also received the *Holy Spirit* into your life. It is the Holy Spirit—sent by Jesus to dwell within all those who believe in Him—who enables you to lead a godly life. He is your sufficiency as you walk in the footsteps of Jesus.

Do you ever feel burned out in your walk with God? Do you wonder if you are on the right track or if there is something more you should be experiencing? Do you wish that God's direction were clearer to you? If so, you may be trying to live the Christian life in your own strength and wisdom rather than by following the leadership of the Holy Spirit. In the Bible, Jesus referred to the Holy Spirit as the "Spirit of truth" (John 14:17). The Holy Spirit leads you to decisions, choices, and an understanding of God's will that is true from God's perspective. He empowers you to both *know* and *keep* God's commandments.

Life Principle 22 teaches, *To walk in the Spirit is to obey the initial promptings of the Spirit.* When you do so, you are equipped by the Holy Spirit and enjoy His perfect guidance. He may lead you in ways you don't

PRINCIPLE IN ACTION
Abraham (Genesis 22:1–18)
Widow of Zarephath
   (1 Kings 17:12–16)
Ahasuerus (Esther 6:1–10)
Joseph (Matthew 1:1–18)
Philadelphians
   (Revelation 3:7–13)

You can live a life free of sin and bold in action because you are empowered by the same Holy Spirit who empowered Jesus.

—CHARLES F. STANLEY

expect—perhaps even far out of your comfort zone— but you always end up squarely in the middle of God's will. And as you learn to trust Him, you come to realize no other paths would have taken you where you needed to go.

Day 64: Who Do You Trust?

The only Guide worth trusting is the Holy Spirit.

To whom do you turn for daily guidance on how to live? The Bible tells you the only Guide worth trusting is the Holy Spirit. He knows your past completely, from the moment you were conceived to the present. He knows what the future has in store for you, from this present day to eternity. He knows God's plan and purpose for you in the current moment and each moment you will have during the course of your life. He knows what is good and right for you.

The Holy Spirit is like an inner compass in your life—always pointing you toward what Jesus would be, say, or do at any given time. As Christ said, "He will guide you into all truth; for He will not speak on His own authority, but whatever He hears He will speak; and He will tell you things to come" (John 16:13). The Holy Spirit will also be quick to convict you of sin. He does this not to make your life miserable under a load of condemnation, but so you might quickly confess, receive God's forgiveness, and repent by seeking to obey God fully.

God has provided the Spirit of truth to be your daily guide.

God desires to make His will known to you. He wants you to know what to do and when to do it. He wants you to know what sinful patterns of behavior you should avoid. He has not left you alone to figure these things out on your own but has provided the Spirit of truth to be your daily guide. Just as the disciples found themselves empowered to live for God and proclaim the message of Christ after the Lord poured the Holy Spirit on them (see Acts 3–4), you will find yourself empowered when you lean on Him and accept His direction.

When [Cornelius] observed him, he was afraid, and said, "What is it, lord?" So he said to him, "Your prayers and your alms have come up for a memorial before God. Now send men to Joppa, and send for Simon whose surname is Peter. He is lodging with Simon, a tanner, whose house is by the sea"
(Acts 10:4–6).

1. Read Acts 10:1–48. At the time this story took place, it was believed in the church that Gentiles (non-Jews) could not receive the Holy Spirit because He was given only for the people of Israel. How would you describe Cornelius's faith (1–5)? What does God tell this centurion in the Roman army to do (5–6)?

   _____

   _____

   _____

   _____

   _____

   _____

   _____

2. One of the things that set the Jews apart from other nations was their dietary laws. God's people were forbidden to eat certain animals that were considered unclean. Given this, why did God's Spirit use those animals in Peter's dream (9–12)?

_____

_____

_____

_____

_____

[Peter] fell into a trance and saw heaven opened and an object like a great sheet bound at the four corners, descending to him and let down to the earth. In it were all kinds of four-footed animals of the earth, wild beasts, creeping things, and birds of the air (Acts 10:10–12).

3. Why did Peter doubt the instructions of the Holy Spirit in the vision (14)? How did the Holy Spirit reveal that He was speaking the truth to Him (19–23)?

_____

_____

_____

_____

While Peter thought about the vision, the Spirit said to him, "Behold, three men are seeking you. Arise therefore, go down and go with them, doubting nothing; for I have sent them" (Acts 10:19–20).

4. What thoughts do you suppose were going through Peter's mind when he realized Cornelius had also been prompted by the Holy Spirit (30–32)?

_____

_____

_____

_____

_____

"I prayed in my house, and behold, a man stood before me in bright clothing, and said, 'Cornelius, your prayer has been heard'" (Acts 10:30–31).

5. What did Peter come to learn about who could receive the Holy Spirit? How did the Holy Spirit lead him to this realization (34–43)?

_____

_____

_____

_____

Then Peter opened his mouth and said: "In truth I perceive that God shows no partiality" (Acts 10:34).

6. What were the immediate results of Cornelius and Peter's obedience to the Holy Spirit's promptings (44–48)? What were the long-term results for all believers?

_____

_____

_____

_____

_____

Those of the circumcision who believed were astonished, as many as came with Peter, because the gift of the Holy Spirit had been poured out on the Gentiles also (Acts 10:45).

> *Cornelius was known as a God-fearer. This meant he ascribed to Jewish worship and morals and believed in the one true God, but he probably wasn't a Jewish convert in the formal sense of being circumcised and undergoing Jewish baptism.*

Day 65: Learning to Yield

He who keeps His commandments abides in Him, and He in him (1 John 3:24).

The apostle John wrote that one of the ways you can know the Holy Spirit dwells within a person is that the person keeps God's statutes (see 1 John 3:24). The Holy Spirit leads in such a way that over time, believing, saying, and doing the right thing becomes as natural as breathing. The more you rely on the Holy Spirit to guide you into all truth, the more you take on the character of Christ and automatically seek to do what is pleasing in God's sight.

You must stay yielded to the Holy Spirit.

Yet there are conditions you must meet to experience the guidance of the Holy Spirit and to get you to that place in your walk with God. The first condition is that *you must stay yielded to the Holy Spirit*. You don't have an override feature that allows you to pick and choose the promptings you will obey. You must say *yes* to the Spirit when He prompts you to take a certain action or say a certain word. You must give mental assent to the Spirit's direction, and then you must actually follow through by doing or saying what He has called you to do or say.

The Holy Spirit will often speak to you in the stillness of your heart with a word of conviction or assurance. When the Holy Spirit is revealing something in your life that is harmful, you will often have a heaviness, a feeling of trouble and foreboding, or an uneasiness in your spirit about it. When the Holy Spirit is directing you toward helpful things, you will tend to feel a deep inner peace, an eagerness to see what God will do, and a feeling of joy.

So the churches were strengthened in the faith, and increased in number daily (Acts 16:5).

7. Read Acts 16:1–10. As the scene opens, Paul and Silas have recently embarked on a missionary journey to visit the churches that Paul previously planted. What was the immediate effect on the churches they visited (5)?

_____

_____

_____

_____

_____

8. What happened when Paul and Silas reached Asia (6–7)? Why do you think the Holy Spirit prevented them from preaching the gospel there?

_____

_____

_____

When they had gone through Phrygia and the region of Galatia, they were forbidden by the Holy Spirit to preach the word in Asia (Acts 16:6).

9. How did Paul and Silas yield to the Holy Spirit (8)? How did He redirect them (9–10)?

_____

_____

_____

So passing by Mysia, they came down to Troas. And a vision appeared to Paul in the night. A man of Macedonia stood and pleaded with him saying, "Come over to Macedonia and help us." Now after he had seen the vision, immediately we sought to go to Macedonia, concluding that the Lord had called us to preach the gospel to them (Acts 16:8–10).

10. When was a time that you didn't understand a prompting from the Holy Spirit but yielded and followed His guidance anyway?

_____

_____

_____

11. How has God used a restlessness in your spirit to direct you to a course of action?

_____

_____

_____

Paul and his companions never let their plans get in the way of the Spirit's leading. Because they obeyed the Lord's direction, they went into Europe with the gospel. Paul planted churches at Philippi, Thessalonica, and Berea, which proved to be strategic in the spread of Christianity.

Day 66: Ever Vigilant

The second condition you need to meet to experience the guidance of the Holy Spirit in your life is to *believe and obey His guidance*. This requires a degree of vigilance on your part, for to obey the Spirit's commands,

You must believe and obey the Holy Spirit's guidance.

you must first *recognize* His promptings. And you are much more likely to recognize His promptings if you are anticipating them. The most surefire strategy for hearing what the Holy Spirit has to say is to actively listen for Him to speak.

The writer of Hebrews states that God is a "rewarder of those who diligently seek Him" (11:6). In practical terms, this can mean putting yourself in the right space—physically, spiritually, and emotionally—to hear what the Holy Spirit has to say. It might mean retreating to a quiet place, away from the interruption and noise of daily life. It will mean clearing your mind of to-do list items, pressing deadlines, and continual distractions. It will mean asking the Lord to prepare your heart to receive His instruction.

The Holy Spirit has come to reveal the truth to you. He has come in His all-knowing ability to impart to you what you need to know in order to live an obedient and faithful life. So acknowledge you need God and the Holy Spirit at all times and in all decisions and choices. Invite Him to be your sufficiency day by day. Then trust Him to guide you—now and always!

Actively listen for the Holy Spirit to speak to you.

The Holy Spirit has come to reveal the truth to you.

I say then: Walk in the Spirit, and you shall not fulfill the lust of the flesh (Galatians 5:16).

12. Read Galatians 5:16–26. Why does Paul say you must be vigilant to walk in the Spirit (16)? What is the result of a life led by the Spirit?

_____

_____

_____

_____

But if you are led by the Spirit, you are not under the law. Now the works of the flesh are evident, which are: adultery, fornication, uncleanness, lewdness, idolatry, sorcery, hatred, contentions, jealousies, outbursts of wrath, selfish ambitions, dissensions, heresies, envy, murders, drunkenness, revelries, and the like (Galatians 5:18–21).

13. What does Paul mean when he says that if you are led by the Spirit, you are not under the law (18)?

_____

_____

_____

14. What are some of the works of the flesh? What is the danger in yielding to these works in your life (19–21)?

_____

_____

_____

_____

The fruit of the Spirit is love, joy, peace, longsuffering, kindness, goodness, faithfulness, gentleness, self-control (Galatians 5:22–23).

15. What are some of the fruit of the Spirit (22–23)? How has the Holy Spirit revealed this fruit in your life?

_____

_____

_____

_____

16. What do you need to do today to more diligently seek the Holy Spirit?

_____

_____

_____

_____

If we live in the Spirit, let us also walk in the Spirit (Galatians 5:25).

When you are in a union with Christ, the Holy Spirit's primary responsibility is to produce His likeness in you. He teaches you how to be totally dependent on God, which then produces an overflow of love, joy, peace, patience, kindness, goodness, faithfulness, gentleness, and self-control in you.

Living the Principle

Have you been ignoring the Spirit's promptings because you're unsure about where He is directing you? Has the Spirit challenged your beliefs like He did with Peter? Is He moving you to change your course? If so, remember that the Holy Spirit can never lead you wrong, because He guides you in doing God's will. Jesus said, "The Spirit . . . will guide you into all truth. . . . He will glorify Me, for He will take of what is Mine and declare it to you" (John 16:13–14).

The Holy Spirit is your Counselor, Comforter, and Helper. He makes sure you have everything you need to accomplish whatever God has called you to do. So don't try to do things in your own power. Obey what the Holy Spirit is guiding you to do right away, then watch and enjoy the wonderful Spirit-filled life that unfolds before you.

How will you live out Life Principle 22 this week? If you sense the Holy Spirit is prompting you in a certain area of your life, discuss it with a trusted Christian friend or your pastor. Consider what action steps you need to take in order to yield to the Holy Spirit and follow His instruction. Step out in faith this week and see where God leads you next. Ask the Lord to continue revealing His will to you as you walk with Him, and thank Him for His guidance in your life. Pray that you will become even more attuned to the Holy Spirit's prompting in your situation.

The Holy Spirit always guides you in doing God's will.

Life Lessons to Remember

❖ You need to stay yielded to the Holy Spirit (see Romans 8:13–14).
❖ You need to trust the Holy Spirit to guide you (see 1 Thessalonians 5:19).
❖ You need to listen for the Holy Spirit's prompting (see Galatians 5:16–18).

Notes AND Prayer Requests

USE THIS SPACE TO WRITE ANY KEY POINTS, QUESTIONS,
OR PRAYER REQUESTS FROM THIS WEEK'S STUDY.

_____

_____

_____

_____

_____

_____

_____

_____

_____

_____

_____

_____

_____

_____

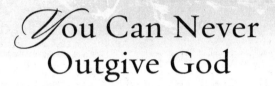

LIFE PRINCIPLE 23

You Can Never Outgive God

God is able to make all grace abound toward you, that you, always having all sufficiency in all things, may have an abundance for every good work.

2 CORINTHIANS 9:8

Life's Questions

Giving is an aspect of discipleship that church leaders are generally hesitant to talk about and believers are less than enthusiastic to hear about. For some reason, the topics of tithing and generosity strike many as too personal to discuss and too difficult to turn over to God. Believers are certainly eager to *receive* God's blessings, but they're hesitant to *obey* Him with the gifts He has given to them. The source of this discomfort is typically due to a lack of trust in God and a refusal to acknowledge His ownership of all that exists.

What's strange about this is that when you look at the Bible, you find it is *filled* from cover to cover with stories about the goodness of God. Your heavenly Father is always giving, always loving, and always generous toward His children. In Genesis, you read how He gives the man and woman a perfect Garden of Eden. In Revelation, you learn about the ultimate home God has prepared for you—a perfect and eternal heaven. In the books in between, you read how He delighted in blessing His people and how He sent His Son as His ultimate gift to you. God has given you an infinite supply that cannot be measured and cannot be depleted.

As Life Principle 23 teaches, *You can never outgive God.* He knows your needs better than and before you do. He has all the power to supply what you need, and He is at work—even now—to meet those needs. For this reason, when God commands you to let go of your wealth and resources,

PRINCIPLE IN ACTION
Israelites (Numbers 14:11)
David (Psalm 108:12)
Matthew (Matthew 9:9–13)
Poor Widow (Luke 21:1–4)
Corinthians (2 Corinthians 8:1–7)

Money is a part of you, both in earning it and in giving it. You must be as generous in your material gifts as you are in every other area.

—CHARLES F. STANLEY

you can be sure it's for a good reason. He doesn't want to deprive you. Rather, He wants to teach you to be more like Him by making you into a generous giver. No one, after all, has God's track record of generosity. As you learn to let go of your possessions, you find you receive back from Him above and beyond all that you've released.

Day 67: Abundant Generosity

King David knew God had prospered him and given him rest from his enemies. One day, he looked around at his comfortable home and said to Nathan the prophet, "See now, I dwell in a house of cedar, but the ark of God dwells inside tent curtains" (2 Samuel 7:2). He wanted to build a temple for God—which was no small undertaking. But God had a much bigger gift in mind for David. He said, "The LORD tells you that He will make you a house. . . . Your house and your kingdom shall be established forever before you" (verses 11, 16).

This story serves as a powerful reminder that your God is abundant in His generosity. While He invites your gifts and offerings, He will always give you *far more* than you could possibly ever give to Him. He is the source of all you need and will never be a debtor to anyone. When you realize the depths of His love for you, it compels you to respond as David did: "You are great, O Lord GOD. For there is none like You, nor is there any God besides You, according to all that we have heard with our ears" (verse 22).

Jesus later declared that anyone who gave one of His followers even a cup of water in His name would be lavishly rewarded (see Mark 9:41). He illustrated God's generosity by describing how a wealthy master rewarded his servants who had doubled the little bit of money he had given them with multiple cities (see Luke 19:11–27). Peter once boasted to the Lord, "See, we have left all and followed You" (Luke 18:28). He probably expected a pat on the back. Instead Jesus told him, "Assuredly, I say to you, there is no one who has left house or parents or brothers or wife or children, for the sake of the kingdom of God, who shall not receive many times more in this present time, and in the age to come eternal life" (verses 29–30).

1. Read Luke 21:1–4. How do you picture the widow in this story? What was it about her that captured Jesus' attention (1)?

_____

_____

_____

_____

2. The "mite" the widow put into the treasury was likely a *lepton,* the smallest and least valuable coin in Palestine at the time. So what did Jesus mean when He said this woman had "put in more than all" (3)?

_____

_____

_____

_____

3. What distinction did Jesus draw between the two types of gifts? Why was it harder for the woman to give her two small coins than it was for the rich to put their more expensive gifts into the treasury (4)?

_____

_____

_____

_____

_____

_____

4. What do you take away from the fact that Jesus noticed the widow's sacrifice—even when no one else did? What does this tell you about what God sees when you give?

_____

_____

_____

_____

_____

5. What does this story tell you about making sacrifices? What lessons can you apply to your own giving habits?

_____

_____

_____

_____

He said, "Truly I say to you that this poor widow has put in more than all; for all these out of their abundance have put in offerings for God, but she out of her poverty put in all the livelihood that she had" (Luke 21:3–4).

Do not forget to do good and to share, for with such sacrifices God is well pleased (Hebrews 13:16).

The word grace *in the New Testament comes from the root word* to rejoice. *It means the* absolutely free benefit or expression of lovingkindness, deeds that cause joy, *and* favor conferred. *When Paul writes, "God is able to make all grace abound toward you" (2 Corinthians 9:8), it means that God shows you a super abundance of kindness that will cause you immense joy.*

Day 68: A Blessing Poured Out

In Luke 6:38, Jesus provides one of the clearest explanations of the principle of giving found in Scripture when He said, "Give, and it will be given to you: good measure, pressed down, shaken together, and running over will be put into your bosom. For with the same measure that you use, it will be measured back to you." God's desire for you is abundance—a pressed-down, shaken-together, and running-over prosperity.

This doesn't mean that Jesus is saying personal gain should be a motive for giving. You give as part of the web of generosity God has established for His people. He gives to you, you give to others, and then you give back to Him. Yet the fact remains that you can *never* outgive God. His resources—not to mention His delight in blessing His children—cannot be equaled.

In the Old Testament, God instructed the people to bring Him the full tithe and said to them, "Try Me now in this . . . if I will not open for you the windows of heaven and pour out for you such blessing that there will not be room enough to receive it" (Malachi 3:10). To *tithe* is to give ten percent of one's income to God. All you have is a gift from God, so it represents a mere portion of what He has already given to you. If you obey God and cheerfully give the portion He has requested, He will bless you and the work of His kingdom.

God's desire for you is abundance.

"Take heed that you do not do your charitable deeds before men, to be seen by them. Otherwise you have no reward from your Father in heaven. Therefore, when you do a charitable deed, do not sound a trumpet before you as the hypocrites do in the synagogues and in the streets, that they may have glory from men. Assuredly, I say to you, they have their reward" (Matthew 6:1–2).

6. Read Matthew 6:1–4. How would you describe someone who does charitable deeds in order to be noticed by others (1)?

_____

_____

_____

_____

7. How might a person "sound a trumpet" (2) today?

_____

_____

_____

8. What does it mean not to "let your left hand know what your right hand is doing" (3)?

_____

_____

_____

_____

9. Why does God bless secrecy on the part of His people when they give (4)? What attitude is He seeking in people's hearts when they bring their gifts to Him?

_____

_____

_____

_____

10. What are some ways that you have done charitable deeds in secret? What impact has your humility in giving had on your life?

_____

_____

_____

_____

> *"But when you do a charitable deed, do not let your left hand know what your right hand is doing, that your charitable deed may be in secret; and your Father who sees in secret will Himself reward you openly"* (Matthew 6:3–4).

You do not need to boast about your Spirit-led good deeds or advertise the things you do that might otherwise be overlooked. God gives the only rewards that matter, and He keeps careful tally.

Day 69: True Blessings

When a pastor talks about giving, you may be tempted to jump to the conclusion that the person wants your money. But the truth is that God has established principles for good financial stewardship for *your* own benefit. God's principles are universal, eternal, and absolute, and the ways He directs you to use your resources will be personal, detailed, and specific. He will bless you as you trust Him to guide your stewardship of the gifts He has entrusted to you.

Once you have accepted Jesus Christ as your Savior and have received God's forgiveness for your sins, you fully qualify for God's promises related to prosperity and blessing. However, keep in mind that prosperity relates to your *entire life*, not just financial gain. A person can be rich and still not be prosperous. So when you think of blessings, think in terms of life's whole—a harmony that has spiritual, mental, emotional, physical, financial, and relational dimensions.

God's greatest desire is for you to be a *whole* person. He desires to bless you and cause you to grow in every area of your life in a balanced and fruitful way. He wants you to fulfill His destiny on earth—and do

God has established principles of financial stewardship for *your* benefit.

God's greatest desire is for you to be a whole person.

Brethren, we make known to you the grace of God bestowed on the churches of Macedonia: that in a great trial of affliction the abundance of their joy and their deep poverty abounded in the riches of their liberality (2 Corinthians 8:1–2).

so as a whole person. He then challenges you to let Him prove Himself and promises to bless you in return. "Honor the Lord with your possessions, and with the firstfruits of all your increase; so your barns will be filled with plenty, and your vats will overflow with new wine" (Proverbs 3:9–10). You truly can never outgive the Lord.

11. Read 2 Corinthians 8:1–15. Paul was spearheading a collection for the beleaguered church in Jerusalem. The believers in Macedonia, who were facing poverty themselves, had stepped up in a big way. In contrast, the believers in Corinth, who were comparatively well off, had pledged their support but neglected to follow through. What words stand out to you in Paul's praise for the Macedonian believers (1–5)?

_____

_____

_____

_____

You know the grace of our Lord Jesus Christ, that though He was rich, yet for your sakes He became poor, that you through His poverty might become rich. And in this I give advice: It is to your advantage not only to be doing what you began and were desiring to do a year ago; but now you also must complete the doing of it (2 Corinthians 8:9–11).

12. How would you explain Paul's words in verse 9—"though He [Jesus] was rich, yet for your sakes He became poor, that you through His poverty might become rich"—to someone who's struggling to understand Christian giving?

_____

_____

_____

_____

13. Why does Paul say that exercising financial stewardship is to the Corinthian believers' advantage (10–11)? What principles is he instilling in them?

_____

_____

_____

I do not mean that others should be eased and you burdened; but by an equality, that now at this time your abundance may supply their lack, that their abundance also may supply your lack—that there may be equality (2 Corinthians 8:13–14).

14. According to Paul, what is a Christian's responsibility to his or her fellow believers (13–15)?

_____

_____

_____

15. How has following God's principles of stewardship blessed your life? How have you seen God return an abundance to you when you have given to others in need?

_____

_____

> *God is not after your time, talents, or bank accounts.*
> *He already owns the world and everything in it*
> *(see Exodus 19:5). His greatest desire is to have a personal*
> *and intimate relationship with you for all eternity.*

Living the Principle

Do you give ten percent of your income for the ministry of the church on a consistent basis? Do you give generously and bless those in need? Perhaps you look at those questions and think, *I can't give to others because I have barely enough to live on myself.* Or maybe your response is, *I've worked hard for what I have, and I don't see why I should have to give it up.*

Both these attitudes represent a failure to comprehend that *everything* you have comes from God. When you give, you show your gratitude for the Lord's provision and your confidence that He will continue to meet all your needs (see Philippians 4:19). Your willingness to give to God declares your level of faith, and when you refuse to obey Him with your time, talents, and tithe, it opens the door for the enemy to consume the fruit of your labors. As God once told His people, "You have sown much, and bring in little . . . and he who earns wages, earns wages to put into a bag with holes" (Haggai 1:6).

How will you live out Life Principle 23 this week? Begin by taking a close look at your giving habits. What does your bank account reveal about your priorities? Are you offering God the firstfruits of your earnings—and thus putting Him first—or are you withholding resources? Are there areas in which you can be more generous? Commit to honoring God with your money by regularly tithing ten percent of your income. Then, look for ways that you can give of your time to your church. Is there a volunteer opportunity that needs to be filled? Is there a need in your congregation that you have the skills to fill? Take steps to give back to God this week.

When you give, you show gratitude for God's provision and confidence He will meet your needs.

Life Lessons to Remember

❖ All you have is a gift from God; therefore, whatever you offer Him is only a portion of what He has already given to you (see Deuteronomy 10:14).

❖ When you obey God by honoring Him with your tithes, He protects your finances and blesses you (see Malachi 3:10).

❖ God supplies all your needs from His limitless wealth (see Philippians 4:19).

Notes AND Prayer Requests

USE THIS SPACE TO WRITE ANY KEY POINTS, QUESTIONS,
OR PRAYER REQUESTS FROM THIS WEEK'S STUDY.

To Live the Christian Life Is to Allow Jesus to Live His Life in and Through You

I have been crucified with Christ; it is no longer I who live,
but Christ lives in me; and the life which I now live in the flesh I live by
faith in the Son of God, who loved me and gave Himself for me.

GALATIANS 2:20

Life's Questions

What troubles your heart today? What concern is consuming you with fear and doubt? What difficult circumstance is burdening your soul? Do you realize it's not your place to worry about that person, situation, or issue? Have you come to the understanding that everything that concerns you is *Christ's* responsibility to care for, rather than yours, and that your job is simply to obey Him? As David wrote in Psalm 138:7–8, "Though I walk in the midst of trouble . . . Your right hand will save me. The LORD will perfect that which concerns me."

Many people daydream of receiving an unexpected inheritance from a wealthy person. However, the fact is that as a believer in Christ Jesus, you are the heir of the most lavish inheritance that any person could ever dream to receive! Paul declared, "Eye has not seen, nor ear heard, nor have entered into the heart of man the things which God has prepared for those who love Him" (1 Corinthians 2:9). The inheritance you have been given in Christ is so glorious, so vast, and so tremendous you cannot even comprehend it with your finite mind. Nothing of benefit or goodness has been withheld from you.

You may be so used to taking care of yourself and/or others that this is a difficult truth for you to accept. However, if you embrace Life

PRINCIPLE IN ACTION
Jeremiah (Jeremiah 14:17)
Centurion (Matthew 8:5–13)
Peter (Matthew 14:28–31)
Judas (John 18:3)
Paul (Galatians 2:20)

Our identity as believers flows from the relationship we have with God through Christ Jesus, His Only begotten Son.

—CHARLES F. STANLEY

Principle 24—*To live the Christian life is to allow Jesus to live His life in and through you*—you will experience all the peace, joy, confidence, and assurance that are rightfully yours in Jesus Christ. If you don't, you'll continue being distracted by issues that were never yours to worry about in the first place—and you will miss the blessings of the abundant life God has planned for you.

Day 70: Beyond Adequate

Don't be content to just lead an "adequate" Christian life.

Many Christians today seem content to live what they think is an adequate Christian life. They believe that if they go to church, read their Bible occasionally, and say their prayers once in a while, they will be all right with God. Occasionally, they may be inspired to go above and beyond their normal routine and volunteer to serve others as an usher or a member of a church committee. They may even go on a short-term missions trip.

Yet while these believers go through the motions of being a "good Christian," they don't enjoy the power, peace, and joy that should come with the abundant life Jesus promised (see John 10:10). Eventually, the counterfeit Christian life they are living becomes a burden and does not comfort them when the storms of adversity assail. This is not the life God intended for His children. He does not call anyone to a marginal Christian life characterized by chores and rituals. He desires to have a daily relationship with His people, where they experience His presence and trust Him for wisdom, courage, and strength in all situations.

God desires to shine in your life.

The Lord wants to glorify Himself through you with every step you take, every decision you make, every conversation you have, and every thought you entertain. He desires to shine in your life—with His love, joy, peace, patience, kindness, goodness, faithfulness, gentleness, and self-control illuminating your unique personality as you walk in obedience to Him.

If we are beside ourselves, it is for God; or if we are of sound mind, it is for you. For the love of Christ compels us, because we judge thus: that if One died for all, then all died (2 Corinthians 5:13–14).

1. Read 2 Corinthians 5:12–21. Paul often had to deal with critics who questioned his motives when it came to his sharing the gospel with unbelievers. What defense does he provide in this passage (12–13)? What compels his actions (14)?

   _____

   _____

   _____

   _____

   _____

2. What does Paul say should characterize the life of a believer (15)?

_____

_____

_____

[Christ] died for all, that those who live should live no longer for themselves, but for Him who died for them and rose again (2 Corinthians 5:15).

3. What does Paul mean when he says, "If anyone is in Christ, he is a new creation" (17)? What are some of the "old things" that pass away?

_____

_____

_____

_____

If anyone is in Christ, he is a new creation; old things have passed away; behold, all things have become new (2 Corinthians 5:17).

4. In what ways are you serving as Christ's ambassador to the world (20)?

_____

_____

_____

We are ambassadors for Christ, as though God were pleading through us: we implore you on Christ's behalf, be reconciled to God. For He made Him who knew no sin to be sin for us, that we might become the righteousness of God in Him (2 Corinthians 5:20–21).

5. How will you allow the Lord to glorify Himself through the actions you take today?

_____

_____

_____

_____

When you are born again, you receive the Holy Spirit, who comes to indwell you and live Christ's life through you. You can never be what you were before because you have been born into His life with a new spirit and nature. Because of this, your desires and goals should be conformed to those God has for you.

Day 71: It Begins with a Relationship

To live the Christian life is to allow Jesus to live in you and through you. This is why Paul wrote, "I have been crucified with Christ; it is no longer I who live, but Christ lives in me; and the life which I now live in the flesh I live by faith in the Son of God, who loved me and gave

You have been "crucified with Christ."

Himself for me" (Galatians 2:20). The key to living the Christian life is never found in the pious acts you perform for the Lord but in the deep and intimate relationship you form with Him.

You build this kind of relationship through Bible study, prayer, worship, and fellowship with other believers. Through these disciplines, you learn not only *about* Jesus, but also how to interact *with* Him and, most importantly, to listen to Him. And when you listen to Him, He teaches you how to love Him, live for Him, and walk in His ways. As David wrote, "Commit your way to the LORD, trust also in Him, and He shall bring it to pass" (Psalm 37:5).

The ways in which Jesus lives in and through a person are as different and unique as each believer who follows Him. This is because He has a special purpose for each life. Therefore, the most important thing you can ever do is simply to obey Him—no matter what He tells you to do. God will allow situations and troubles in your life that only He can solve so He can demonstrate His glory, His power, His love, and His wisdom through you.

> When you listen to Christ, He shows you how to love Him, live for Him, and walk with Him.

> When Peter had come to Antioch, I withstood him to his face, because he was to be blamed; for before certain men came from James, he would eat with the Gentiles; but when they came, he withdrew and separated himself, fearing those who were of the circumcision. And the rest of the Jews also played the hypocrite with him (Galatians 2:11–13).

6. Read Galatians 2:11–21. What was Peter doing that offended Paul (11–13)?

_____

_____

_____

7. What signals was Peter (perhaps inadvertently) sending to other Christians who looked to him for guidance?

_____

_____

_____

> We who are Jews by nature, and not sinners of the Gentiles, knowing that a man is not justified by the works of the law but by faith in Jesus Christ (Galatians 2:15–16).

8. What did Paul say about what it means to be a believer? What is required (14–16)?

_____

_____

_____

_____

> I have been crucified with Christ; it is no longer I who live, but Christ lives in me (Galatians 2:20).

9. What does Paul mean when he says he has been "crucified with Christ" (20)? How does this concept shape the identity of a believer in Jesus?

_____

_____

_____

_____

10. Why does it sometimes seem easier to go back to living under the law (obeying rules and regulations) instead of letting Christ live in and through you?

_____

_____

_____

_____

_____

I do not set aside the grace of God; for if righteousness comes through the law, then Christ died in vain (Galatians 2:21).

When you trust in Jesus and receive eternal life, you don't somehow "get around" the law. Rather, Jesus fulfilled the whole law, and by identifying with Him in His death and resurrection, you do as well (see Romans 8:2–4).

Day 72: Identity Exchanged

The Bible says that before you accepted Christ as your Savior, you were "in Adam." You were a natural heir of Adam, descended from the first man and woman created by God, who rebelled against God in their disobedience and became subject to sin and spiritual death. You were born naturally with a sinful state of heart—your inclination was to sin, and your desire was to sin.

In this state, you were in absolute darkness. You were blinded to the truth about God, separated from a relationship with Him, and in bondage to sin's impulses without genuine freedom to live a righteous life. You were headed for eternal death—the ultimate consequence of an unchanged sinful heart. But when you accepted the work that Jesus Christ did on the cross, you exchanged your old identity "in Adam" for a new identity "in Christ." This was all that was required. In fact, no substitution for this requirement will work—no amount of good works, self-help techniques, thinking good thoughts, or striving to be a good person.

So, if today you are worried you're not doing enough to deserve a relationship with Christ, remember your salvation comes through faith in Christ and not by works. There is absolutely *nothing* you can do to earn God's salvation or be worthy of it, and there is nothing you can do or fail to do that would cause you to forfeit it. You are a new creature with a new life ahead—a life reconciled to God and set on a path toward fulfillment in Christ Jesus.

You were born naturally with a sinful state of heart.

Salvation comes through faith in Christ, not by works.

You He made alive, who were dead in trespasses and sins, in which you once walked according to the course of this world (Ephesians 2:1–2).

11. Read Ephesians 2:1–10. How does Paul describe your spiritual state before you came to Christ? Whom did you serve (1–3)?

_____

_____

_____

_____

[God], when we were dead in trespasses, made us alive together with Christ (by grace you have been saved) (Ephesians 2:5).

12. What did God do to save you from this existence? What motivated Him to do this for you (4–7)?

_____

_____

_____

_____

_____

By grace you have been saved through faith, and that not of yourselves; it is the gift of God, not of works, lest anyone should boast (Ephesians 2:8–9).

13. What did you have to do to receive this gift from Him (8)? What does this say about your ability to "earn" God's salvation (9)?

_____

_____

_____

_____

For we are His workmanship, created in Christ Jesus for good works, which God prepared beforehand that we should walk in them (Ephesians 2:10).

14. What does it mean to be God's "workmanship" (10)? How should this define your walk with Him?

_____

_____

_____

_____

15. In what ways have you been tempted to "work" for God's approval? What insights does this passage provide about the way God sees you?

_____

_____

_____

_____

God has designed you for a specific, fulfilling purpose, but you cannot find it or achieve it on your own. Rather, it is only by abiding in Him that it will come to fruition in your life.

Living the Principle

The Jewish believers in the early church who insisted the non-Jewish believers had to follow the Law of Moses were likely doing so out of a strong conviction that they were guarding the faith. However, what they were really doing was allowing themselves to be distracted by issues that weren't important. They were also creating a great deal of conflict in the process.

What is distracting you from letting Jesus live His life in you and through you? What are you allowing to take your focus off the deep relationship that God wants to have with you? Are you settling for an adequate life when something extraordinary is within your reach? In many cases, it all comes down to a matter of control. You have to be fully convinced the life Jesus will live in you and through you will bring fulfillment and happiness. You have to let go of the idea that you're better qualified to handle the reins of your life than Jesus is.

How will you live out Life Principle 24 this week? Think about some of the distractions that have gotten in the way of your relationship with God. Take these to the Lord in prayer, and ask Him to help you see beyond these distractions so you can focus on what truly matters. Also, ask Him to make you aware of times when you allowed Christ to live in you and through you, as well as times when you refused to do so. Seek His forgiveness for anything He reveals, then brainstorm strategies for how you will relinquish control to Him in the future.

Certain men came down from Judea and taught the brethren, "Unless you are circumcised according to the custom of Moses, you cannot be saved" (Acts 15:1).

Life Lessons to Remember

❖ God desires an intimate relationship with you in which you experience His presence, trust His wisdom, and rely on His strength (see Isaiah 58:2).

❖ The Spirit-filled life is marked by purpose, power, and effectiveness (see Romans 8:14–17).

❖ There is nothing you can do to earn the gift of God's salvation and your new identity in Christ (see Ephesians 2:8–10).

God was motivated by love to save mankind, and He did for man what man could not do for himself—He completely and eternally bridged the gap created by man's sin so that all who believe in Christ Jesus might be forgiven and have eternal life.

Notes and Prayer Requests

USE THIS SPACE TO WRITE ANY KEY POINTS, QUESTIONS,
OR PRAYER REQUESTS FROM THIS WEEK'S STUDY.

_____

_____

_____

_____

_____

_____

_____

_____

_____

_____

_____

_____

_____

_____

_____

_____

God Blesses You So That You Might Bless Others

Let him who stole steal no longer, but rather let him labor, working with his hands what is good, that he may have something to give him who has need.

EPHESIANS 4:28

Life's Questions

Does your love for God motivate you to serve others? Does your relationship with Him inspire you to comfort other people just as He has done for you? Every person needs encouragement at times, but for the most part this world is experiencing a drought of comforting words, uplifting examples, genuine heroes, "good news" stories, and genuine expressions of appreciation. You are far more likely to hear negative words of criticism, blame, and ridicule on a daily basis than you are to hear positive words of praise, recognition, and thankfulness.

There are many ways you can minister to others with the abilities and resources God has given to you. If you know Jesus Christ as your Lord and Savior, you can share your faith with those who have never experienced forgiveness for their sin and don't know where they will spend eternity. If God has given you talents or provided you with a good income, you can help others with what you have received. If God has taken you through a difficult situation and carried you to the other side, you can share your story with someone facing those same circumstances. You may not feel you have much to offer others, but you always do.

This is at the heart of Life Principle 25: *God blesses you so that you might bless others*. It is a truth you must embrace if you want to experience the abundant life that God has in store for you. First Peter 4:10 states, "As each one has received a gift, minister it to one another, as good stewards of the manifold grace of God." If you want to be a good steward of what God has provided to you, look for opportunities to bless others.

PRINCIPLE IN ACTION
Ruth (Ruth 2:11–12)
David (1 Samuel 30:6)
Disciples (Matthew 10:8)
Unforgiving Servant
   (Matthew 18:23–35)
Barnabas (1 Corinthians 9:6)

God's praise and blessing are reserved for those who serve others without expectation of praise or recognition from people.

—CHARLES F. STANLEY

Day 73: Blessing Other Believers

When Jesus left this earth, He entrusted the work of His ministry to a band of followers who came to be known as the *church*. Luke describes this early group of believers in Acts 4:32: "Now the multitude of those who believed were of one heart and one soul; neither did anyone say that any of the things he possessed was his own, but they had all things in common." The early believers recognized the incredible blessings they had received from God and shared those blessings with others in the fellowship.

The church was designed from the beginning to function as the living body of Christ on earth. This is why one of the most important spiritual disciplines you can develop is faithful involvement with other believers. No Christian has ever been called to "go it alone" in his or her faith. You cannot survive—let alone prosper—without the sincere prayers, love, support, and encouragement of other believers offered on your behalf. God has designed the Christian life as a community event, not as a solo endeavor.

This is one reason why you need to be in regular fellowship with other believers: so you can receive the benefit of *their* spiritual gifts. Another reason is so that the believers in your community can receive the benefit of *your* spiritual gifts. The members of a church are always made stronger when each person both receives and gives. And as this occurs, it brings unity to the body of Christ and makes it more effective as a whole.

1. Read Ephesians 4:1–16. What are some of the traits that Paul asks believers to exhibit in the body of Christ (1–3)? Why are these traits important in building unity?

_____

_____

_____

_____

_____

2. Why does the notion of "us" versus "them" have no place in the church?

_____

_____

_____

_____

_____

Jesus has entrusted the work of His ministry to the church.

The church functions as the living body of Christ on earth.

The church is stronger when each person gives and receives.

I . . . the prisoner of the Lord, beseech you to walk worthy of the calling with which you were called, with all lowliness and gentleness, with longsuffering, bearing with one another in love, endeavoring to keep the unity of the Spirit in the bond of peace (Ephesians 4:1–2).

3. According to the "all for one and one for all" nature of the Christian body (4–6), what happens when you endeavor to bless someone else?

_____

_____

_____

There is one body and one Spirit, just as you were called in one hope of your calling; one Lord, one faith, one baptism; one God and Father of all, who is above all, and through all, and in you all (Ephesians 4:4–6).

4. What are some of the gifts that Jesus gave to the church (11)? What was Jesus' purpose in providing these gifts to believers (12)?

_____

_____

_____

He Himself gave some to be apostles, some prophets, some evangelists, and some pastors and teachers, for the equipping of the saints (Ephesians 4:11–12).

5. What are some ways you have used your God-given gifts to enable growth to take place in the church and edify others (16)?

_____

_____

_____

_____

Speaking the truth in love, may [we] grow up in all things into Him who is the head—Christ— from whom the whole body, joined and knit together by what every joint supplies, according to the effective working by which every part does its share, causes growth of the body for the edifying of itself in love (Ephesians 4:15–16).

Jesus poured out His life so others could be saved (see Luke 19:10). If you're going to represent Him (see 2 Corinthians 5:20), shouldn't you be like Him in character and purpose?

Day 74: Blessing the World

Perhaps you believe the only reason for salvation is so you can go to heaven when you die. While it is true that eternal life is part of God's plan of forgiveness, it is not the *only* reason for your salvation. God saved you so that you might reflect His nature. You are His representative on earth, doing the kinds of works that Jesus Himself would do if He were walking in your shoes. He desires to manifest His character through your personality and your gifts.

Jesus made it clear that His followers are to be involved in active ministry to those who do not know Him. He sent out His disciples two by two, giving them authority over all demons and power to cure

God saved you so that you might reflect His nature.

diseases (see Luke 9:1–2). On one occasion, Jesus sent out seventy of His disciples (again two by two) and said to them, "The harvest truly is great, but the laborers are few; therefore pray the Lord of the harvest to send out laborers into His harvest. . . . Heal the sick there, and say to them, 'The kingdom of God has come near to you'" (10:2, 9).

If you desire to be a follower of Jesus, you must acknowledge that He is sending you out as well. He is saying the same things to you as to those disciples: You are to heal the sick and proclaim the kingdom of God. When you allow the Holy Spirit to work in you and through you, you become a vessel of His love in action. You begin to reflect His compassion, love, and mercy, and in so doing, become His witnesses. You bring credit, honor, and glory to Him.

When you allow the Holy Spirit to work in you and through you, you become a vessel of His love in action.

6. Read Philippians 2:1–18. What should your motives be when you seek to bless others (1–3)?

_____

_____

_____

_____

_____

_____

Let nothing be done through selfish ambition or conceit, but in lowliness of mind let each esteem others better than himself (Philippians 2:3).

7. What did Jesus do to reach this lost and hurting world (5–8)? How did this represent the ultimate act of service?

_____

_____

_____

_____

_____

_____

Jesus, who, being in the form of God, did not consider it robbery to be equal with God, but made Himself of no reputation, taking the form of a bondservant (Philippians 2:5–7).

8. What was the result of Jesus' humility (9–11)?

_____

_____

_____

Therefore God also has highly exalted Him and given Him the name which is above every name (Philippians 2:9).

9. In what ways are Christians to serve as light bearers to the world (14–16)?

_____

_____

_____

_____

_____

Do all things without complaining and disputing, that you may become blameless and harmless, children of God without fault in the midst of a crooked and perverse generation (Philippians 2:14–15).

10. How is God calling you to serve those who do not know Him? In what ways are you using the gifts He has provided to share about Christ?

_____

_____

_____

_____

_____

"Pray the Lord of the harvest to send out laborers into His harvest" (Matthew 9:38).

When Paul says you are to work out your salvation with "fear and trembling" (Philippians 2:12), he means you are to give careful attention to your actions and behavior, making sure that you represent the One who saved you with honor and humility.

Day 75: Called to Serve

Some believe that a person is most like Jesus when he or she preaches like Jesus preached, teaches like Jesus taught, heals like Jesus healed, or performs miracles like Jesus performed them. They look at the outward manifestation of a person's witness and ministry to determine how similar he or she is to Christ. However, the foremost characteristic of the life of Christ was *service*. A person is most like Him when he or she *serves as Jesus served*.

Jesus was the supreme servant, and His motivation for service was always love. He preached, taught, healed, and performed miracles to help others—never to call attention to Himself. We often think of Jesus' ministry as being the final three years of His life; but for nearly thirty years before, He served His family. Christian tradition states that Joseph, Jesus' earthly father, died when Jesus was a young man. As the eldest son in the family, Jesus became responsible for the general well-being of His mother and His earthly brothers and sisters. In all likelihood, Jesus filled this role in a practical way by providing the family income and helping in the training of his younger siblings.

It was in serving His family that Jesus no doubt developed a great deal of the compassion we see Him exhibit during His ministry years—reaching out to children, touching lepers, and embracing outcasts. This was a pattern He had developed throughout His years of caring for His own family, and God calls you to serve others in this same way. He didn't save you or call you to service so that you might be exalted, praised,

You are most like Jesus when you serve as He served.

God calls you to serve others with compassion.

glorified, or put on a pedestal. Rather, He saved you so you could serve Him and others. When you do this, you bring Him honor.

God has set the members, each one of them, in the body just as He pleased. And if they were all one member, where would the body be?
(1 Corinthians 12:18–19).

11. Read 1 Corinthians 12:12–31. Why is your set of spiritual gifts absolutely unique? Why are your gifts absolutely essential to the church (15–19)?

_____

_____

_____

The eye cannot say to the hand, "I have no need of you"; nor again the head to the feet, "I have no need of you"
(1 Corinthians 12:21).

12. What happens when someone in the church refuses to use his or her unique gifts? What does that do to the unity in that fellowship (20–22)?

_____

_____

_____

If one member suffers, all the members suffer with it; or if one member is honored, all the members rejoice with it
(1 Corinthians 12:26).

13. What happens when someone in the church thinks his or her gifts are superior to the gifts of others (24–26)? How does that bring disunity to the fellowship?

_____

_____

_____

God has appointed these in the church: first apostles, second prophets, third teachers, after that miracles, then gifts of healings, helps, administrations, varieties of tongues
(1 Corinthians 12:28).

14. How would you encourage someone who is struggling with feelings of envy or inferiority because his or her spiritual gifts aren't the kinds that draw attention (28–30)?

_____

_____

_____

15. What are some examples of the diversity of spiritual gifts you see in your small group or church congregation? How do those gifts work together in unity?

_____

_____

_____

While a church can and should "desire spiritual gifts" (1 Corinthians 14:1), you—as an individual believer—are never encouraged to request specific gifts. The Spirit gives the talents that are necessary for you to complete the tasks He wants you to accomplish. God always assumes the responsibility of enabling you to do whatever He has called you to do.

Living the Principle

Jesus came as a servant, not as a superstar. His three-year ministry was a powerful example of servanthood, from His first miracle of changing water to wine at a wedding feast to His sacrificial death on the cross. He chose the servant role for Himself—which was actually the heavenly Father's role for Him—and called His followers to do the same. He said, "Greater love has no one than this, than to lay down one's life for his friends" (John 15:13).

Does your love for God motivate you to minister to others for His glory? Does your relationship with Him inspire you to give freely of the blessings you have received so others can know His salvation, comfort, and joy? Can you be *trusted* with the blessings God has given you? Only you can stop God's goodness from flowing through your life and into the lives of others . . . and you do so by hoarding His gifts. Therefore, count your blessings and look for opportunities to shine His light into others' lives. You will find it truly is much more blessed to give than to receive.

How will you live out Life Principle 25 this week? Take an inventory of the blessings God has poured into your life. How are you sharing those blessings with others in your church? How are you using those blessings to show the light of Christ to the world? Consider talking with the ministry leaders in your church about how you can use your gifts in a greater capacity, and reach out to someone you see in need in your community. Then, watch as God uses you to bring His blessings to the people in your world.

Jesus came as a servant, not as a superstar.

Life Lessons to Remember

❖ God provides spiritual gifts to equip individuals in the church for His work and to His glory (see Ephesians 4:12).
❖ God has called you to bring His light to the world and proclaim His kingdom (see Luke 9:1–2).
❖ You are most like Jesus when you serve others (see Matthew 20:27–28).

The Lord doesn't ask us to succeed in the eyes of others, but He does ask us to live a life that is acceptable to Him. Jesus never said, "Do your best." He said, "Follow Me." If we truly desire to please the Lord, we will follow Him and become His disciples.

Notes AND Prayer Requests

USE THIS SPACE TO WRITE ANY KEY POINTS, QUESTIONS,
OR PRAYER REQUESTS FROM THIS WEEK'S STUDY.

$\mathscr{A}$dversity Is a Bridge to a Deeper Relationship with God

That I may know Him and the power of His resurrection,
and the fellowship of His sufferings, being conformed to His death,
if, by any means, I may attain to the resurrection from the dead.

PHILIPPIANS 3:10-11

Life's Questions

There's nothing lonelier than suffering because it feels like no one understands what you're going through. When you have accomplishments and prosperity, loved ones will gather around to share in your joy and celebrate your success. But with grief, people feel distant—even when they are trying to support and comfort you—because they cannot reach into that profound place where your pain has made its home.

During those times, you may wonder, *Where is God? Why has He allowed this? Has He left me alone to struggle with this? Has God abandoned me?* In fact, just the opposite is true. In Psalm 34:17–18, David writes, "The righteous cry out, and the LORD hears, and delivers them out of all their troubles. The LORD is near to those who have a broken heart, and saves such as have a contrite spirit." Adversity isn't a time when God is far from you. On the contrary, it's when He is closest to you, teaching you His ways.

Life Principle 26 teaches, *Adversity is a bridge to a deeper relationship with God.* The reason for this is because when everything goes well, you will have a tendency to forget that you need God. But when trouble strikes, it quickly reminds you that He is the only One who can comfort you to the depth of your soul. It is during times of adversity that He has your full attention and can teach you the joy of His wonderful presence.

PRINCIPLE IN ACTION
Joseph (Genesis 50:19–21)
Jehoiada (2 Kings 11:17)
Job (Job 2:10)
Joel (Joel 2:13)
Smyrnaeans (Revelation 2:8–11)

We can learn valuable lessons from adversity that prepare us to be the people God created us to be.
—CHARLES F. STANLEY

Day 76: God's Goal for Adversity

God's basic objective in adversity is to draw us closer to Himself.

What is God's goal in allowing you to experience adversity? His basic objective is to draw you closer to Himself. He does not find pleasure in your sorrow but uses painful situations to teach you about His love and faithfulness. Adversity, trials, and heartaches operate as lessons in the school of experience. They bring you new insight and understanding, alter your perception of the world and of God, and lead you to change your behavior.

The Lord is the ultimate Teacher, and He is the One to whom you must look for the meaning of any lesson related to adversity. Pain, disappointment, and trials are effective tools He will use to drive you to Himself and the cross, where you will discover your personal need for a Savior. You will be struck with a defining thought: *I need God*. You need His strength, wisdom, and forgiveness.

God always has a purpose for allowing adversity in our lives.

Whenever you are confronted by adversity, remember that God has a purpose for allowing it. It may be to get your attention. Or it may be to lead you into self-examination. Or it may be to help you change your beliefs or your behaviors. Your circumstances, no matter how dire they may seem, are never out of God's control. He has a plan and a goal, not just for a particular situation, but also for your entire life. In times of difficulty, He is your immovable strength, and He has promised never to abandon you.

From the Jews five times I received forty stripes minus one. Three times I was beaten with rods; once I was stoned; three times I was shipwrecked (2 Corinthians 11:24–25).

1. Read 2 Corinthians 11:23–31. What types of adversity did Paul experience at the hands of his fellow Jews (24–25)?

_____

_____

_____

_____

In perils of waters, in perils of robbers, in perils of my own countrymen, in perils of the Gentiles, in perils in the city, in perils in the wilderness, in perils in the sea, in perils among false brethren (2 Corinthians 11:26).

2. What types of adversity did Paul face when He went on His missionary journeys to proclaim the message of Christ (26–28)?

_____

_____

_____

_____

If I must boast, I will boast in the things which concern my infirmity (2 Corinthians 11:30).

3. Why do you think Paul states he can *boast* in these adversities (30)?

_____

_____

_____

4. What are some of the ways that God has used trials to bring you new insights and new understanding?

_____

_____

_____

_____

5. How has God used adversity to bring you closer to Himself?

_____

_____

_____

_____

Blessed be the God and Father of our Lord Jesus Christ, the Father of mercies and God of all comfort, who comforts us in all our tribulation, that we may be able to comfort those who are in any trouble (2 Corinthians 1:3–4).

For I consider that the sufferings of this present time are not worthy to be compared with the glory which shall be revealed in us (Romans 8:18).

Day 77: When Adversity Strikes

When adversity strikes, one of the first things you should do is turn to the Lord and ask Him to show you what you need to learn in the situation. You may initially battle feelings of disbelief or denial, but the overriding thought needs to be one of trust and faith in God's ability. The second step is to affirm your commitment to God and set your focus on Him—not on your circumstances. You see these traits portrayed in the lives of the men and women of the Bible.

Next, realize that the most vital outcome of adversity is the formation of your character. That outcome is eternal and is most important to your heavenly Father, for what happens to you on the inside will count forever. Your response to adversity must be intentional—If you go with the flow, you will never grow. Furthermore, if you refuse to benefit from adversity, you will actually choose to be destroyed by it.

Adversity that you allow to go unchecked and unmediated by the Lord will only lead to more adversity. You will lose ground rather than advance if you fail to learn and grow through life's toughest times. For this reason, when adversity strikes, you must make a decision that you will—with God's help—come through your time of hardship better, not bitter.

When adversity strikes, turn to God and ask what He wants you to learn through it.

You will lose ground if you fail to learn and grow through adversity.

There was a man in the land of Uz, whose name was Job. . . . This man was the greatest of all the people of the East (Job 1:1, 3).

6. Read Job 1. If there was ever a person in the Bible who knew a bit about adversity, it was Job. How had God blessed Job for his faithfulness (1–3)?

_____

_____

_____

_____

_____

_____

The LORD said to Satan, "Behold, all that he has is in your power; only do not lay a hand on his person" (Job 1:12).

7. What brought about the change in Job's situation (9–12)? Why do you think God allowed Satan to bring affliction on Job?

_____

_____

_____

_____

_____

Job answered the LORD and said: "I know that You can do everything, and that no purpose of Yours can be withheld from You. You asked, 'Who is this who hides counsel without knowledge?' Therefore I have uttered what I did not understand, things too wonderful for me, which I did not know. Listen, please, and let me speak; You said, 'I will question you, and you shall answer Me.' "I have heard of You by the hearing of the ear, But now my eye sees You. Therefore I abhor myself, and repent in dust and ashes" (Job 42:1–6).

8. Read Job 42:1–6. Job lost his family, his possessions, and his health—and then endured counsel from friends who tried to convince him that he had brought God's punishment on himself. In the end, what conclusion did Job reach about God's ways (2–3)?

_____

_____

_____

_____

_____

9. Why do you think Job's view of his situation was so limited (5)? What kept him from seeing the bigger picture in the midst of his adversity?

_____

_____

_____

_____

_____

_____

_____

When tragedy strikes, believers hurt just as much as anyone else. They grieve, but not "as others who have no hope" (1 Thessalonians 4:13). You can worship, even in tragedy, because nothing can separate you from God and His love.

10. How do you tend to respond when adversity strikes? What can you do to turn to God *first* in times of crisis and ask Him to reveal His will in the situation?

_____

_____

_____

_____

_____

_____

_____

Come to Me, all you who labor and are heavy laden, and I will give you rest (Matthew 11:28).

Day 78: Advancing Through Adversity

Many times, there will be no quick solution to the trials you face. However, there is one sure way through the difficulties of life, and that is through obedience and the surrender of selfish feelings and desires. Adversity has a way of pushing you beyond yourself to where you find God waiting to gather you in His arms. It stirs you to pray like nothing else can. And it is in prayer that you find shelter from the storms of life. Held under the canopy of God's presence, you discover a sense of security and hope that you thought had evaded you.

When adversity strikes, reaffirm your relationship with God, then pray for Him to remove the trial from your life. Yield to God's timetable and reaffirm His promise of sustaining grace. Say to the Lord, "I trust that You are with me and that You will carry me through this ordeal." Resist any temptation to deny God and begin to explore ways you might grow through the experience. Deal with your adversity in a godly way by loving your enemies, blessing those who curse you, and doing good to those who don't deserve it (see Matthew 5:44-45). Finally, reflect on ways you might minister to others in your adversity, and ask the Lord to give you courage as you stand strong in faith and remain true in your relationship with Him.

Never forget that God knows the future. He understands the advantage of adversity and how it can be used to strengthen your faith, refine your hope, and settle your heart into a place of contentment and trust. He will guide you through your greatest difficulties, and then you will know what it means to live in His place of blessing.

11. Read 2 Corinthians 1:3-11. The apostle Paul experienced terrible trials on his missionary journeys, but he never lost his trust in the Lord. In fact, the Lord used those very hardships to strengthen his

The surest way through trials is obedience to God.

In prayer we find shelter from the storms of life.

Reflect on ways you might minister to others during times of adversity.

Blessed be the God and Father of our Lord Jesus Christ, the Father of mercies and God of all comfort, who comforts us in all our tribulation that we may be able to comfort those who are in any trouble, with the comfort with which we ourselves are comforted by God. For as the sufferings of Christ abound in us, so our consolation also abounds through Christ. Now if we are afflicted, it is for your consolation and salvation, which is effective for enduring the same sufferings which we also suffer. Or if we are comforted, it is for your consolation and salvation. And our hope for you is steadfast, because we know that as you are partakers of the sufferings, so also you will partake of the consolation. For we do not want you to be ignorant, brethren, of our trouble which came to us in Asia: that we were burdened beyond measure, above strength, so that we despaired even of life. Yes, we had the sentence of death in ourselves, that we should not trust in ourselves but in God who raises the dead, who delivered us from so great a death, and does deliver us; in whom we trust that He will still deliver us, you also helping together in prayer for us, that thanks may be given by many persons on our behalf for the gift granted to us through many (2 Corinthians 1:3–11).

faith. What does Paul say is the relationship between the adversity that believers experience and God's comfort during those trials (3–5)?

_____

_____

_____

_____

_____

12. What purpose does Paul see in his own sufferings as it relates to the work he has been doing among the believers in Corinth (6–7)?

_____

_____

_____

_____

_____

13. How had Paul learned to advance through adversity? What had God revealed to him through all the trials he had faced (8–10)?

_____

_____

_____

_____

_____

14. What part did the believers' prayers play in Paul's deliverance from adversity (11)?

_____

_____

_____

_____

_____

15. How have the trials in your life taught you to not trust in yourself "but in God who raises the dead" (9)? What has adversity revealed about your walk with God?

_____

_____

_____

_____

_____

*God allows your faith to be refined by fire—just as gold is—
so that every impurity, doubt, anxiety, and frustration bubbles to
the surface. Then, when He answers your desperate prayers, all
of those hindrances to your trust in Him are removed,
leaving only purified confidence in His holy ways.*

Living the Principle

Have you ever seen a precious metal in the process of refinement? The metal, such as gold or silver, is heated to extremely high temperatures so it becomes liquid. Anything that is an impurity (or dross) floats to the top of the cauldron. The dross is skimmed away, leaving the metal pure and nearly translucent. Only when the metal is in this state is it poured into molds, where it cools and becomes precious bullion. The Lord uses adversity in a similar way in your life to purify your faith. He wants you to have both a perfect and a proven faith.

God uses adversity to purify your faith.

Your trials may be prolonged, intense, confusing, complicated, and stressful. At times, you may get frustrated, impatient, and even angry with God. However, the more fiercely you insist on pushing through your trial in your own strength, the longer it will take God to teach you that only He can heal your soul. The wisest response to your troubles is to surrender your will completely to God and seek to grow in your relationship with Him. As you keep your focus on Him and trust His love, wisdom, and strength, you will come to know Him more deeply and intimately. You will see His glory in a way you never thought possible.

How will you live out Life Principle 26 this week? Ask God to use the troubles you are facing as a bridge to a deeper relationship with Him, and express to Him any feelings of anger or bitterness that you have. Look for ways God has provided His profound comfort and peace during your time of adversity, and thank Him for the work He is doing in your life. Share your experiences with trusted Christian friends and ask for them to pray for you as well.

Life Lessons to Remember

❖ God's objective in adversity is to draw you closer to Himself (see 2 Corinthians 1:3–7).
❖ When adversity strikes, immediately turn to God (see Psalm 40:1–3).
❖ Adversity is a tool God uses to shape you for service (see 1 Peter 1:6–7).

Notes AND Prayer Requests

USE THIS SPACE TO WRITE ANY KEY POINTS, QUESTIONS,
OR PRAYER REQUESTS FROM THIS WEEK'S STUDY.

_____

_____

_____

_____

_____

_____

_____

_____

_____

_____

_____

_____

_____

Prayer Is Life's Greatest Time-Saver

Finally, brethren, pray for us, that the word of the Lord may run swiftly and be glorified, just as it is with you.

2 THESSALONIANS 3:1

Life's Questions

Imagine it is Monday morning, and the alarm on your nightstand has just awakened you from a peaceful slumber. You get out of bed knowing you can't waste a second because there are so many demands on your life. The kids need to get their lunches, homework, and backpacks together so they can catch the school bus. You need to get yourself together so you can make it to work on time. Your heart and mind begin to race.

There just isn't enough time to get it all done, you tell yourself. As your feet hit the floor, you are tempted to take off running—to get a head start on the day—so you can engage the frenzy of activity that awaits you. But that's exactly the *wrong* thing to do. Before you throw yourself into the melee of busyness and nonstop competition for your attention, you need to take a moment to focus on your heavenly Father and engage with Him in prayer.

Chances are prayer is one of the things you've decided to sacrifice to squeeze a few more minutes into your day. You may think, *I'm sorry, God, I just can't stop.* But consider this a wake-up call. No matter how insane your schedule looks, or how much you need to do before you leave the house, you cannot afford to leave God out of your planning. As Life Principle 27 teaches, *Prayer is life's greatest time-saver.* If you want to make the most of every moment, you must begin your day with the One who holds every second of your life in His hands.

PRINCIPLE IN ACTION
Joshua (Joshua 9:14–27)
Samuel (1 Samuel 12:23–25)
Solomon (1 Kings 3:1–14)
Hezekiah (2 Kings 20:5)
James (James 4:2)

Each of us has a need to communicate with God built into us by our Creator. It is part of God's design, part of His imprint on our lives. We desire to be in touch with our Maker.
—CHARLES F. STANLEY

Day 79: Minimizing the Risk

The ancient Greek philosopher Heraclitus said, "The only thing that is constant is change." No matter in what stage of life you find yourself, you can rest assured that change is never far away. Some of these changes will be minor and require little more than an adjustment on your part. Others will cause seismic shifts in your life. These life-altering changes will require you to make important decisions—which will introduce the possibility of making mistakes.

As a believer in Christ, it is important to recognize that the quicker you turn a change-related situation over to God in prayer—whether that happens to be great or small—the sooner you will minimize the risk of making a wrong decision. Of course, at times the temptation to hold your own counsel and make a gut decision can be overwhelming. You may be compelled to charge ahead without thinking and just do what *feels* right.

However, in doing so, you not only take a needless risk but also squander the most precious resource you have at your disposal: *God's wisdom.* You also incur the cost—in terms of time, spent energy, and frustration—in having to go back later and fix any mistakes you made in your haste. When you make decisions without seeking the Lord's leadership, you court disaster. But when you commit yourself to His will through prayer, you open the door to His blessings.

1. Read Joshua 9. The Israelites had entered into the Promised Land and had been victorious in their battles against Jericho and Ai. In response, the tribes in the region—except one—began to gather together to confront the threat (1–2). What tactics did the inhabitants of Gibeon employ to deal with the Israelites (3–6)?

   _____

   _____

   _____

   _____

2. What question did the Israelites ask to test the Gibeonites' story (7)? What proof did the men provide (9–13)?

   _____

   _____

   _____

   _____

Change is never far away.

You court disaster when you make decisions without seeking the Lord's counsel.

When the inhabitants of Gibeon heard what Joshua had done to Jericho and Ai, they worked craftily, and went and pretended to be ambassadors (Joshua 9:3–4).

"These wineskins which we filled were new, and see, they are torn; and these our garments and our sandals have become old because of the very long journey" (Joshua 9:13).

3. What did Joshua fail to do before signing a treaty with the men (14–15)?

_____

_____

_____

_____

_____

Then the men of Israel took some of their provisions; but they did not ask counsel of the LORD (Joshua 9:14).

4. What were the consequences of this hasty decision (16–23)?

_____

_____

_____

_____

It happened at the end of three days, after they had made a covenant with them, that they heard that they were their neighbors who dwelt near them. Then the children of Israel journeyed and came to their cities on the third day. Now their cities were Gibeon, Chephirah, Beeroth, and Kirjath Jearim. But the children of Israel did not attack them, because the rulers of the congregation had sworn to them by the LORD God of Israel. And all the congregation complained against the rulers (Joshua 9:16–18).

5. What life-changing decision are you facing today? What does this story reveal to you about the need to take *every* decision to God first in prayer?

_____

_____

_____

_____

_____

Certainly God has heard me; He has attended to the voice of my prayer. Blessed be God, who has not turned away my prayer, nor His mercy from me! (Psalm 66:19–20)

Day 80: Failure to Communicate

Communication—or rather, failure to communicate—is a major problem in the world today. All too often people don't say what they mean or have difficulty putting their feelings into words, leaving people with misunderstanding. They have problems communicating in their families, workplace, and church. Many people also have problems communicating with God. They are uncomfortable talking with God, wonder if He heard what they said, and are frustrated with their lack of ability to say what they mean.

The foremost problem in communication, however, is none of the situations mentioned above. The main problem in people's relationships

Many people are uncomfortable talking with God.

with others and with God is a *failure to try* to communicate. Often, this is because people feel they do not have the time needed to engage in a dialogue, so they "put it off until later." All too frequently, "later" never happens. The result is that communication is stymied, and no growth occurs in the individual's ability to express himself or herself to others.

As mentioned previously, God will often bring adversity into your life to get your attention and teach you how to better trust in Him. Sometimes you will find yourself in a prison of your own making—one marked by your sin or error, relationship problems with others, self-created financial problems, or self-inflicted health problems. In such situations, the key is to stop and talk to God, remembering that prayer is the shortest distance between problems and solutions, difficulties and remedies, and questions and answers.

Prayer is the shortest distance between problems and solutions, difficulties and remedies, and questions and answers.

Is anyone among you suffering? Let him pray. Is anyone cheerful? Let him sing psalms. Is anyone among you sick? Let him call for the elders of the church, and let them pray over him, anointing him with oil in the name of the Lord. And the prayer of faith will save the sick, and the Lord will raise him up. And if he has committed sins, he will be forgiven. Confess your trespasses to one another, and pray for one another, that you may be healed. The effective, fervent prayer of a righteous man avails much (James 5:13–16).

6. Read James 5:13–18. What does James call you to do when times are good? What does he call you to do when times are bad (13–14)?

_____
_____
_____
_____
_____

7. What does James mean when he states "the prayer of faith will save the sick" (15)? What inspiration do you draw from this promise?

_____
_____
_____
_____

8. What is the importance of praying with other believers? How does this foster a spirit of openness, honesty, and caring within the community (16)?

_____
_____
_____
_____
_____

9. When in your life have you seen the truth of James's statement that "the effective, fervent prayer of a righteous man avails much" (16)?

_____
_____
_____
_____

10. Do you believe your prayers could ever have the impact that Elijah's prayer had when he prayed for God to bring rain (17–18)? Why or why not?

_____

_____

_____

_____

Elijah was a man with a nature like ours, and he prayed earnestly that it would not rain; and it did not rain on the land for three years and six months. And he prayed again, and the heaven gave rain, and the earth produced its fruit (James 5:17–18).

> *Elijah was no different than any believer.*
> *He did not have any special control over nature. Rather, the power*
> *rested with the One to whom he prayed. And because the prophet*
> *trusted wholeheartedly in the Lord, he saw the answers to*
> *his requests. The same can be true for you.*

Day 81: Active Listening in Prayer

Before you can receive direction from God when you go to Him in prayer, you have to be able to hear and receive what He says to you. To do this requires you to listen to God actively. Note that there is a difference between *active listening* and *passive hearing*. Hearing is something you do with your ears. If your hearing is normal, you can't help but hear sounds that are within a certain range. Listening involves your mind. It requires you to put your brain in gear to not only hear what is said but also to determine its meaning.

People often make the mistake of not coming to God with anticipation of His response. The result is the same as in not opening your heart and mind to the Lord in the first place: a failure to communicate. When you assume God is not speaking to you, it leads to the same issue of not receiving God's guidance and wisdom in your situation. You end up wasting time, energy, and resources by moving ahead in your own strength instead of the Lord's.

The Lord knows exactly what you need, and He will always answer your prayers in the ways that are absolutely best for you. It's important, then, for you to spend time actively listening to Him, drinking in His presence and power. Be quiet before Him, rest in Him, and allow Him to order your steps. No matter what you face, commit yourself to His schedule, His wisdom, His provision, and His guidance through prayer. As you do, you will find that your time with Him is the best investment you make every day.

Receiving direction from God requires you to listen to Him actively.

God will answer your prayers in the ways that are absolutely best for you.

If you receive my words, and treasure my commands within you, so that you incline your ear to wisdom, and apply your heart to understanding; yes, if you cry out for discernment, and lift up your voice for understanding, if you seek her as silver, and search for her as for hidden treasures; then you will understand the fear of the Lord, and find the knowledge of God. For the Lord gives wisdom; from His mouth come knowledge and understanding; he stores up sound wisdom for the upright; he is a shield to those who walk uprightly (Proverbs 2:1–7).

11. Read Proverbs 2:1–9. What are the characteristics of a person who wants to receive wisdom and understanding from God (1–5)?

_____

_____

_____

_____

_____

12. What is the reward for those who actively listen to God and obey His commands (6–7)?

_____

_____

_____

_____

_____

_____

He guards the paths of justice, and preserves the way of His saints. Then you will understand righteousness and justice, equity and every good path (Proverbs 2:8–9).

13. How does a pattern of listening to God enable you to understand "righteousness and justice, equity and every good path" (9)?

_____

_____

_____

_____

_____

14. What are some ways that you are actively seeking to be led by God today?

_____

_____

_____

_____

15. In what ways are you committing to abide by God's schedule instead of your own? What steps are you taking to prioritize talking to God and listening for His response?

_____

_____

_____

_____

_____

_____

My sheep hear My voice, and I know them, and they follow Me.
And I give them eternal life, and they shall never perish; neither shall
anyone snatch them out of My hand (John 10:27–28).

Living the Principle

The apostle Paul knew Christ's command that believers were to be His witnesses "to the end of the earth" (Acts 1:8). In his day, the persecution of believers was spreading, and many thought that Jesus' return was imminent. There was so much for Paul to do, so many people to reach and churches to plant, that he must have felt overwhelmed. However, he knew God could get it done. If he stayed in constant communication with the Lord through prayer, God would maximize his time and give him the energy he needed to accomplish his mission.

Whatever you need to accomplish may likewise seem overwhelming and unfeasible to you. But remember that "things which are impossible with men are possible with God" (Luke 18:27). God knows everything that will happen to you today, and He knows the best way for you to handle your tasks. If you ask Him to help you, He will slow you down to accomplish the activities that require caution and precision and give you the speed to move through the things that are less important. He will also steer you clear of the time traps you should avoid.

How will you live out Life Principle 27 this week? Begin by asking yourself if you are willing to stop and listen to God. Are you ready for Him to make you as fruitful as you can possibly be? If so, commit yourself to His schedule and spend some quality time with Him in prayer—both talking with Him and waiting on Him for His response. Ask God to continually draw you into intimate communication with Himself and to transform your life so you can affect the world for the sake of His kingdom.

All who desire to live godly in Christ Jesus will suffer persecution (2 Timothy 3:12).

Life Lessons to Remember

❖ Go to God first before making a life-changing decision (see Matthew 6:33).
❖ Commit to seeking God's instructions each day (see Daniel 6:10).
❖ Listen for God's direction when you pray (see Jeremiah 33:3).

Notes AND Prayer Requests

USE THIS SPACE TO WRITE ANY KEY POINTS, QUESTIONS,
OR PRAYER REQUESTS FROM THIS WEEK'S STUDY.

_____

_____

_____

_____

_____

_____

_____

_____

_____

_____

_____

_____

_____

_____

No Christian Has Ever Been Called to "Go It Alone" in His or Her Walk of Faith

And let us consider one another in order to stir up love and good works,
not forsaking the assembling of ourselves together,
as is the manner of some, but exhorting one another, and so much
the more as you see the Day approaching.

HEBREWS 10:24-25

Life's Questions

Perhaps you've heard someone say, "Oh, I don't go to church very often. I'd rather stay at home and watch sermons on television, download a podcast from a favorite speaker, or go online and listen to a message." Maybe you've heard someone say, "I only go to church when I can work it into my family's schedule." Or you might have heard a person say, "I go to church *as often as I can*," which usually means not often at all.

There are many reasons that people give for not attending church. Some refuse to join because they've had a terrible experience with "religious" people. Others live so far from a biblically sound fellowship that they feel it isn't feasible for them to be active members. Some people are shy and find it difficult to open up to others. Others object to the hypocrisy they perceive in organized congregations. And there are those who are so frightened of being rejected they isolate themselves from others—including other Christians.

PRINCIPLE IN ACTION
Adam and Eve (Genesis 2:18)
Ruth and Boaz (Ruth 4:13–22)
David and Jonathan (1 Samuel 18:1)
Barnabas and Saul (Acts 13:2)
Early Church (Hebrews 10:25)

Imagine how much would be accomplished in our churches if believers banded together against their true enemy, rather than wasting time and energy bickering with one another.

—CHARLES F. STANLEY

God created you for fellowship with Himself and with other believers.

The reality is that God created you for fellowship with Himself and with other believers. This is why Life Principle 28 emphasizes, *No Christian has ever been called to "go it alone" in his or her walk of faith*. No matter what reason you might have for separating yourself from the body of Christ, it pales in comparison to why God wants you involved in the church. You need love, encouragement, fellowship, accountability, and a spiritual outlet—and it's through other believers that God provides all these things.

Day 82: Spurred Along

The writer of Hebrews knew that his audience, made up mainly of Jewish believers who had just come to faith, was struggling with how to incorporate their Jewish heritage into their walk with Christ. He therefore spent a great deal of time explaining to them that Jesus Christ prepared the way for their uninterrupted fellowship with the Father. He was their great High Priest whose death provided the means for them to have personal access to God without going through a human agent.

Jesus prepared the way for your uninterrupted fellowship with the Father.

The author instructed his readers to *help one another* hold fast to their faith in God. He knew they would be tempted by the trials and persecution they faced to drift from the truth that God had plans for their lives. So he said, "Let us consider one another in order to stir up love and good works" (Hebrews 10:24). The Greek term translated *stir up* literally means "to irritate" or to pressure one another to consider what the Lord has done in the past.

God will not abandon the work of His hands in your life.

God is faithful and will not abandon the work of His hands in your life. In times of joy, He blesses you with happiness and contentment. In times of difficulty, sorrow, rejection, or other distresses, you can know without doubt that He will provide the wisdom and resources you need. He will often do this through the encouraging words of another person in the body of Christ. This believer can spur you along, help you refuse to become ensnared by negativity, and compel you to take responsibility for your life in Christ.

Therefore, brethren, having boldness to enter the Holiest by the blood of Jesus, by a new and living way which He consecrated for us, through the veil, that is, His flesh, and having a High Priest over the house of God (Hebrews 10:19–21).

1. Read Hebrews 10:19–25. What is the significance of Jesus being your "High Priest" who allows you access into the presence of God (19–21)?

_____

_____

_____

_____

_____

2. Why is it sometimes difficult to "hold fast the confession of our hope without wavering" (23)? How does meeting regularly with fellow believers make this easier?

_____
_____
_____
_____
_____

Let us draw near with a true heart in full assurance of faith, having our hearts sprinkled from an evil conscience and our bodies washed with pure water. Let us hold fast the confession of our hope without wavering, for He who promised is faithful (Hebrews 10:22–23).

3. When was a time that a group of believers stirred up "love and good works" in you (24)?

_____
_____
_____
_____
_____

4. What is the problem with you not assembling with other believers? Why does the author add, "and so much the more as you see the Day approaching" (25)?

_____
_____
_____
_____
_____

Let us consider one another in order to stir up love and good works, not forsaking the assembling of ourselves together, as is the manner of some, but exhorting one another, and so much the more as you see the Day approaching (Hebrews 10:24–25).

5. What is the best strategy for encouraging a fellow believer to not stop meeting regularly with other believers?

_____
_____
_____
_____

The term stir up in the New Testament means to incite or stimulate. You are to encourage and motivate others to be faithful to God. In the same way, Paul admonished Timothy to "stir up the gift of God which is in you . . . for God has not given us a spirit of fear, but of power and of love and of a sound mind" (2 Timothy 1:6–7).

Day 83: Beyond Worship

To give up meeting together allows Satan the opportunity to draw believers away.

Believers need one another. To give up meeting together spells disaster because it gives Satan the opportunity to draw them away from the Lord. In meeting together, believers give and receive the mutual encouragement to keep going. This is why God wants you to regularly meet with other believers. He wants His people in church.

Many believers don't take this admonition seriously because they don't know the reason behind it. They feel they can worship God at home and don't need to go to church. They believe the sole reason God calls His children to meet together is to worship. This is understandable . . . after all, we do call it a "worship service." But worship is not the sole reason for meeting together. Nor is it the reason for being taught God's truth.

The writer of Hebrews says the reason is to safeguard against drifting. When you meet with other believers, you are doing what comes naturally and what you will do for eternity—be together in His presence. You and your fellow Christians make up the church, and together you will provide strength to one another. As Solomon wrote, "Though one may be overpowered by another, two can withstand him. And a threefold cord is not quickly broken" (Ecclesiastes 4:12).

Christians make up the church and provide strength to one another.

6. Read 1 John 3:10–23. How can believers find—and build on—the common ground they have against the devil when they meet together (10–13)?

_____

_____

_____

_____

In this the children of God and the children of the devil are manifest: Whoever does not practice righteousness is not of God, nor is he who does not love his brother (1 John 3:10).

7. How does having love for your fellow believers in Christ reveal that you have "eternal life" abiding within you (14–15)?

_____

_____

_____

_____

Whoever hates his brother is a murderer, and you know that no murderer has eternal life abiding in him (1 John 3:15).

8. How do you lay down your life for Christian brothers and sisters (16)? Do you feel this standard of love that Jesus set is too high to follow? Explain.

_____

_____

_____

_____

By this we know love, because He laid down His life for us. And we also ought to lay down our lives for the brethren (1 John 3:16).

9. In what ways are you to show love to your fellow believers (18)? When was a time that a fellow believer showed Christ's love in such a real and profound way?

_____

_____

_____

_____

10. Why is the fellowship of believers pleasing in God's sight (22)?

_____

_____

_____

_____

Your relationship with God is usually reflected in your relationships with other people. The more loyal you are to God, the more loyal you will tend to be with friends and family members. God considers loyalty an important trait.

Day 84: Not Alone

Enemy forces are always at work around you, seeking to blow you off course. Sheer individual commitment is really not enough to keep you in line. You need the presence and accountability of other believers who love you, are willing to laugh and cry with you, and who regularly check on you. It is in the atmosphere, worship, and fellowship in God's house where you discover you are not alone.

When you gather together with other believers, you hear them tell about how the Lord has miraculously provided for them. One person may describe the pain he's suffered as a result of a loss. A new believer may tell her story of redemption, rejoicing in God's grace. As you listen to others recount God's work in their lives, something happens inside of you. You are spurred on to faithfulness and to praising God for His goodness. The accountability found in church anchors you against the tides that work to sweep you away. To neglect the regular assembly of fellow Christians is to miss out on this essential element in the development of your faith.

Throughout the Bible, you find that one of God's principle desires is to have a close relationship with people. As you are active in a local church, you safeguard against missing out on all that God has for you.

It is in the atmosphere, worship, and fellowship in God's house you discover you are not alone.

One of God's principle desires is to have a close relationship with people.

Your participation in a body of other believers compels your personal fellowship with God. Remember, when you drift away from the family of God, it is only a matter of time until you drift away from fellowship with God.

Be diligent to come to me quickly; for Demas has forsaken me, having loved this present world, and has departed for Thessalonica—Crescens for Galatia, Titus for Dalmatia (2 Timothy 4:9–10).

11. Read 2 Timothy 4:9–18. When Paul wrote this letter to his loyal coworker, he was likely in prison in Rome. The end of his life was near—and he knew it. Why did he request Timothy's presence at this time (9–10)?

_____

_____

_____

12. Paul's comment about Demas underscores one of the challenges of interacting with other believers—not all relationships run smoothly (10). In terms of Christian fellowship, why is it still better to have loved and lost than never to have loved at all?

_____

_____

_____

Only Luke is with me. Get Mark and bring him with you, for he is useful to me for ministry (2 Timothy 4:11).

13. Mark had failed Paul in the past. He had even caused a split between Paul and Barnabas (see Acts 15:36–41). What is significant about Paul's request to have Timothy bring Mark along (11)? What does this say about how Paul viewed his fellowship with other believers—even those whom had disappointed him in the past?

_____

_____

_____

The Lord stood with me and strengthened me, so that the message might be preached fully through me, and that all the Gentiles might hear. Also I was delivered out of the mouth of the lion. And the Lord will deliver me from every evil work and preserve me for His heavenly kingdom. To Him be glory forever and ever. Amen! (2 Timothy 4:7–18).

14. How had the Lord proved faithful to Paul in spite of those who sought to cause him harm (17–18)? Why do you think Paul still needed the fellowship of other believers?

_____

_____

_____

15. What specific things can you do to be one who builds others up in the body of Christ rather than tear them down? How can you make yourself "useful" in ministry?

_____

_____

_____

As in Paul's life, believers may forsake you during your time of need. However, you must remember Paul's example and not count it against them. You must forgive them, being confident that the Lord will not desert you—no matter what happens.

Living the Principle

Do you find it easy or difficult to open up to other people? Do you consider yourself a loner, or are you naturally drawn to others? Regardless of your personal makeup, understand how important it is for you to be part of the church. This will be more challenging for some than for others, but being involved in a Bible-believing congregation is indispensable for *all* Christians.

You are bombarded by worldly pressures and ungodly influences on a daily basis, and you will not be able to stand on your own for long. Either you will be destroyed by the stress, or you will drift away from the faith. You will also miss out on the abundant life God planned for you because an important part of expressing that life is showing love to other believers and receiving it from them in return. You need to be involved in a local church—one that will encourage you, keep you accountable, challenge you to grow, help you to express your spiritual gifts, and feed you the meat of God's Word. The body of Christ isn't complete without you.

How will you live out Life Principle 28 this week? Consider your level of involvement in the local church. On your list of priorities—the things that receive the lion's share of your time, energy, and attention—where does church rank? What can you do to make it a higher priority? Also, look for tangible ways to engage in fellowship with other believers. Call up a friend in your church and go out for coffee or lunch during the week. Seek to get to know a new person in your church or someone with whom you are less familiar. You never know the blessing these connections might bring or how you will impact that person's life.

> It is important for you to be a part of the church.

Life Lessons to Remember

❖ Meeting regularly with other believers helps to spur you in your faith (see Hebrews 10:24).

❖ Fellowship with other Christians will help to safeguard you against drifting (see Hebrews 3:13).

❖ Interacting regularly with other believers also stirs up good works (see James 2:14–17).

Notes AND Prayer Requests

USE THIS SPACE TO WRITE ANY KEY POINTS, QUESTIONS,
OR PRAYER REQUESTS FROM THIS WEEK'S STUDY.

_____

_____

_____

_____

_____

_____

_____

_____

_____

_____

_____

_____

_____

_____

LIFE PRINCIPLE 29

You Learn More in Your Valley Experiences Than on Your Mountaintops

My brethren, take the prophets, who spoke in the name of the Lord, as an example of suffering and patience.

JAMES 5:10

Life's Questions

Perhaps you've noticed that many of the Life Principles have focused on how to respond to adversity. You could say this reflects the amount of adversity that believers face in today's culture. However, it's primarily due to the precept found in Life Principle 29: *You learn more in your valley experiences than on your mountaintops.* In other words, the low points in your life are much better teachers than your high points.

In Psalm 23:4, David wrote, "Yea, though I walk through the valley of the shadow of death, I will fear no evil; for You are with me." When you are in the valley, you don't have the vantage point you need to see your way out. It may seem as if the walls or the mountains are closing in around you and there is no escape. The challenges may seem so immense and your choices so limited that you feel weak—and completely unable to claw your way out. You may be tempted to think, *Is this it? Is this all there is? Is this the end of my story?*

Be encouraged: the valley is not the end of your story. In fact, God may be taking you through the valley to instruct you on what you need to know so you can reach—and truly appreciate—the mountaintops. Things *will* change because God's will for you is "good and acceptable

PRINCIPLE IN ACTION
Naaman (2 Kings 5:1–19)
The Preacher (Ecclesiastes 7:14)
Mary of Bethany (John 11:32–37)
Simon (John 21:15–19)
Paul (Acts 9:1–18)

Make your position in Christ the perspective from which you view trouble.

—CHARLES F. STANLEY

and perfect" (Romans 12:2). And you can know that "goodness and mercy" shall follow you all the days of your life when you allow God to be your shepherd (Psalm 23:6).

Day 85: The Source of Adversity

The book of Job tells how one day Satan came and stood before the throne of God. When God pointed out to him the righteousness of Job, the devil answered, "Stretch out Your hand and touch all that he has, and he will surely curse You to Your face" (Job 1:11). The episode should raise two important questions for you. First, is Satan responsible for all the adversity you face? Second, to what extent will God allow adversity in your life?

The Bible is clear that while the enemy will try to discourage you from serving God or tempt you to sin, he is limited both in *power* and the *ability* to persecute you. The reality is that you live in a fallen world that is passing away (see 1 Corinthians 7:31). All people—believers and nonbelievers alike—may suffer hardships that seem senseless. These disasters, accidents, and tragedies that occur in your world are a constant reminder that no one is promised tomorrow (see James 4:14). They remind you that life on this earth is fragile and short, and you must be ready at all times to stand before God (see Hebrews 9:27).

As previously discussed, God allows some adversity for your betterment. He is ultimately concerned with your spiritual growth, not with your happiness or momentary pleasures. He wants you to be free from sin and grow in faith, endurance, ministry, and relationship with Him. He always has the big picture in mind whenever He allows or sends adversity into your life. So David wrote, "I know, O LORD, that Your judgments are right, and that in faithfulness You have afflicted me" (Psalm 119:75).

1. Read 1 Samuel 19. David had become famous throughout Israel after word spread of his victory over Goliath—a little *too* famous as far as King Saul was concerned. How did Saul's jealousy bring adversity into the life of David and Jonathan (1–3)?

_____

_____

_____

_____

_____

_____

_____

"You have blessed the work of his hands, and his possessions have increased in the land. But now, stretch out Your hand and touch all that he has, and he will surely curse You" (Job 1:10–11).

Satan is limited in power and ability to persecute you.

God allows some adversity for your betterment.

Saul spoke to Jonathan his son and to all his servants, that they should kill David; but Jonathan, Saul's son, delighted greatly in David. So Jonathan told David, saying, "My father Saul seeks to kill you. Therefore please be on your guard until morning, and stay in a secret place and hide" (1 Samuel 19:1–2).

2. What do you think it means that "the distressing spirit from the LORD came upon Saul" (9)? What did this compel Saul to do (10)?

_____

_____

_____

_____

The distressing spirit from the LORD came upon Saul as he sat in his house with his spear in his hand. And David was playing music with his hand. Then Saul sought to pin David to the wall with the spear, but he slipped away from Saul's presence; and he drove the spear into the wall (1 Samuel 19:9–10).

3. What do you take away from the fact that God would allow David to endure *years* of this kind of adversity at the hands of Saul?

_____

_____

_____

_____

4. Read Psalm 59:1–4, 14–17. David wrote this psalm after King Saul sent men to watch his house in order to kill him (see 1 Samuel 19:11). What is David's complaint to God in his valley experience (1–4)?

_____

_____

_____

_____

Look, they lie in wait for my life; the mighty gather against me, not for my transgression nor for my sin, O LORD (Psalm 59:3).

5. What did David reveal that he had learned through this experience? How had it strengthened his trust in God (14–17)?

_____

_____

_____

_____

I will sing of Your power; yes, I will sing aloud of Your mercy in the morning; for You have been my defense and refuge in the day of my trouble. To You, O my Strength, I will sing praises; for God is my defense, my God of mercy (Psalm 59:16–17).

Sometimes God will allow you to go without any earthly or human comfort so that you will turn completely to Him.

Day 86: A Look Inside

At times, God will allow adversity in your life to motivate you to self-examination. These winds of adversity will blow away the surface issues and force you to cope with things on a deeper level. They will remove the cloak of denial and reveal who you really are, as well as what you believe about God, His deity, and His faithfulness. Nothing has the ability to drive you closer to God than trials and tribulations.

Trials and tribulations drive you closer to God.

Times of adversity allow you to examine your faith.

When these crises strike, they should compel you to declare, as David did, "My heart is steadfast, O God, my heart is steadfast" (Psalm 57:7). Times of adversity allow you to examine your faith and your level of discipline. Are you committed to standing firm in your trust in Christ, or are you blown off course by every ill wind that blows your way? As Paul wrote, "Let a man examine himself" (1 Corinthians 11:28). In other words, you need to take a straightforward look inside and discover what is driving you, motivating you, and enticing you. If it is anything other than God, it is not right. He needs to be your motivating factor at every turn in life.

The Lord wants you to free yourself of anything that might keep you in bondage. When you become complacent and accept the hurts of the past as a part of who you are, you have accepted the wrong view and the wrong game plan. You are a new creation in Christ. He has sealed you with His Spirit. That newness of life gives you hope, even in hopeless times.

O LORD, You have searched me and known me. You know my sitting down and my rising up; you understand my thought afar off. You comprehend my path and my lying down, and are acquainted with all my ways. For there is not a word on my tongue, but behold, O LORD, You know it (Psalm 139:1–4).

6. Read Psalm 139. It is not known for certain when David wrote this psalm, but it quite likely occurred during King Saul's persecution of him. What does David confess about God's power and authority (1–6)?

   _____

   _____

   _____

   _____

If I ascend into heaven, You are there; if I make my bed in hell, behold, You are there (Psalm 139:8).

7. What does David acknowledge about God when he makes his "bed in hell" (8)? What does this say about God's constant presence during your times of adversity?

   _____

   _____

   _____

   _____

My frame was not hidden from You, when I was made in secret, and skillfully wrought in the lowest parts of the earth. Your eyes saw my substance (Psalm 139:15–16).

8. What lessons has David learned through his trials about God's knowledge of him and his situation (15–16)?

   _____

   _____

   _____

   _____

9. What is David's concluding plea to the Lord (23–24)? In what way is this your prayer when you go through valley experiences?

_____

_____

_____

_____

Search me, O God, and know my heart; try me, and know my anxieties; and see if there is any wicked way in me, and lead me in the way everlasting (Psalm 139:23–24).

10. What is driving you, motivating you, and enticing you? How will you submit these things to God today?

_____

_____

_____

_____

When you cannot understand yourself or comprehend your feelings, God invites you to take your internal struggles to Him and ask Him for insight. He understands what you do not and knows what to do when you don't.

Day 87: Emerging from the Valley

Of course, you can't escape the fact that some suffering will come as a result of your own actions and personal sin. Each sin you commit carries some consequence that results from your disobedience. In cases like this, you can't blame God, the devil, or others. You must follow David's example and say, "I know my transgressions, and my sin is ever before me. Against You, You only, I have sinned and done what is evil in Your sight" (Psalm 51:3–4).

Ultimately, the lessons God teaches you through adversity are intended to change your behavior—or change the belief that prompted the behavior. You must therefore allow His Spirit to have free access to every area of your life. As you learn to watch, listen, and look for His guidance and direction, you learn how to change a wrong response or behavior. This is critical because you will never benefit from adversity or grow as a result of it if that adversity does not prompt true introspection and change.

Jesus came to bear the burdens that plague your life. He will help you carry your burdens to the cross and deal with them there, once and for all. He alone knows that pain paves the path to complete spiritual

Each sin carries some consequence for you.

Jesus came to bear the burdens that plague your life.

healing and restoration. If you are willing to go through the valley, allow God to surface the inner rubbish of your life, and then change what needs to be changed, you will emerge on the mountaintop closer to Christ, more mature as His child, and with far greater potential to reflect His love to the world around you.

David's anger was greatly aroused against the man, and he said to Nathan, "As the LORD lives, the man who has done this shall surely die! And he shall restore fourfold for the lamb, because he did this thing and because he had no pity" (2 Samuel 12:5–6).

11. Read 2 Samuel 12:1–14. The adversity David faced in this situation was different in that it had occurred as a result of his own actions. David had sinned by committing adultery with a woman named Bathsheba and then conspired to have her husband killed. How did Nathan's story force David to confront his sin (1–6)?

_____

_____

_____

_____

_____

_____

"Thus says the LORD: 'Behold, I will raise up adversity against you from your own house'" (2 Samuel 12:11).

12. What were to be the consequences for David's actions (7–12)?

_____

_____

_____

_____

David said to Nathan, "I have sinned against the LORD." And Nathan said to David, "The LORD also has put away your sin; you shall not die" (2 Samuel 12:13).

13. What important step did David take when confronted with his sin (13)? How did this impact the judgment against him (14)?

_____

_____

_____

_____

Create in me a clean heart, O God, and renew a steadfast spirit within me. Do not cast me away from Your presence, and do not take Your Holy Spirit from me (Psalm 51:10–11).

14. Read Psalm 51:10–13. David wrote this psalm after Nathan had confronted him with his sin. What does David request of God to help him emerge from the valley (10–11)?

_____

_____

_____

_____

I will teach transgressors Your ways, and sinners shall be converted to You (Psalm 51:13).

15. How did David's adversity enable him to "teach transgressors [God's] ways" (13)? How have you seen God use the adversity in your life to help others in their faith?

_____

_____

_____

_____

Living the Principle

Any time God allows you to go through a valley experience, it is because He wants to show you His power and love when He takes you to the mountaintop. He may be using the trial to get your attention and free you from some emotional bondage or destructive habit. He may be seeking to eliminate an attitude or behavior in your life that is hindering His work. Perhaps there is some precious quality that He wants to develop in you.

Whatever the reason for the time God has you spend in the valley, remember that He never means it for your harm. Rather, He intends it for your good, so you can become everything you were created to be and experience His abundant blessings. Therefore, respond to adversity in the way that honors Him. Stay close to Him in prayer and through His Word—obeying whatever He tells you to do. Learn through your valley experiences so God can prepare you for the mountaintops because your story is not over. The best is still to come.

How will you live out Life Principle 29 this week? Identify the valleys you've been experiencing lately—those situations where the walls seem to be surrounding you and you can't see your way out. Ask God to give you His perspective as you travel through it, to search your heart for any wrongful thinking you have, and teach you what you need to learn from the trial. Remember that God has put the body of Christ in your life to give you encouragement and support, and reach out to a few trusted individuals for their help.

> God allows you to go through valleys to show you His power and His love.

Life Lessons to Remember

- ❖ Adversity leads to trusting in God (Psalm 56:3–4).
- ❖ Adversity leads to self-examination (see Psalm 77:6–12).
- ❖ Adversity leads to change in behavior (see Psalm 119:67).

Notes AND Prayer Requests

USE THIS SPACE TO WRITE ANY KEY POINTS, QUESTIONS,
OR PRAYER REQUESTS FROM THIS WEEK'S STUDY.

An Eager Anticipation of the Lord's Return Keeps You Living Productively

And behold, I am coming quickly, and My reward is with Me,
to give to every one according to his work.

REVELATION 22:12

Life's Questions

What would you do if you knew that Jesus was returning in just a few hours? The question is not a frivolous exercise in speculation—it may be the prompt you need to examine your Christian walk. Would you be happy about Christ's return and prepare for the celebration? Or would you want to clean up some aspects of your life before He arrived?

The early church lived in eager anticipation of Jesus' return. Some of these believers had been close followers of Christ or had seen and heard Him. They knew how wonderful it was to be with Him, and they were eager to be in His presence again. Others had contact with Jesus' disciples and followers. They had heard the apostles speak of being with Jesus, and they could hardly wait for their turn to be in His presence. There was great enthusiasm in the early church for Christ's return, and His return was frequently the topic of the believers' conversations.

The second coming of Christ should also be a joyous time for believers today. After all, as Paul writes in 1 Thessalonians 4:16–17, "For the Lord Himself will descend from heaven with a shout. . . . Then we who are alive and remain shall be caught up together with them in the clouds to meet the Lord in the air. And thus we shall always be with the Lord."

PRINCIPLE IN ACTION
Timothy (1 Timothy 6:12)
Wise Virgins (Matthew 25:1–13)
Thessalonians
   (1 Thessalonians 5:1–10)
Wise Servant (Matthew 24:45–51)
All Believers
   (Revelation 22:12–21)

For the Christian, the return of Jesus is great and glorious news! It will be the most exciting, exhilarating experience of our lives.
—CHARLES F. STANLEY

When the Lord returns, He is coming to take you to your new home in heaven—to the place He has prepared especially for you (see John 14:1–3). It is going to be a wonderful time, and you don't want any regrets to taint your happy reunion with the Lord. That is why Life Principle 30 states, *An eager anticipation of the Lord's return keeps you living productively.*

Day 88: Watch Faithfully

You are to watch for Jesus' appearing because no one knows the hour of His return.

Throughout the Gospels, Jesus offered the repeated admonishment that you are to watch for His coming because no one knows the day or hour of His appearing (see Matthew 24:42; 25:13). Jesus gave this specific instruction to His followers: "Watch therefore, and pray always that you may be counted worthy to escape all these things that will come to pass, and to stand before the Son of Man" (Luke 21:36).

In addition to praying as you watch, you are also called to stand fast in the faith with bravery and strength (see 1 Corinthians 16:13). You are instructed to watch *soberly*, arming yourself with faith, love, and salvation (see 1 Thessalonians 5:8). You are also to remain particularly aware of false prophets, for their lies can do incalculable damage. You have a responsibility to discern the spirits and reject soundly all who do not confess that Jesus Christ is God in the flesh (see 2 Peter 2:1; 1 John 4:1–2).

Anticipation of Jesus' return will create an urgency in you to reach lost souls.

In John's vision recorded in the book of Revelation, Jesus gave this great promise to those who remain watchful: "Behold, I am coming as a thief. Blessed is he who watches" (16:15). An eager anticipation for the Lord's return will create an urgency within you to reach lost souls, an increased focus on doing things that count for eternity, a purity of heart, and exceedingly great joy as you realize Jesus' return will bring an end to pain and sorrow.

"The kingdom of heaven shall be likened to ten virgins who took their lamps and went out to meet the bridegroom" (Matthew 25:1).

1. Read Matthew 25:1–13. In Jesus' day, a man and woman were legally betrothed to each other long before the wedding took place. During this time, the groom prepared a home for his bride and set things in order for their life together. The groom might come at any time, and the bride's responsibility was to be ready. How is that similar to what God expects of you as you wait for Jesus' return?

   _____

   _____

   _____

   _____

   _____

2. What is the distinction between the five wise virgins and the five foolish ones (2–4)?

_____

_____

_____

_____

3. Both the wise and the foolish virgins slept while the bridegroom was delayed (5). What happened when the cry suddenly went out that he had arrived (6–9)?

_____

_____

_____

_____

4. What happened to those who were not prepared for the bridegroom's return (10–12)? How does this relate to you being ready for Jesus' return?

_____

_____

_____

_____

5. What do you need to put in order to eagerly anticipate and be watching for Jesus' second coming to this world?

_____

_____

_____

_____

"Now five of them were wise, and five were foolish. Those who were foolish took their lamps and took no oil with them, but the wise took oil in their vessels with their lamps" (Matthew 25:2–4).

"Then all those virgins arose and trimmed their lamps. And the foolish said to the wise, 'Give us some of your oil, for our lamps are going out'" (Matthew 25:7–8).

"While they went to buy, the bridegroom came, and those who were ready went in with him to the wedding; and the door was shut. Afterward the other virgins came also, saying, 'Lord, Lord, open to us!' But he answered and said, 'Assuredly, I say to you, I do not know you.' Watch therefore, for you know neither the day nor the hour in which the Son of Man is coming" (Matthew 25:10–13).

God acts in His timing, not yours. This is why it is so important for you to be prepared and walking in the center of His will at all times.

Day 89: Work Diligently

Why does Jesus leave you here on earth after He saves you? Why aren't you immediately taken into the Lord's presence after you're born again? Wouldn't an express trip to heaven save you from a lot of temptation, pain, disappointment, and misery? It would . . . but then again, it would also cause you to miss out on one of the fundamental purposes of the

Christian walk. The reason for your continuing earthly sojourn is that you still have work to do!

God calls you to win souls.

For one thing, God calls you to win souls. You are to be the Lord's witness—telling of the love of God and the atoning death of Jesus Christ. You are to testify about what Christ has done in your life, both with your words and by your example. As long as there remains a soul on earth who hasn't heard the gospel of the Lord Jesus Christ, you have work to do.

God calls you to develop increasing intimacy with Him.

In addition, Jesus leaves you on earth so you can develop an ever-increasing intimacy with God. *Everyone* has room to grow, and in those areas where you discover you are unlike Christ, you must work with the Spirit to become conformed to His likeness. Your mind must be renewed (see Romans 12:2). Your inner hurts and emotions must be healed. You must grow in spiritual discernment and in the wisdom of God. Your faith must be strengthened and used so your prayers and actions more effectively build up the Lord's kingdom.

"What man of you, having a hundred sheep, if he loses one of them, does not leave the ninety-nine in the wilderness, and go after the one which is lost until he finds it?" (Luke 15:4).

6. Read Luke 15:1–7. What does this parable teach about the way in which God seeks out those who don't yet know Him (4)?

_____

_____

_____

"And when he has found it, he lays it on his shoulders, rejoicing. And when he comes home, he calls together his friends and neighbors, saying to them, 'Rejoice with me, for I have found my sheep which was lost!'" (Luke 15:5–6).

7. What is God's attitude toward the lost when they come to Him (5–6)?

_____

_____

_____

8. How do you feel about the responsibility of "searching for lost sheep"—that is, being the Lord's witness and actively trying to bring others to Him?

_____

_____

_____

_____

"There will be more joy in heaven over one sinner who repents than over ninety-nine just persons who need no repentance" (Luke 15:7).

9. Do you share God's enthusiasm when a sinner repents (7)? Why or why not?

_____

_____

_____

_____

10. How does focusing on the fact that Jesus could return at any time motivate you to fulfill His command to "go therefore and make disciples of all the nations" (Matthew 28:19)?

_____

_____

_____

_____

"Repentance and remission of sins should be preached in His name to all nations" (Luke 24:47).

Jesus could not talk about heaven and about the redeemed who populate it without talking about joy and gladness. Heaven is a very happy place because believers have been reconciled to the Lord (see Romans 5:11) and have the privilege of enjoying His wonderful presence.

Day 90: Wait Peacefully

Waiting isn't easy for most people. Impatience often leads to frustration, and it also causes fear to build up in people. The longer they wait for something they anticipate to occur, the greater their concern grows with what will happen. This can quickly degenerate into worry over what might happen—and then fear is only a step away.

However, the Lord does not call you to fear but to peace as you await His return. The angels spoke peace to the earth at His first coming (see Luke 2:14), and more than 400 times in Scripture, we are instructed not to fear but to enjoy peace. To the woman with an issue of blood Jesus said, "Go in peace" (Mark 5:34). To a stormy sea He said, "Peace, be still!" (4:39). To His disciples He said, "My peace I give to you" (John 14:27).

Apart from Jesus, there can be no peace in this world. However, with Jesus, you experience a type of peace that surpasses your rational capacity and settles deep within (see Philippians 4:7). You are to seek and find this peace as you await the Lord's return. So, when the Lord comes, will He find you among those who love Him and call Him Savior and Lord? Will He find you doing what He has commanded you to do? Will He find you eager to see Him?

11. Read Psalm 27. How do you keep the desire to dwell with the Lord kindled while you wait for His return (4)?

_____

_____

_____

When worry sets in, fear is only a step away.

Seek God's peace as you await Jesus' return.

One thing I have desired of the LORD, that will I seek: that I may dwell in the house of the LORD (Psalm 27:4).

When You said, "Seek My face," My heart said to You, "Your face, LORD, I will seek" (Psalm 27:8).

12. How can you seek God's face in your daily routine (8)? Why is that an important part of waiting for Jesus' return?

_____

_____

_____

_____

I would have lost heart, unless I had believed that I would see the goodness of the LORD In the land of the living (Psalm 27:13).

13. What role does courage play in waiting on the Lord (13)?

_____

_____

_____

_____

Wait on the LORD; be of good courage, and He shall strengthen your heart; wait, I say, on the LORD! (Psalm 27:14).

14. What does it mean to you to "wait on the LORD" (14)? How has God strengthened your heart as you look forward to Jesus' return?

_____

_____

_____

_____

15. What worries and fears do you have as you look at the state of the world today? What areas of your life do you need God to invade with His perfect peace?

_____

_____

_____

_____

Jesus' peace keeps you from fear and worry because it brings you straight to Him and teaches you to depend on Him in everything you face.

Living the Principle

When Jesus returns, will He find you eager to see Him?

When Jesus comes again to this earth, will He find you eager to see Him and ready for His return? Will He find you seeking Him, serving Him, and focused on the reward that awaits you? Will He find that you have been keeping His second coming at the forefront of your mind so that when you finally do meet, you are as glad to see Him as He is to see you?

You have it within your will to answer these questions. And you need to answer them, because the Bible is clear that Jesus *is in fact* coming again. As Paul writes, "Behold, I tell you a mystery: We shall not all sleep, but we shall all be changed—in a moment, in the twinkling of an eye, at the last trumpet. For the trumpet will sound, and the dead will be raised incorruptible, and we shall be changed" (1 Corinthians 15:51-52). Jesus has prepared a great reward and a wonderful home for you in heaven. So be strong—diligently working and expectantly watching—because one day, you are going to see Him face to face.

How will you live out Life Principle 30 this week? Talk with some trusted Christian friends about your feelings in regard to the second coming of Christ. Share your thoughts, questions, and frustrations about balancing excitement over His return with the daily responsibilities of living a life that is faithful and pleasing to Him. Spend some time in prayer, asking God to help you watch faithfully, work diligently, and wait peacefully as you look for Jesus' return.

When will Jesus return? No one can say. Yet Christ's return should not be merely a far-off hope for you. Rather, it should be a daily reminder that God is always active in your life.

—CHARLES F. STANLEY

Life Lessons to Remember

❖ You are to watch for the Lord's return (see Ezekiel 33:7; Mark 13:32–33).
❖ You are to work as if the Lord were returning soon (see Matthew 9:37–38; 24:45–47).
❖ You are to eagerly anticipate the Lord's return (see Isaiah 62:11–12).

The purpose of Christ's coming as our Savior was to destroy the devil's authority and power over our spirits, souls, and bodies; Jesus came to restore man to God. In His second coming, Christ will restore all of creation and all of the world's systems to God in both the spiritual and natural realms.

Notes AND Prayer Requests

USE THIS SPACE TO WRITE ANY KEY POINTS, QUESTIONS,
OR PRAYER REQUESTS FROM THIS WEEK'S STUDY.

_____

_____

_____

_____

_____

_____

_____

_____

_____

_____

_____

_____

_____

_____

30 LIFE PRINCIPLES

BIBLE STUDY

· ·

LEADER'S GUIDE

· ·

Thank you for your willingness to lead your group through the *30 Life Principles Bible Study*. The rewards of being a leader are different from those of participating; and as you lead, you will find your own walk with Jesus deepened by this experience. During this study, you and your group members will explore thirty Life Principles in the Bible and how you should respond to them as followers of Christ. There are several elements in this leader's guide that will help you as you structure your study and reflection time, so follow along and take advantage of each one.

Before You Begin

Before your first meeting, make sure the group participants have a copy of this study guide so they can follow along and have their answers written ahead of time. Alternately, you can hand out the guides at your first meeting and give the group members some time to look over the material and ask any preliminary questions. During your first meeting, be sure to send a sheet around the room and have the members write down their names, phone numbers, and email addresses so you can keep in touch with them during the week.

Generally, the ideal size for a group is between eight to ten people, which will ensure everyone has enough time to participate in the discussions. If you have more people, you might want to break up the main group into smaller subgroups. Encourage those who attend the first meeting to commit to attending for the duration of the study, as this will help the group members get to know each other, create stability for the group, and help you know how to prepare each week.

Each lesson begins with a brief introduction to the principle that you and your group members will be studying that week. As you begin your time together, consider opening with an "icebreaker" question to get the group members thinking about the topic you will discuss. Ask people to share their initial thoughts on the subject, but ask them to keep their answers brief. Ideally, you want everyone in the group to get a chance to answer the question, so try to keep the responses to a minute or less. If you have talkative group members, make sure to state up front that everyone needs to limit his or her answer to one minute.

Give the group members a chance to answer, but tell them to feel free to pass if they wish. With the rest of the study, it's generally not a good idea to have everyone answer every question—a free-flowing discussion is more desirable. But with the opening icebreaker questions, you can go around the circle. Encourage shy people to share, but don't force them.

Before your first meeting, let the group members know the sessions are broken down into three days' worth of reading material. The goal of structuring the material in this format is to encourage group members to spend time each day in God's Word. During your group discussion time, the participants will be drawing on the answers they wrote down during the week, so encourage them to always complete these ahead of time. Also, invite them to bring any questions and insights they uncovered while reading to your next meeting—especially if they had a breakthrough moment or didn't understand something they read.

Weekly Preparation

As the leader, there are a few things you should do to prepare for each meeting:

❖ *Read through the lesson.* This will help you become familiar with the content and know how to structure the discussion times.

❖ *Decide which questions you want to discuss.* Each session contains fifteen Bible study questions (five per day), so you might not be able to cover every question. Instead, select two to three questions in each day's reading that especially stood out to you.

❖ *Be familiar with the questions you want to discuss.* When the group meets you'll be watching the clock, so you want to make sure you are familiar with the Bible study questions you have selected. You can then spend time in the passages again when the group meets. In this way, you'll ensure you have the passages more deeply in your mind than your group members.

❖ *Pray for your group.* Pray for your group members throughout the week and ask God to lead them as they study His Word.

❖ *Bring extra supplies to your meeting.* The members should bring their own pens for writing notes, but it's a good idea to have extras available for those who forget. You may also want to bring paper and additional Bibles.

Note that in many cases, there will not be one "right" answer to any question. Answers will vary, especially when the group members are being asked to share their personal experiences.

Structuring the Discussion Time

You will need to determine with your group how long you want to meet each week so that you can plan your time accordingly. Generally, most groups like to meet for either sixty minutes or ninety minutes, so you could use one of the following schedules:

SECTION	60 MINUTES	90 MINUTES
WELCOME: Members arrive and get settled	**5 minutes**	**10 minutes**
ICEBREAKER: Discuss an opening icebreaker-type question with the group	**10 minutes**	**15 minutes**
DISCUSSION: Discuss the Bible study questions you selected ahead of time	**35 minutes**	**50 minutes**
PRAYER/CLOSING: Pray together as a group and dismiss	**10 minutes**	**15 minutes**

As the group leader, it is up to you to keep track of time and keep things moving along according to your schedule. You might want to set a timer for each segment so both you and the group members know when your time is up. (Note: There are excellent phone apps for timers that play a chime instead of a disruptive noise.) Don't feel pressured to cover every question you have selected if group discussion is going well. Again, it's not necessary for each group member to share.

Don't be concerned if the members are quiet or slow to share. People are often quiet when they are pulling together their ideas, and this might be a new experience for them. Just ask a question and let it hang in the air until someone shares. You can then say, "Thank you. What about others? What came to you when you meditated on the passage?"

Group Dynamics

Leading a group through the *30 Life Principles Bible Study* will prove to be highly rewarding, both for you and your group members—but that doesn't mean you will not encounter any challenges along the way. Discussions can get off track. Group members may not be sensitive to the needs and ideas of others. Some might worry they will be expected to talk about matters that make them feel awkward. Others may express comments that result in disagreements. To help ease this strain on you and the group, consider the following ground rules:

❖ When someone raises a question or comment that is off the main topic, suggest that you deal with it another time; or, if you feel led to go in that direction, let the group know you will be spending some time discussing it.

❖ If someone asks a question you don't know how to answer, admit it and move on. At your discretion, feel free to invite group members to comment on questions that call for personal experience.

❖ If you find one or two people dominating the discussion time, direct a few questions to others in the group. Outside the main group time, ask the more dominating members to help you draw out the quieter ones. Work to make them a part of the solution instead of the problem.

❖ When a disagreement occurs, encourage group members to process the matter in love. Encourage those on opposite sides to restate what they heard the other side say about the matter, and then invite each side to evaluate if that perception is accurate. Lead the group in examining other Scriptures related to the topic and look for common ground.

When any of these issues arise, encourage your group members to follow the words from the Bible: "Love one another" (John 13:34), "If it is possible, as much as depends on you, live peaceably with all men" (Romans 12:18), and "Be swift to hear, slow to speak, slow to wrath; for the wrath of man does not produce the righteousness of God" (James 1:19–20).

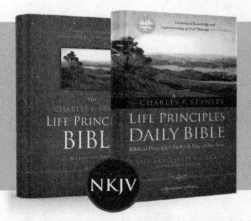

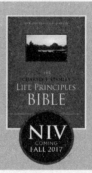